ECONOMICS IN AMERICA

ECONOMICS IN AMERICA

AN IMMIGRANT ECONOMIST
EXPLORES THE LAND OF INEQUALITY

ANGUS DEATON

PRINCETON UNIVERSITY PRESS

PRINCETON & OXFORD

Published by Princeton University Press
41 William Street, Princeton, New Jersey 08540
99 Banbury Road, Oxford OX2 6JX

press.princeton.edu

All Rights Reserved

Library of Congress Cataloging-in-Publication Data

Names: Deaton, Angus, author.
Title: Economics in America : an immigrant economist
    explores the land of inequality / Angus Deaton.
Description: Princeton : Princeton University Press, [2023] |
    Includes bibliographical references and index.
Identifiers: LCCN 2023011502 (print) | LCCN 2023011503 (ebook) |
    ISBN 9780691247625 (hardback) | ISBN 9780691247854 (ebook)
Subjects: LCSH: Income distribution—United States. | Consumption
    (Economics)—United States. | Poverty—United States. |
    Capitalism—Social aspects—United States. | BISAC: BUSINESS &
    ECONOMICS / Economic History | HISTORY / United States /
    21st Century
Classification: LCC HC110.I5 D438 2032 (print) | LCC HC110.I5 (ebook) |
    DDC 339.2/20973—dc23/eng/20230518
LC record available at https://lccn.loc.gov/2023011502
LC ebook record available at https://lccn.loc.gov/2023011503

British Library Cataloging-in-Publication Data is available

Editorial: Joe Jackson, Emma Waugh
Jacket: Karl Spurzem
Production: Danielle Amatucci
Publicity: James Schneider, Kate Farquhar-Thomson

Jacket image: Union Jack and American flag in PD, superimposed
on bowtie from RKF / Shutterstock

This book has been composed in Arno and Balboa

Printed in the United States of America

10 9 8 7 6 5 4 3 2 1

For Anne, with love and gratitude

CONTENTS

PREFACE

I WAS BORN in Scotland, was educated there and in England, and moved to Princeton, New Jersey, in 1983. Like many other immigrants, I thought I could do better for myself and my family in the United States. Princeton University seemed like it would be a splendid place to work, as indeed it was, and I'd been poor enough as a child and young man to appreciate the security that an American salary offered. I was in awe of the accomplishments of American scholars and writers, and of the wealth and opportunities that America promised, especially to immigrants and even more so to their children. I am still in awe.

But there is also a dark side. Inequalities of all kinds are wider in America than almost anywhere else on earth. Some of them are good; the opportunities are real, and some people take more advantage of them than do others. The United States is less interested than is Europe in providing for people who could not or who did not benefit from those opportunities. Indeed, many argue that the two things are connected: the opportunities work best when there is no safety net to distract people from seizing them, and that with so many opportunities, we do not need a safety net. The lack of a safety net, today and throughout history, has much to do with race, an ever-present issue that is viewed quite differently in the United States than in other rich countries. Even so, I was shocked by the lack of provision for the not so fortunate and by the harsh politics that accompany it.

I was appalled when one of my new colleagues (publicly) proclaimed that "government is theft." I had grown up in a country where I, my parents, and our friends saw the government as benevolent, a friend in times of trouble, and I found it hard to believe that a distinguished academic could be so cynical and so libertarian. I still do not agree with his sentiment, but I have come to understand the extent to which state and federal government in the United States often work, not to protect ordinary people but to help rich predators make ordinary people poorer. Yet the system is far from entirely rigged, and it provides an immensely productive and good life to some, even if those some no longer include most of the population.

For the last quarter century, I have written regular bulletins for Britain's Royal Economic Society, reflecting on what I have seen, both good and bad. Sometimes in awe, and sometimes in shock. I have used these reflections as the starting point for this book, though I have updated the original material and added a great deal that is new.

I have divided the book into sections, each associated with a specific topic. The original pieces were written over a twenty-five-year period, but I have not kept the chronological order. Instead, I have edited to try to make them of current interest, but without changing the arguments. Each is written from the viewpoint of the end of 2022. In some cases, where the commentary is about a specific historical event (for example, associated with the Bush, Obama, or Trump presidency, or about a policy that was relevant at the time, like Star Wars), I have noted the historical context but make no apology for retaining content given that the underlying questions remain as relevant as ever. Each section starts with a guide that explains its contents and how it relates to the overarching themes of the book.

I found myself returning again and again to the same set of issues, above all to inequality in its many manifestations. With a constant eye on inequality, I write about healthcare, pensions, the stock market, and poverty at home and abroad. I am an economist who works with and cares about numbers, about how data can and should shape our understanding, but also about how data affect politics and how politics affect data, what I think of as the politics of numbers.

Economists are deeply involved in policy, more so than other academics. They are listened to (sometimes for good, sometimes for ill), they often take policymaking positions, and they are often influential without being active policymakers. The current secretary of the Treasury, Janet Yellen, is a distinguished economist, as is Larry Summers, who was Treasury secretary from 1999 to 2001. Ben Bernanke, who shared the Nobel Prize in Economics in 2022 and was once my colleague at Princeton, was chairman of the Federal Reserve System from 2006 to 2014 during the Financial Crisis and was succeeded in that office by Janet Yellen. There are many other economists who staff the president's Council of Economic Advisers and who have senior roles at the World Bank and the International Monetary Fund (IMF). Working alongside politicians and their advisers, albeit usually in a subsidiary role, economists have influence on policies that affect the country and the world.

Dead economists may have even more influence than live economists. John Maynard Keynes wrote that "practical men who believe themselves to be quite exempt from any intellectual influence, are usually the slaves of some defunct economist. Madmen in authority, who hear voices in the air, are distilling their frenzy from some academic scribbler of a few years back."[1] Among those dead economists is surely Keynes himself, on what is now seen as the left; on the right are Milton Friedman and Friedrich von Hayek. Keynes's dictum frequently comes to mind when thinking about economics and politics in Washington.

I have never held a policymaking position, but I know and talk to many who have. I have been a teacher and researcher for more than fifty years, but I have almost always worked on topics that were relevant for policy. I have also worked with international organizations, such as the World Bank, the IMF, and the Organisation for Economic Co-operation and Development (OECD), which collects data and makes policy recommendations. I have been a member of several panels at the National Academy of Sciences, working on topics of national importance, including poverty, prices, and mortality. My work on health and wellbeing has been funded for many years by the National Institutes of Health. I also served a spell as editor of *Econometrica*, the leading mathematical and statistical journal in economics.

Because economics and economists are important for what happens to the livelihoods and wellbeing of so many, they have (properly) attracted attention and criticism, and several excellent recent books argue that reform is needed, that much of what economists believe is wrong, and that their prescriptions over the last half century bear much of the responsibility for the erosion of democratic capitalism as well as the loss of trust in expertise.[2] Economists were given too much power over the world, these arguments go, and they broke it.

I have much sympathy for the critics, even if I do not always recognize the profession they portray. Academic economics also has much to be proud of: it has made real discoveries, and, in the past thirty years, it has become more applied, less focused on abstract theory, and more focused on trying to interpret the world. Yet, as the critics argue, we have our blind spots. I hope this book will help noneconomists understand how my profession works and what economists do from day to day as they break the world and try to put it back together. I talk about both the triumphs and the disasters. And I try to be honest about our failings, our overenthusiasm for markets and for globalization, and our decidedly odd way of thinking about the ethics of what we are doing.

The last two chapters of the book, "Did Economists Break the Economy?," and "Is Economic Failure a Failure of Economics?" attempt to answer the question and to explain just how and where I think that we have gone wrong.

The book is part biographical: I write about myself and about other economists. I write about what it was like to win a Nobel Prize, as well as about my experiences as president of the American Economic Association, the leading professional society of economists in the United States. I write about my own encounters with America's sometimes impressive but deeply flawed and destructive healthcare system, as well as about how the costs of that system bear heavy responsibility for today's economic and political troubles. I write about pensions, including my own adventure with the Social Security Administration, and how pensions and inequality are deeply linked. I write about how to measure things that matter and about the impossibility of measurement being detached from politics.

The United States has become a darker society since I arrived in 1983. The hopes of the immigrant have been tempered by reality, but even more by the corruption of the American economy and its politics, a corruption that threatens our democracy.

ECONOMICS IN AMERICA

CHAPTER 1

BEGINNINGS

FAST-FOOD RESTAURANTS, GANGSTERS, AND THE MINIMUM WAGE

I PERMANENTLY relocated to Princeton, New Jersey, from England in the summer of 1983 but had earlier spent a year in Princeton with my family in the 1979–1980 academic year. The anecdote that begins this chapter, recalled many years later, is about an immigrant's fears about the mafia in New Jersey and his anxiety about whether the United States was a good place to bring up a family and to spend a life of intellectual inquiry. America is famous, not just for its science and scholarship but also for its recurrent bouts of anti-intellectualism.

Princeton in the late 1980s was an exciting place to be an economist. My then young colleagues David Card and Alan Krueger were beginning their subsequently famous work on the minimum wage, looking at fast-food restaurants in New Jersey and Pennsylvania. Some years later, in a piece written in 1996, I described their work, which I admired, and the reaction to it, which I did not. I began to experience American anti-intellectualism. The Card and Krueger study, which was much cited in the official write-up for Card's 2021 Nobel Prize[1] (Alan

Krueger died in 2019), not only is an early example of a style that is heavily used in economics today but also shows what happens when research challenges vested interests and triggers hardball politics. Especially when, as here, the policy recommendations, if implemented, would redistribute income from the rich to the poor, from capital to labor, and from those with great power to those with much less.

I returned to the topic in a piece written in 2019, and that and the original piece are adapted here as the second and third sections of the chapter. The final section is an entirely new postscript written after Card won the Nobel Prize in 2021.

An Immigrant's First Impressions

America can seem very strange to foreigners. When I first set foot in New Jersey with my family in the summer of 1979, I half believed that the place was infested with gangsters. This idea did not come from watching *The Sopranos*, which lay far in the future, but more likely from reading *Tintin in America* to my kids or from versions of the Al Capone story in the *Reader's Digest* that had scared me as a child. In Scotland in the 1950s, in a home with few books and one television station, the *Reader's Digest* was my window into America.

In New Jersey, I took my family to a Burger King near Princeton (the town itself was then too snooty to allow such places). Coming from Britain, where *ham*burgers were made of *ham*—though only a small amount of the patty was ham; most of it was filler— we believed that American hamburgers were a health food. As I carried our heavily laden tray to a table, we were startled by what I took to be a gunshot. I looked up, and a man across the room had his hands over his face, viscous red liquid welling between his fingers. Just as I had supposed.

Apart from gangsters and the safety of New Jersey, my other worry was more personal. I often wondered about anti-intellectualism, or rather my puzzle over trying to reconcile the coexistence of anti-intellectualism and great universities. Years later, especially when Donald Trump was president, anti-intellectualism seemed more of an issue than did a relatively quiescent mafia. Populists are the new mob; they terrorize us more than gangsters, and populists hate immigrants and intellectuals in equal measure. Trump is an ardent (and apparently genuine) supporter of mercantilism—the long-discredited view that we get rich by exporting more than we import—and if Trump had ever had a science adviser, which he never managed to get around to selecting, he or she would likely have recommended leeches or alchemy (or perhaps bleach) as a cure for COVID-19. The tax bill of December 2017 not only redistributed from poor to rich but also imposed a tax on university endowments and, in an early version, proposed to tax as salaries the tuition relief that graduate students nominally receive as an accounting counterpart for the teaching that they are required to do. Universities are generally unpopular, with 59 percent of Republicans in 2019 saying that colleges and universities have a *negative* effect on the way things are going in the country. Only 18 percent of Democrats agree, but taken together, the numbers are not encouraging.[2] In February 2022, the lieutenant governor of Texas, Dan Patrick, proposed eliminating tenure at Texas public colleges and universities.

Many Americans view immigrants even less favorably than intellectuals, and during the Trump administration they were especially antagonistic toward immigrants from Muslim-majority or terror-prone countries, a designation that included three of the four American Nobelists in 2015. One of my fellow American Nobel laureates was Aziz Sancar, who was born in

Turkey; another, Bill Campbell, who found a cure for river blindness, was born in Ireland. My own country, Britain, was long classified as terror-prone because of the activities of the Irish Republican Army. In what now seems like the good old days, Nobel laureates who were American citizens were warmly welcomed to the White House—in my case by a well-informed and curious President Obama. In 2017 and later years, the Nobel visit to the White House did not happen, perhaps by mutual agreement, given that several laureates were no keener to meet the president than the president was to meet them. After all, what could Trump possibly learn from economics laureate Richard Thaler, whose work, among other things, is about self-control?

One immigration measure put on the table in February 2017 was the RAISE Act, proposed in the Senate by Republicans Tom Cotton and David Perdue, and supported by President Trump. It aimed to cut immigration by half and to subject potential immigrants to a test that would select only those whose skills were thought to benefit the country. The *New York Times* published a version of the test, on which a score of thirty points was needed to qualify. I scored thirty-one, just scraping by. The decisive factor for me was not my degrees from Cambridge in England, which did not count, but my high income, which I would not have had had I not already been in the United States. Catch-22.

But I had missed a footnote. A Nobel Prize scores thirty bonus points, which elevated me to sixty-one. However, it is not just *any* Nobel Prize—peace and literature are apparently not useful in today's United States. I was surprised only that Nobel Prizes in Economics counted, perhaps because Milton Friedman had won one.

Anti-intellectualism is not hardwired into America. The Puritans who started the Massachusetts Bay colony greatly valued

learning and founded Harvard within a few years of their arrival. Richard Hofstadter, in his history of anti-intellectualism
in America, quotes Moses Coit Tyler: "Only six years after John
Winthrop's arrival in Salem harbor, the people of Massachusetts
took from their own treasury the fund from which to found a
university; so that while the tree-stumps were as yet scarcely
weather-browned in their earliest harvest fields, and before the
nightly howl of the wolf had ceased from the outskirts of their
villages, they had made arrangements by which even in that
wilderness their young men could at once enter upon the study
of Aristotle and Thucydides, of Horace and Tacitus and the He-
brew Bible."[3] Harvard was teaching young men while Galileo
was still at work in Pisa. Shortly after its founding, Oxford and
Cambridge recognized Harvard's degrees as equivalent to their
own. Of course, neither Trump nor his populist acolytes are
Puritans.

Hofstadter's story is one of cycles, of periods of commitment
to scholarship, and periods of turning away, largely associated
with changes in religion. In more modern times, the United
States made a large commitment to education after Sputnik in
the early 1960s. And we might hope that, once populism has
waned, and the pandemic has gone, Americans will once again
understand the value of higher education. There may even
come a time when the educated elite in general and academic
economics in particular is no longer seen as partly responsible
for the declining fortunes of less educated American workers.

As for immigrants, we are often reminded that the United
States is a nation of immigrants, but here, too, attitudes change
over time and are different from place to place. California, with
more than a quarter of its population foreign born compared
with 15 percent in the country as a whole, likes its immigrants,
and at the beginning of the Trump administration was locked

in a legal battle with Attorney General Jeff Sessions, a longtime opponent of immigration and at one time a senator from Alabama, where there are few immigrants.

But what about New Jersey and the mafia at Burger King? As it turned out, I was the shooter. I had dropped a plastic packet of tomato ketchup from my tray, then stepped on one end, causing the packet to explode and to shoot ketchup into my fellow patron's face. Sometimes, the blood is only fake blood. And it is good to let your prior beliefs meet experience and data. If there were still mafioso in New Jersey, they were not the cause of the incident in Burger King that day. And as I was to learn over the subsequent half century, the predators, the shakedown artists, and the protection rackets were less of a problem in New Jersey than they were, and are, in the nation's capital.

The Economics and Politics of Fast-Food Restaurants

On August 20, 1996, President Clinton signed into law a two-stage increase in the minimum wage, the first such increase passed since 1989. In Congress, the measure attracted bipartisan support, as had previous minimum wage hikes. In the Senate, the bill was so *popular* that Republican majority leader Trent Lott held the measure back as a reward for his colleagues if they completed other, less palatable measures before the summer recess. The enthusiasm of the voters, 80 percent of whom favored an increase, and of a majority of Republican lawmakers was not universal: House majority leader Dick Armey of Texas, a onetime economics professor in Montana and Texas, had sworn to "fight it with every fiber of my being."[4]

Armey's opposition to an increase in the minimum wage was shared by most of the American economics profession, even including several on the left, including in Joe Stiglitz's 1993 text-book *Economics*.[5] Although many economists supported an increase, including Stiglitz in his role as chief economist in the Clinton administration, 90 percent believed that increases in the minimum wage would increase unemployment. But there were dissenters, including, most notably, my then colleagues David Card and Alan Krueger, whose empirical work—cited by Labor Secretary Robert Reich (for whom Krueger had been chief economic adviser), by Senator Edward Kennedy, and (without naming the authors) by President Clinton—became the intellectual battleground for the policy.

The substance of Card and Krueger's work is summarized in their 1995 book *Myth and Measurement*.[6] They examine several episodes when the minimum wage changed and, through careful analysis of their own and others' data, build a consistent picture that modest increases in the minimum wage have little or no effect on the numbers of low-wage workers that are employed. Perhaps the most famous case was Card and Krueger's own comparison of employment levels in fast-food restaurants in the adjacent states of New Jersey and Pennsylvania, only one of which (NJ) raised its minimum wage in April 1992.[7] But that was only one of the many similar findings in the book. The results were (and continue to be) intensively debated. The nature and rhetoric of that debate in 1996 provided insights into the American economics profession, into the way in which empirical evidence is received when it challenges conventional beliefs, and into the relationships among research, methods, and policy.

In 1996, economic research had begun to be revolutionized by the widespread availability of previously unimaginable amounts of data. Research became more empirical and less dependent on theory. When data are scarce, we must rely more on our previous knowledge about how the world works and accept the risk that the knowledge may not be right or applicable. With lots of data, we can discard scaffolding that seems weak or outdated. Card and Krueger were among the very best practitioners of such methods, and the empirical results of their study were convincing and straightforward, so much so that their import was clear to policymakers and to the media.

Many of us who were pleased by this turn to the evidence and who had assumed that our views were shared by the profession were disquieted by the level of public and private vituperation that greeted Card and Krueger's conclusions. The reception accorded to Card and Krueger's Princeton colleagues when visiting economists in other institutions was what might be expected by the friends and defenders of child molesters, and the public outcry was even more extreme.

My prize for nastiness went to Paul Craig Roberts, a leading conservative commentator who used his regular column in *Business Week* to lambast the American Economic Association for awarding its John Bates Clark Medal—its most prestigious award—to Card, "an economist who does not believe in the law of demand, the cornerstone of economic science."[8] Roberts impugned the review process at the *American Economic Review*, claiming that both the publication of the paper and Card's selection for the medal had been contaminated by political correctness, and asking whether the honoring of Card was "because the laughable findings have friends in high places like the Oval Office." Roberts's maligning of the American Economic Association and of Card were repeated by Thomas Sowell in *Forbes*; in an article entitled "Repealing the law of gravity" Sowell likened Card and Krueger's results to "cold fusion."[9]

Card and Krueger's study of fast-food restaurants was also attacked by the Employment Policies Institute (EPI), which supplied payroll data to economists David Neumark and

William Wascher that showed that the increased minimum wage had indeed reduced employment. Judging from media reports and conversations with other economists, the EPI's attack— reiterated by *Business Week, Forbes,* and the *Wall Street Journal*— was extraordinarily successful in discrediting the quality of Card and Krueger's data. Rarely mentioned, however, is that the EPI was, and is, funded by business groups, that its then director was a lobbyist against the minimum wage, that the data (which were not available to other researchers) were not comparable to Card and Krueger's and came from different establishments, and that new data collected by Neumark and Wascher themselves did not actually contradict Card and Krueger's findings.

Among the leaders of the attack was the late Finis Welch, a distinguished empirical labor economist at Texas A&M. He provided some fine quotes: "The Clinton administration used sloppy statistical studies to support its argument and the so-called evidence they're citing has been killed big-time" (*Nation's Restaurant News*) and "Alan (Krueger) ought to consider the old saw: If you drop an apple and it rises, question your experiment before concluding that the laws of gravity have been repealed" (*Time*). In a similar vein, June O'Neill, then director of the Congressional Budget Office, the agency charged with assessing the effects of government policies, reminded the audience at an American Enterprise Institute meeting that theory is also evidence. Welch's review of Card and Krueger's book (in the *Industrial and Labor Relations Review*) is largely an attempt to discredit their data, using arguments that would apply to government (and perhaps all?) data, and it ends with the recommendation that economists should not attempt to collect their own data.[10]

What was at stake was less the political correctness of the American Economic Association than the theoretical incorrectness of the evidence. That evidence may have to be discarded in favor of "science" could hardly be better argued than in Nobel laureate James Buchanan's words in the *Wall Street Journal*: "Just as no physicist would claim that 'water runs uphill,' no self-respecting economist would claim that increases in the minimum wage increase employment. Such a claim, if seriously advanced, becomes equivalent to a denial that there is even minimum scientific content in economics, and that, in consequence, economists can do nothing but write as advocates for ideological interests. Fortunately, only a handful of economists are willing to throw over the teaching of two centuries; we have not yet become a bevy of camp-following whores."[11] The citadel of orthodoxy is exceedingly well defended.

Minimum Wage Revisited a Quarter Century Later

After many years, the debate on the minimum wage has lost none of its relevance or capacity to divide and upset. The EPI is still in business and still bemoans state-ordered increases in minimum wages. Card and Krueger's work continues to polarize both economists and politicians. Jason Furman, who served as the chair of President Obama's Council of Economic Advisers, has recently noted that their results changed the mind of half of the profession.[12]

Alan Krueger died by suicide in March 2019 at the age of fifty-eight. Over his sadly shortened career, he made lasting and creative contributions to economics over a wide range of fields. He also had a high-level career in policy, in the Department of Labor, in the Treasury, and as President Obama's head of the Council of Economic Advisers, then a cabinet-level position. David Card, his coauthor on the minimum wage studies, now at UC Berkeley, continues a career of extraordinary productivity. Unlike Krueger, he has been less involved with policy. Perhaps not exactly policy, but of intense public interest, was his testimony on behalf of Harvard University in the lawsuit alleging that its admissions policies discriminate against Asian Americans. (Harvard won, but as of spring 2023, the case awaits a decision by the Supreme Court, which is widely anticipated to reverse the judgment and perhaps permanently disable affirmative action in university admissions.)

Card and Krueger's work, together with that of others—particularly Joshua Angrist, who was a graduate student at Princeton around the same time—changed empirical economics. The field moved away from the theory-based modeling that was the standard at the time and toward a reliance on natural experiments, such as that created by the change in the minimum wage in New Jersey but not in nearby Pennsylvania. Card, Krueger, and Angrist were creative in finding other such natural experiments, and from there developed a general approach that looked for the causal effects of policy by trying to find two groups that were arguably identical except for the policy. The minimum wage work, and its use of natural experiments, seemed like magic at the time, setting the stage for new possibilities of investigation. As with all new methods, its problems have become more apparent over time, but the history since 1995 is important and instructive, not just for the minimum wage but for the way that economics is practiced today.

When it comes to assessing the ultimate impact of this empirical revolution, as Zhou Enlai said in 1972 about the French Revolution, it is too early to tell. Yet there is no doubting the impact of the work on the minimum wage as well as on economists' thinking about it. Although the federal minimum wage of $7.25 an hour has not been increased since July 2009, many individual states have made increases. Twenty-nine states have higher rates, ranging from $8.25 in Illinois to $12 in Washington (state), and the cities of Seattle and San Francisco have minimum wage levels of $15 an hour. Using the city or state changes as natural experiments, many studies have by now used methods akin to those pioneered by Card and Krueger.[13] My reading is that these mostly replicate Card and Krueger's findings. There has also been extensive experience with (relatively high) minimum wages in Britain, where there is a raft of studies—none of which finds a reduction in employment.

Even so, the defenders of textbook orthodoxy have not given up. About seven out of ten Americans think the federal minimum wage should be raised, and the failure of Congress to pass such legislation is a testament to the power of lobbying in Washington—in this case by the fast-food industry. The industry also continues to commission studies that buttress the conservative position that trying to help people in this way can only hurt them. The EPI continues its battle; the lead story on its website in the spring of 2023 was titled "Businesses are closing because of the fight for $15" ($15 being the current target for those pressing for a higher minimum wage).

My friend Anthony Appiah, who writes the Ethicist column in the *New York Times,* is a philosopher who thinks about and comments on public policy, as well as the private affairs of his correspondents. He recently asked me, with some irritation, why economists *still* had not managed to settle what seemed like a straightforward question. But perhaps Appiah's question cannot be answered, or at least not in general. Why do we economists—as well as noneconomists—suppose that the effect of a policy change should always be the same, or even act in the same direction? Even water runs uphill when in a pipe with sufficient pressure behind it, apples float up in a tub of water, and no one claims that the law of gravity has been repealed.

Recent work has gone back to theory and asked whether there might be circumstances under which increasing the minimum wage will not decrease employment. Those conditions were laid out in Card and Krueger's book *Myth and Measurement* and had been understood for many years, though often seen as an odd case that was unlikely to apply in the real world. If hamburger flippers or cashiers have limited opportunities to find other work, their employers can exploit the situation. They can pay them less than they contribute to the firm's bottom line, behavior that takes money out of the workers' pay and adds it to the restauranteur's profits. Raising the minimum wage, if the increase is not too large, will reduce this transfer from the worker to the employer, but the employer will not fire the worker, because the employer still makes a profit from each worker, just a little less than before. In this situation, in economics language, the employer has "market power" over the worker; the firm is a "monopsonist," a term coined in 1933 by the formidable British economist Joan Robinson.[14] Such an account also explains the fast-food industry's fierce opposition to higher minimum wages. In many cases, higher wages come straight out of profits, and there is a zero-sum game between capital and labor.

In the 1990s, monopsony in the labor market, particularly the fast-food industry, was generally dismissed. I remember trying to use the monopsony story to defend Card and Krueger's original results and being told "no one believes *that*." But the past decade has seen a revival of interest in the idea, particularly in places with a low population density and relatively few employers—a few fast-food places, a chicken processing plant, or a state prison. Geographical mobility has fallen in America, in part because of the high cost of housing in successful cities, and people may find it difficult to move as a family when several family members are working and must do so to get by. In such a world, it is not unlikely that fast-food restaurants have market power and would use it to keep wages low in at least some places. Such behavior is consistent with practices like noncompete clauses, which limit the ability of workers to find other work.[15]

A charge frequently leveled against Card and Krueger's original work was its neglect of theory. While this charge could reasonably be leveled against much empirical work that uses natural or actual experiments, it cannot be leveled against *Myth and Measurement.* There is vindication today as not only the results but the theory are being taken seriously as part of the current reevaluation of the role of market power in the American economy. Monopoly is one example of market power, where producers can artificially raise prices above their free market level, while monopsony is another, where employers can artificially lower wages. This is not just water flowing uphill but a different world altogether, one in which parts of the economy are not well described by competitive markets in which no one has power, but are more like a class struggle in which capital and labor fight over the surplus. If workers have difficulty moving, they are open to predation by powerful employers. Such an economy is one in which working people have good reason to mourn the decline of unions. The intense political reactions to Card and Krueger's work from deeply interested parties, especially the fast-food industry, and indeed the EPI, would not have been a surprise to Adam Smith when he wrote about the harm done by "the clamour of our merchants and manufacturers . . . for the support of their own absurd and oppressive monopolies."[16]

In December 2021, the Nobel Prize in Economics was divided, one half to David Card "for his empirical contributions to labour economics" and the other half divided between

Joshua Angrist and Guido Imbens "for their methodological contributions to the analysis of causal relations."[17] The citation listed the work on minimum wages as part of Card's contribution, and the Nobel Foundation's website contains a detailed and nicely illustrated description of the New Jersey and Pennsylvania study.[18] Alan Krueger could not be included because the Nobel Prize can only be awarded to living recipients.

The minimum wage work has come a long way from its pariah status in 1996, even if only half of the profession is currently convinced, among whom were presumably the members of the Nobel Prize committee. Card, a very serious man who grew up milking cows in Canada, was seen to smile when receiving his medal, not in Stockholm (because of the pandemic) but in Irvine, California, a sad substitute for the magnificent ceremonies in Sweden. Alan Krueger would, I believe, have been much more expressive.

I will return to Nobel Prizes in chapter 9. But what I like most about this story, and the way that it has developed over the years, is that it moved from name-calling (no doubt entertaining) to serious science in the public interest. Instead of dismissing a finding because it contradicts what we think should happen, we need to check whether the contradiction happens elsewhere, then go back to work to think about why it might happen, not necessarily universally, but under what circumstances. This is what led to the work on monopsony, an account that, in turn, still requires more testing and more debate. It also gives one answer to Appiah's question, because it identifies circumstances where we would expect higher minimum wages not to hurt employment. When might an apple float up, or when might water run uphill? Today, when it is often hard for people to move to a new place, and where the courts have rarely prosecuted monopsony—even though it is illegal—the idea that some employers could be keeping wages artificially low could well be one of the reasons for the long-term decline in living standards of less educated working-class Americans.

Card and Krueger's original paper has become one of the flagships of the natural experiment movement. Despite its iconic status and the fact that it is so easy to explain (see, for example, the nice map of New Jersey and Pennsylvania on the Nobel Prize website), it is hardly definitive. Some of the restaurants in the two states are many miles from one another, and there is a lot going on besides a change in the minimum wages. It was New Jersey that raised its wage, not Pennsylvania, so the conventional wisdom is that employment should have fallen in New Jersey relative to Pennsylvania. That wisdom was contradicted, not by what happened or did not happen in *New Jersey*, where there was a small increase in employment, but by the fact that employment fell substantially in *Pennsylvania*. The argument is that the two states are similar enough that whatever caused the fall in Pennsylvania would have caused a parallel fall in New Jersey had the minimum there not increased. That, of course, is a strong assumption about a counterfactual on which there is no direct evidence.

What makes the work so important is not the original study by itself but the many subsequent replications together with a credible story in terms of the market power of at least some employers in the industry. Replications by themselves are never enough, because we can never know whether the next one might be different; remember when it was thought that all swans were white? But replication together with an understanding of what is going on provides a scientific basis for predicting when minimum wages will or will not reduce employment. For example, employers will have market power where there are few other job opportunities or in poor areas where many employees find it difficult to move because they have family members who must work to make ends meet.

As to the politics, most of the name-calling came from the side of the employers, either their own trade group or politicians and economists beholden to them. Their outrage comes not because their interests were being threatened but because economists, as well as economic theory, were supposed to be on their side and had long been so. The minimum wage work was not just wrong, not just bad science ("cold fusion"), but a betrayal. Of course, there have always been economists on the side of labor as well as on the side of capital. But at least some of the recent criticism of economics has been that so much of its conventional wisdom, and its textbook material, is weighted toward capital and against labor, that it takes efficiency much more seriously than it takes equity, that power differentials are ignored, and that economics' widespread acceptance bears some responsibility for the diminishing fortunes of workers.

CHAPTER 2

ADVENTURES IN AMERICAN HEALTHCARE

Why Is Healthcare Such a Big Deal?

To an immigrant from a wealthy country anywhere in the world, the American healthcare system is a shock. I came from Britain, where everyone has health insurance from birth, and I was appalled that so many Americans had (and still have) no insurance. When I took my kids to the doctor, I didn't know the difference between a pediatrician and a podiatrist or why I should choose a specialist in internal medicine as my family doctor. Then there was the thicket of incomprehensible bills.

To an economist as well as to a patient, the system is bewildering. Healthcare eats up almost one in five dollars of American national income. No other rich country spends as much, despite making healthcare a right that is available to all, and despite their citizens having better health than Americans. True, health depends on more than healthcare; drug use, smoking, drinking, and obesity can harm your health and don't have much to do with your doctor. Even so, American healthcare does a poor job for the part of health for which it can be reasonably held responsible, especially among the nonelderly.

If America spent the same share of national income on health as Switzerland, which has the second most expensive system in the world, we would save a *trillion* dollars a year. A trillion dollars—and I am talking about just the *savings*, not the total—would comfortably cover America's military expenditure with cash to spare. Or we could give every person in America the Swiss healthcare system, with its five more years of life expectancy, together with an annual check for $3,000.

Its enormous cost is why healthcare gets its own chapter in a book that is about economics and economists. The vignettes in this chapter illustrate big themes of this book: how economists' thinking contributes to the solution of public problems, how little power economists have compared with politicians and lobbyists for the healthcare industry, how markets work or do not work, and how policy shapes who gets what, sometimes accidentally and sometimes deliberately, affecting who gets to be in the top 1 percent and who labors near the bottom.

We will meet one of the greatest economists of all time, Kenneth Arrow, who was one of the first economists to win a Nobel Prize. It was he who, with others, figured out the necessary conditions for markets to work in the public interest, as Adam Smith long ago argued they would. He also showed just how difficult it is for societies to make collective choices that take into account the needs and desires of their individual members. In this chapter, he will appear as the creator of the key ideas that inform economists' thinking about healthcare.

Because so much money is involved, and because it is impossible for the government *not* to be involved in healthcare, healthcare is a magnet for lobbyists and is one of the main industries from which money pours into politics. There are six healthcare lobbyists in Washington for each member of Congress. Because America's healthcare system cannot remain viable as currently set up, reform is continually being discussed. Politicians must represent their constituents, but they have an endless need for money to campaign, and the public interest will often buckle to the interests of healthcare providers. The providers then have even more money to preserve the system that works so well for *them*.

This chapter illustrates these themes through specific historical episodes, both personal and public. "Trying to Become a Good Hip-op Consumer" was first written after I had a hip replaced in 2006 and is about my first encounter with an American hospital. At that time, the administration of George W. Bush was trying to turn me and other patients into better consumers. "Setting the Hook" is about the early days of President Obama's attempt to reform the healthcare system, how it was complicated by America's vast electoral inequalities, which led him to Montana to fish for trout and for a key senatorial vote. Obama caught no trout, but he got his reform, albeit by buying off the predators (the Washington variety, not the grizzlies and mountain lions in Montana). More people were insured, and the industry got richer; the providers and their lobbyists won. "Adverse Selection, the Mandate, and Broccoli" details how Obamacare set rules to try to stop healthy people free riding on the system by refusing to buy insurance. The rules were designed to deal with an issue that was identified and emphasized by economists. Perhaps we were wrong. "Madmen in Authority" is about what happened after President Trump came to town. In concert with the Republicans on the Hill, who had majorities in both houses, the White House settled on its two highest priorities: tax cuts, standard operating procedure in modern Republican administrations, and the abolition of Obamacare.

Finally, in "Crime, Punishment, and Tobacco," I turn to the large part of health that is *not* determined by healthcare, and to the economics and politics of trying to change people's behavior—in this case, smoking. As often happens, worthy attempts to improve population health led, as if by an invisible, if inevitable, hand, to a transfer of money from the poor to the rich.

Trying to Be a Good Hip-op Consumer

Although I read and write about health, I had managed to live in the United States for twenty-five years with little direct experience with the American healthcare system. So, when I was advised in June 2006 that I needed a hip replacement, a routine procedure but one classified as medium risk, I was apprehensive on both financial and medical grounds. The mortality rate is about 1 percent within ninety days of surgery, about a fifth of which is associated with unpredictable postsurgical deep vein thrombosis, familiar to long-haul airline passengers as "economy-class syndrome." But there was also a modest opportunity to do empirical research on a topic that then, as many times before and since, had become central in American policy discussions.

The George W. Bush administration, populated by officials who believed in the power of markets, embraced the idea of "consumer-directed" healthcare, and they put in place schemes that incentivized people to seek out good value. If people are spending their own money, the argument goes, the magic of the market can help make healthcare better and cheaper. Saving money was hardly my main consideration, but I was happy enough to try to be a good consumer, though not if it increased my risk. Hip and knee replacements are big business in the United States. By 2010, 2.5 million Americans had an artificial hip, ten times more than in 1980; the prevalence of artificial knees has risen even more rapidly.[1] Americans are aging so there are more worn-out joints, but many recipients are young, perhaps because of avid exercising. The increase in gym membership and the decline in church attendance might suggest that genuflection is easier on knees than are elliptical trainers. The cost of a hip replacement varies widely from place to place, but the 2022 average is estimated to be around $40,000; at about half a million replacements each year, the total spending is around $20 *billion*.[2]

To make good choices, I needed good information, and information on either quality or price was remarkably hard to come by.

Although *U.S. News and World Report* ranks hospitals along various dimensions (as it does universities and university departments), there are no such reports on orthopedic surgeons. Although individual surgeons advertise and promote themselves, and although there is lots of gossip ("He's the guy who did the Pope, but he's past it now" or "He used to have the fastest hands in the business, but now his nurse has to hold his coffee"), the medical profession has successfully resisted the publication of any official guide. It might be reasonable to suppose that just as it is possible to find out from colleagues who are the top people in, say, economics or American history, one could talk to one orthopedic surgeon about the others. But this is not true, and while I eventually found a senior night nurse who, when sufficiently bored at 2:30 a.m., was prepared to tell me which of the surgeons in my hospital knew what they were doing, that conversation took place during my recovery and was of limited use for decision making (at least until I needed another replacement or my new one failed). I also wonder which factors the nurse valued—speed, volume, personal hygiene, playing the right music in the OR, or being nice to nurses—and whether her advice would be good for *me*. After all, impressing nurses is not the surgeon's main business.

Of the several surgeons I talked to in advance, I could tell whether I liked or felt comfortable with each, but that seemed of limited relevance for an acquaintanceship during which I planned to be unconscious, and neither they nor my primary care physician nor friends and acquaintances could tell me more. Indeed, the only useful information that I had before the surgery (and the validity of which was strongly confirmed by my own experience) is the well-known and well-researched rule to go to a hospital and a surgeon that do the procedure frequently. I lined up a surgeon who had done ten thousand hip replacements and who works in a hospital that is highly ranked by *U.S. News and World Report*; on the morning that I was having my hip replaced, several dozen other hips were being replaced. (I probably should have been more concerned about how old a surgeon would have to be to have clocked ten thousand replacements, but that did not occur to me at the time.)

Information on the price of the procedure, surely, would be simpler to find. Not so. The surgeons were forthcoming with *their* fees, between $7,000 and $8,000, although from the beginning it was clear that these were somehow negotiable, if not with me then at least with my insurers. Much less straightforward was the price list for the other associated services: anesthesiologists, physical therapists, pain management specialists, and what turned out to be the largest item of all, "board and lodging" in a semiprivate room (shared with one other person). This last item, incredibly, cost more than $10,000 per day. Admittedly, my room was large, with a bath and a splendid view of one of New York's rivers, with its constantly moving shipping that provided fine entertainment, whose perceived quality was perhaps enhanced by the self-controlled morphine pump. Telephone and television were extra.

None of these prices is what it seems. Each insurance company negotiates its own prices with each of the hospitals and physicians with which it deals, and these prices are closely guarded secrets. Of course, the insurance company tells its customers what it will and will not pay for, but that contract, like the hospital's price list, is much less useful than it appears. If the provider is "in network," the company will reimburse a large fraction of the charges. For "out of network" providers, the reimbursement is a smaller fraction, although still usually 80 percent or more. So, it would seem that my personal liability was fairly limited. Again, not so, because my insurance company pays 90 percent of the "secret" price, not of the full price. So if, for example, the anesthesiologist (who seems like the wrong person to antagonize, and who, in my case, sent me a letter two days before the surgery stating that he did not accept my insurance and then, on the day of the surgery, asked me to sign an "informed consent" form for an experimental in-surgery procedure immediately before rendering me unconscious) bills me for $6,000 and the insurance company believes that the appropriate price is $4,500, the reimbursement is 90 percent of the latter, making my exposure not $600 (10 percent of $6,000) but more than three times as much, $1,950 (the uncovered $1,500 plus 10 percent of the covered amount). If there is a way of knowing these amounts in advance, I could not discover it. Nor at any stage before, during, or after my hospital stay did anyone ask me whether I wanted any of the many procedures and services that I "purchased." I felt like punching the anesthesiologist instead of signing the "consent" form. Signing in anger is the last thing I remember.

So much for informed choice based on price, or more seriously, for informed consent. My late Princeton colleague Uwe Reinhardt compared the choice situation to shopping blindfolded in a department store and then months later being presented with a bill in which some items are charged at full price and others at some fraction of full price, but with no advance knowledge of either what one has bought or what it will cost. And this is for those who are fortunate enough to have insurance. The nearly 10 percent of the American population that has no insurance is charged the much higher list or "chargemaster" price. Reinhardt gives the example of someone who spends many years paying off a debt of $30,000 for a procedure that would have cost Medicare $6,000. Hospital debt recovery procedures involve relentless persecution by collection agencies, something that is threatened on almost every one of the blizzards of bills that come to (even insured) patients for many months after the surgery. The bills are often wrong, and rectification requires much time dealing with phone robots.[3]

The favored instrument of the Bush administration for controlling the rapid increase in health spending was the health savings account. Consumers (and their employers) are permitted to make annual contributions of tax-free dollars into these accounts on the condition that they purchase a health insurance policy with high deductibles. Health expenses can be paid out of the accounts and remaining balances rolled forward, ultimately providing a retirement nest egg for people who have not been too sick. Because people are spending their own money, they have an incentive to find out about prices and to pick providers who offer the best value. The hope among the proponents of the scheme was that the very existence of the accounts would put pressure on providers to give the sort of information that would permit comparison shopping.

Certainly, that information was not available to me in 2006, and hospitals were only (reluctantly) forced to list their prices in 2021. Opponents of the scheme point out that a large fraction of health expenditures are incurred by a small fraction of people whose expenditures are so large that they could not conceivably be covered by their health savings account. So even if people were to shop around more effectively, total savings would likely be small. The accounts would also reward good health and penalize the sick. Glenn Hubbard, a distinguished economist and George W. Bush's first chairman of the Council of Economic Advisers, argued that health savings accounts "are probably the best thing to happen to healthcare in a generation" and that they would "give people a way to profit financially from their own good health."[4] Or, equivalently, to be penalized financially for their own poor health—not such an attractive way of putting it. None of the proponents explained how this was consistent with one of the administration's other avowed aims, which was to reduce the gap in health status between the rich and the poor. Indeed, health savings accounts would seem to be uniquely well designed to make the healthy wealthy and the sick poor, even if that were not otherwise the case. Even enthusiasts might balk if the scheme were presented as one in which the government gives you a large lump sum when you retire, provided you have managed to stay healthy.

Two decades later, the relentless rise in the price of health insurance has induced employers and employees to provide or to choose less expensive plans, which have high deductibles and substantial cost sharing, and so, for most people, health savings accounts no longer have the bite that they once did.[5] People are already well incentivized to keep down costs. On the other side of the ledger, it is possible that even small increases in co-payments can deter people from using cheap, life-saving drugs.[6]

And how is my hip? Just fine. And it remains so sixteen years later. Like almost everyone else who has had the procedure, I would be happy to recommend my surgeon and my hospital, for what that is worth. How about my wallet? It is about $7,000 lighter, some of which probably reflects a quality premium for the providers I selected. I would have been interested in knowing how much my insurance paid, but that was one of the secrets to which I was not privy.

There was no wait, and I could schedule the surgery at my convenience; for comparison, the Organisation for Economic Co-operation and Development reported that in 2000, the average wait in the United Kingdom for a hip replacement was 250 days, though it fell to around 100 days by 2015, slightly less than the median wait in 16 rich countries.[7] Because my employer offered a modified version of a health savings account (but with no rollover of unspent funds), some of the $7,000 came out of pretax earnings, though that was only because I knew well in advance when I was going to have the surgery. If I were poor, unemployed, or uninsured, I could have been financially ruined or, more likely, still hobbling around on an arthritic and increasingly painful hip.

When I had my other hip replaced nearly ten years later, in a different hospital close to home, I was old enough to qualify for Medicare, and the procedure was financially painless. More like what would have happened in Europe, although without the wait.

Setting the Hook

Anne Case and I spend August in southwest Montana, one of America's more remote and most beautiful states. We rent a small house on a bluff overlooking the floodplain of the Madison River, rightly famed for its abundance of wild trout, and where the loudest noise is the trumpeting of the two sandhill cranes whose annual visit is synchronized with our own. In

August 2009, both we and the cranes were mightily surprised
when a fighter jet screamed down the valley, at about eye level
with our deck, followed by a flight of three identical helicopters
that flew much more slowly. Having cleared the Madison, Grav-
elly, and Tobacco Root Ranges of mountain men and militias,
the local counterparts of the Taliban and ISIS, the Madison
River was deemed safe for President Obama's fly-fishing les-
son. As a married couple and dedicated aficionados, we had no
trouble understanding why the president should want to be a
fly-fisherman, although if we had even one helicopter at our
disposal, we should have been high in the mountains fishing
virgin lakes for giant cutthroat trout that had never seen an artificial fly. But although Obama did indeed go fishing, trout
were perhaps less on his mind than healthcare reform, courtesy
of America's wildly unequal system of political representation.

The term "inequality" is often associated with inequality of
income or of wealth—the United States ranks high in both. But
the country also excels in *political* inequality. Each of the fifty
states has two senators but wildly different populations. There
are 580,000 people in Wyoming, the least populous state, and
just over a million people in Montana, which is the ninth least
populous despite its enormous area (fourth after Alaska, California, and Texas). The four largest states by population are
California with 40 million, Texas with 30 million, Florida with
22 million, and New York with 19 million. It is perhaps disre-
spectful to put a price on a senator (though for some current
senators, the disrespect would surely be well earned), but just
for the moment, suppose each is worth $100 million to the state
that he or she represents. Each resident of Wyoming then gets
a "senator income" of $345 each year, compared with $200 in
Montana, $10.50 in New York, and only $5 in California. The 40
million people in California are extremely poor in senator

income, and the 580,000 people in Wyoming extremely rich. There are various standard measures of income inequality, and if we apply these to "senator" income, it turns out that inequality in senator income and inequality in actual income are pretty much the same.

So much for "one person, one vote." Of course, the House of Representatives is more closely related to population, and so, overall, electoral politics is less unequal.

Electoral inequality had much to do with Obama's visit to Montana, which, with less than one-third of 1 percent of the U.S. population, has 2 percent of the votes in the Senate and is thus overrepresented by a factor of six. Alaska and Wyoming would have done even better in their Senate shares—and the fly-fishing is outstandingly good in both—but neither would have been so welcoming to the president (think Sarah Palin and Dick Cheney). More importantly, the senior senator for Montana in 2009 was Max Baucus, a Democrat who chaired the Senate Finance Committee and was a member of the "gang of six" senators who had emerged as the likely "deciders" on healthcare reform. These senators, three Republicans and three Democrats, all declared moderates, were members of the Senate Finance Committee. Between them, they represented 2.8 percent of the American population, and a much smaller percentage of African Americans and Hispanics.

The way that healthcare reform was pursued, leading to what eventually became Obamacare, owed much to the failure of the earlier attempt by the Clintons. Academics and healthcare experts—including several economists—were well represented on Hillary Clinton's task force, which presented a plan to a Congress that it had had little role in shaping and less interest in passing. This time around, the White House presented only loose guidelines and let the politicians work it out for themselves.

Because financing reform is the hardest issue, and because the Senate is historically the place where reform is made or unmade, the Senate Finance Committee was key. All this certainly contributed to something being accomplished, but it also minimized the role of the extensive research on healthcare reform by academics and policy analysts over the long years in the desert of no reform. Of course, the many economists in DC who were working for the administration were involved in the negotiations behind the scenes.

As to Obamacare, the dominant role of the Senate meant that the negotiations were wide open to the lobbyists from the hospitals, doctors, health insurance companies, pharmaceutical companies, and device manufacturers. With such well-funded feeders in attendance, there was no chance of effective cost control. Neither a single-payer system nor even a system with a public option was allowed to be discussed, though either one would have had some chance of controlling costs, if only through eliminating most of the current administrative expenses of the insurance companies. According to the Center for Responsive Politics, Baucus had received a cumulative $3.1 million since 1989 from health groups opposed to the public option,[8] although he is certainly not the only senator to be so funded, and both Obama and McCain, the presidential candidates in 2008, accepted much more. Polls also show that Montana's democrats are broadly in favor of public healthcare.

The triumph of Obamacare was that it brought coverage to millions of previously uninsured people. Its tragedy was that all the providers and insurers had to be bought off, and so it did nothing to control the outrageous costs that are crippling the American economy.

Also not discussed was the scheme developed by Vic Fuchs, America's most prominent health economist. The plan involved giving people vouchers that could be spent on care, something that would have broken the stranglehold of employer-provided care and provided incentives for cost control. And although proposals to end tax breaks for employer-provided healthcare have been debated, they had little chance of implementation in a reform designed by politicians, whose constituents believe that employer-provided healthcare is a free good, even in the face of evidence that healthcare costs have been a major limitation on the growth in median wages. It is ironic that the Fuchs plan was developed jointly with Zeke Emanuel, an oncologist and bioethicist, with doctorates in both medicine and philosophy, who was uniquely well placed to influence the reform. At the time he was special advisor for health policy to Peter Orzag, director of the administration's Office of Management and Budget, and is a brother of President Obama's then chief of staff, Rahm Emanuel, two of the central players in the negotiations. (According to the *New York Times*, Rahm Emanuel also paid a fly-fishing visit to Montana, but presumably without the fighter jet or the helicopters.)

And what of the president's fishing trip? The weather was bad, so he had to abandon the Madison River and go instead to the East Gallatin, a lesser but more sheltered stream. His guide for the afternoon, Dan Vermillion of the Sweetwater Fly Shop in Livingston, reported that Obama, a talented neophyte who made contact with several fish, brought none to the net. According to Vermillion, "You could say he pardoned all the fish but, honestly, Obama couldn't set the hook."[9] On health reform he did better, landing a very large fish that, by providing subsidies, has provided affordable health insurance to around 20 million Americans. Still, nearly 9 percent of Americans had no insurance at any point in 2020, including during the pandemic. As for cost control, the fish remains an enormously swollen creature that is more likely to eat the population than to nourish it.

Given the history, Obama's achievement was real. But the odds remain stacked against taming the monstrous fish that, even before the pandemic, was eating nearly one dollar in five and depriving Americans of so much else that they need. Reform will have to battle America's deep political and financial inequality, in which so many people count for so little while so few count for so much, and where, relative to the payoffs, amazingly few dollars from the industry can buy them so much influence in a Congress that is addicted to money.

Adverse Selection, the Mandate, and Broccoli

Downton Abbey, the interminable British soap opera, was broadcast in the United States on public television and is the network's all-time greatest hit. For viewers in the New York area, the showing was preceded by a sixty-second commercial on behalf of New York (previously Columbia) Presbyterian hospital. One advertisement for the hospital featured the boxer Daniel Jacobs, a rising star in 2011 when he was brought down by, in his own words, a "massive tumor that had wrapped itself around my spine." But his doctor at NY Presbyterian "aced it; they resurrected me and resurrected my career," and so "on August 9th, 2014, I became the WBA middleweight champion of the world."

The audience for public television in New York is well heeled (the next ad was for Viking River Cruises) but likely contains few professional boxers, fewer still who have a cancer wrapped around their spine and who are free to choose their healthcare in the same way as they choose between Budapest and Bangkok for their Viking River cruise. The same can be said for the audience for the ad on the cover of the program for a Metropolitan

Opera run of *Don Giovanni*, featuring a young woman "told by doctors" that amputation of her legs was the best treatment but who, thanks to the same hospital, now needs braces only for her teeth. Broadcasts of New York Yankees baseball in 2022 were sponsored by Montefiore, a competitor of NY Presbyterian, whose ads, set among the mesas of the southwest, feature Barbara Higgins, who gave birth at age fifty-seven. Most baseball fans are male.

Yet the hospital ads are indeed aimed at consumers, who are being implicitly incited to pressure their employers and the insurance companies that organize their healthcare to provide plans that cover treatment at NY Presbyterian, or Montefiore as the case may be. When insurance companies negotiate secret discounts from chargemaster hospital prices, they are influenced by pressure from employers and employees who want to be eligible for the miracles that they see in the commercials. The purpose of the ads is to keep the discounts smaller than those of its competitors, an area in which NY Presbyterian has reputedly been very successful, as is suggested by the later imitation by Montefiore. The story of *Downton Abbey* is set in a time when falling land rents were threatening the incomes of the landholding British aristocracy. On American television, the ads were also helping change fortunes, now by working to recruit an audience to help raise prices for U.S. healthcare, prices that are creating great wealth among successful hospital entrepreneurs, including doctors turned CEOs. They have turned from repairing bodies to destroying wallets, from the pursuit of health to the pursuit of wealth.

Market fundamentalists attribute the high prices of healthcare to the fact that the market for healthcare is undermined by moral hazard, by the overuse, overprovision, and lack of price discipline that comes with insurance, or at least with too much insurance. They believe that if consumers bore all or at least a larger direct share of their healthcare costs—a favorite phrase is "if they had more skin in the game"—market forces would bring down the cost of MRI machines, proton-beam scanners, and hip replacements, just as they have brought down the cost of the flat screen televisions on which they enjoy *Downton Abbey*. Everyone would then be able to afford cheap, high-quality healthcare, just as everyone owns a smartphone and a flat screen television, and insurance would cover only catastrophically expensive events. Such arguments have a germ of truth, and the scandal of high-cost healthcare is clearly exacerbated by insurance, as well as by the implacable opposition of providers, device manufacturers, and the pharmaceutical industry (as well as the market fundamentalists) to the kind of cost-benefit evaluation of medicines, procedures, and machines that is done in other countries—for example, by the National Institute of Health and Care Excellence in the UK.

Ever since the publication of a famous paper by Arrow in 1963,[10] economists have been aware that health insurance markets are dogged by adverse selection, that healthy people are unwilling to participate because their premiums are high relative to what they expect to spend, leaving only the sick as participants, whose expenses are very large, so that, in the end, the cost of insurance can rise to prohibitive levels. This is the infamous "death spiral" in which premiums spiral up and coverage spirals down. We need to have everyone in the scheme, sick and healthy alike, or it will self-destruct. Yet, it has been hard to explain that idea to the public. Politicians of the right, who understand about original sin, appreciate moral hazard, that people faced with subsidized prices will overuse healthcare. But they are (perhaps willfully) blind to adverse selection, that if market prices are high, only those who anticipate high health expenditures—those with pre-existing conditions—will use the market. To them, markets are perfect and it is people who are imperfect. During the primaries for the 2008 election, Hillary Clinton favored a "mandate" that would require people to have insurance, a proposal that Barack Obama denounced as unnecessary and (presumably) unlikely to appeal to voters. But the Congressional Budget Office had predicted that, without it, adverse selection would make the premiums higher.

After Obama won the primary and the election, his administration passed the Affordable Care Act, without a single Republican vote, but with the mandate. But cures for adverse selection are not so easily sold. The first potentially crippling challenge to the whole of Obamacare focused on the mandate and argued that it was unconstitutional for the federal government to require anyone to buy anything; Supreme Court Justice Antonin Scalia asked if the state could force people to buy broccoli. (Perhaps he thought you didn't need health insurance if you ate enough broccoli?)

The Supreme Court decided in June 2012—on the surprise vote by Chief Justice John Roberts—that the mandate was not in fact a mandate, which five of the nine justices would have ruled unconstitutional, but a perfectly constitutional tax, something that the Obama administration had consistently denied, if only because it would have had consequences for the evaluation of the law and the likelihood of its passage. Chief Justice Roberts was excoriated by conservatives for not killing Obamacare when he had the chance. He joked afterward that his end-of-term preplanned trip to teach on the island of Malta, "an impregnable island fortress . . . seemed like a good idea."[11]

When the distinguished MIT economist Jonathan Gruber, who had advised on the law but was not one of its central architects, said that the law was deliberately obscure, that its lack of transparency was a political advantage that, given "the stupidity of the American voter," was critical to its passage, he was only expressing something that many economists have often thought. Unfortunately, he was caught on video.[12] That summer, in Montana, a fishing guide expressed his hope that, although we were economists, we were not friends of Gruber.

Market fundamentalists believe that people should be free to choose to be uninsured or to buy any insurance that they like, including deceptive policies that are attractive only because most healthy people have no idea what hospitals will charge them if they fall ill. These policies were outlawed under Obamacare, and so some people had to give up insurance that they were happy with, at least as long as they did not have the ill fortune to try to use it. This interference with freedom of choice has been much criticized on the right and was made worse by Obama's false claim that no one would have to give up their existing insurance. Yet the market fundamentalists cannot admit that markets can fail. But they dare not give up the requirement (popular among both consumers and the industry) that prevents insurance companies from discriminating against preexisting conditions. Economists are tortured by their inability to demonstrate how insurance works and find it hard to explain its flaws in a way that can make them widely and intuitively understood. Market-fundamentalist politicians are trapped between, on the one hand, their own beliefs that getting the government out of healthcare and healthcare regulation will bring down prices, increase access, and give people freedom to choose, and on the other, the demands of both the industry and consumers that no one be denied insurance because of preexisting conditions.

At the time of writing (2023), the mandate still exists—people are required to have health insurance—but the penalty has been reduced to zero since 2018, though some states have instituted mandates with penalties. Yet there is no sign of the death spiral or of large increases in premiums, at least up to the pandemic. Perhaps it takes time for people to adjust their behavior, or perhaps they take seriously the requirement to have insurance, even without a penalty. Adverse selection is real enough and has destroyed other insurance schemes, so it would be unwise to pretend it does not exist. And in the meantime, no one is being forced to buy broccoli.

"Madmen in Authority"

The Trump administration, blessed with Republican majorities in the House and Senate, took up healthcare reform in 2017 as its first major legislative task. Republicans had wanted to repeal Obamacare ever since it was passed against their united opposition, and they campaigned on repealing it in 2016. As the debate progressed, news came of the death of Kenneth Arrow, at the age of ninety-five, who had written wisely and insightfully about healthcare and what would happen if societies tried to use markets to provide it.

John Maynard Keynes's "madmen in authority" could hardly be bettered as a description of Washington during the Trump administration. Healthcare often involves great uncertainty, and patients rely on physicians who know much more than they do. They cannot rely on repeat purchases to discover what works for them. People need disinterested advice, not the advice of providers whose incomes depend on what is decided. As experience around the world has shown, and as Arrow anticipated, there is no ideal delivery system for healthcare, though it is only in the United States that policy has consistently tried to prove that Arrow was wrong about

markets, and Trump and the Republican Congress were determined to try again.

Early in the Trump administration, economists were largely
excluded from positions of authority. The Council of Economic
Advisers was demoted from cabinet status and there was a long
delay in appointing a chairman. The health reformers, led by
Republican House leader Paul Ryan, were driven in part by
their unshakable political commitment to the repeal of Obamacare, which by then had insured an additional 16 million
people. But they also shared a genuine intellectual belief that
healthcare would be better with more market and less government; Ryan often noted his intellectual indebtedness to Ayn
Rand and said that it was her *Atlas Shrugged* that got him interested in economics. Ayn Rand, not Ken Arrow, is the "defunct
scribbler" to whom these politicians were slaves. Rand is not
part of the canon of economics, and I doubt that her books appear on many economics reading lists. Yet, as one of her biog-
raphers argues, "Rand's approach to freedom and capitalism has
helped to fuel contemporary enthusiasm for free markets and
social indifference to widespread inequality."[13] Rand, who glo-
rified greed, despised both losers and altruism, and if Arrow's
ideas are the first that should be consulted in constructing a
socially desirable healthcare system, Rand's are surely the last.

Trump himself displayed an unsurprising ignorance. His
response—"Nobody knew health care could be so complicated"—
fit someone who promised that he would give everyone higher-
quality coverage at lower cost. The American public has long
greatly disliked and distrusted their healthcare system, providing
fertile ground for those who would blame Obamacare. There
is a long-standing unwillingness among the white population
to pay for healthcare for African Americans, an unwillingness that is exploited by unscrupulous politicians. Of course,

because people don't know when they will need medical care, or what kind they will need, it is unclear what people really want or would pay for. When asked at the time, 46 percent of Americans were opposed to Obamacare, while only 26 percent were opposed to the Affordable Care Act, which is its official title.[14]

There are arguments for the free market case. If there were no subsidies and no government programs, we would benefit from the fierce and effective cost control that competitive markets yield for other technologically complicated commodities, like TVs or phones. The absence of government might also help eliminate the gigantically expensive industries that live off and lobby for government favors and government programs. Yet pervasive insurance would still stand in the way of cost control—spending other people's money removes the brakes on both patients and providers—and nonmandated insurance tends to destroy itself over time as the low-cost healthy exit the scheme and the high-cost sick remain. Some have even proposed banning insurance, except for catastrophically expensive treatment, though such a policy would hardly appeal to those who believe in the magic of markets. Arrow's truth—that markets are incapable of delivering healthcare in a socially acceptable way—lurks around every corner.

Republicans promised choice, arguing that people should be able to choose the healthcare plans that they want and not have the government interfere. Ryan talked about giving people "access to quality, affordable health care," meaning that they can purchase it; in that sense, I have access to a private jet or, like Jeff Bezos, Elon Musk, or Richard Branson, a spaceship. Jason Chaffetz, then chairman of the House Oversight Committee, noted that "Americans have choices . . . and so, maybe rather than getting that new iPhone that they just love . . . maybe they should invest in their own health care. They've got to make those decisions themselves."[15] In this light, healthcare is a commodity like any other—but with an annual cost about twenty times that of an iPhone—and if people choose not to purchase it, they should be free to do so. Choice is unproblematic, and little recognition is given to the possibility that people might choose poorly or not have the information to choose well. Nor is there any concession to the idea that we might have some collective responsibility to help those of us who are in distress.

Trump's administration wanted to allow the deceptively attractive insurance policies that Obamacare had banned. Presumably, well-informed consumers will recognize and drive out such policies. Permitting these schemes—sold as "deregulation"—is a sop to the insurers or advisers who are enriched by the deception. Not everyone agrees, and indeed, much of the Chicago economics of George Stigler, Ronald Coase, and Milton Friedman can be thought of as arguments that the problems that bothered Arrow are either not so bad or have cures that are worse than the disease. As in that literature, Trump's reformers said little about income distribution and who does and does not have the ability to pay.

Another great American health economist, Victor Fuchs, who played a role in urging Arrow to write the 1963 paper, and who is happily (and productively) still with us at the age of ninety-eight, has long noted that there are good reasons why different countries should have different healthcare systems. Americans are less egalitarian than Europeans and are much less trusting of government. So perhaps the American healthcare system ought to be more market based. Yet Fuchs also believes that, at an *excess* price of around a trillion dollars a year, we are paying far too much for our tastes. Life expectancy in the United

States is among the lowest in all rich countries, and even before the pandemic, it was *falling*, uniquely so among comparably rich countries. Working-class people are dying from an epidemic of suicides, drug addiction, and alcoholism and are facing rising death rates from heart disease. The mixed system of government and private provision has generated a machine that is spectacularly well designed for enriching a few under the protection of politicians who enable them, but appallingly designed for improving or even maintaining health. And because so many Americans have health insurance "provided" by their employers, and believe it to be free to them, they do not see how the cost of healthcare is holding down their wages or destroying working-class jobs.

At the end of his paper, Arrow writes, "It is the general social consensus, clearly, that the *laissez-faire* solution for medicine is intolerable."[16] This is perhaps one of the few sentences in the paper that has *not* stood the test of time, though there is nothing at all wrong with it.

Crime, Punishment, and Tobacco

As I write, in late 2022, there is an ongoing legal battle over the penalty that the Sackler family should pay for their misleading marketing of Purdue Pharmaceutical's blockbuster painkiller, OxyContin, which has been directly or indirectly responsible for the addiction and deaths of hundreds of thousands of people. As of February 2022, the Sacklers offered to pay $6 billion, which is likely less than half of the family's profits. But we have been here before, or something very like it. Settlement of opioid lawsuits echoes tobacco manufacturers' settling of lawsuits with the states in November 1998. The manufacturers agreed to a stream of future payments totaling more than $200 billion to forty-six states, the other four states having received separate, earlier settlements.

As far as I could judge, there was widespread support for the tobacco settlement. Noneconomist friends argue that the manufacturers behaved in a way that merits severe punishment, and think that, if anything, they got off easily. This view is typically not much affected by pointing out that the settlements are not coming out of the pockets of tobacco executives or even in large part from their shareholders, but from future smokers who will pay higher prices. The general view is that smokers too deserve what they get and indeed should be grateful for the incentive to quit that is provided by the settlement-induced increase of about forty-five cents a pack.

Tobacco consumers have been demonized along with tobacco manufacturers (an odd contrast with today's moves toward the legalization of marijuana, an arguably more dangerous substance[17]). Some state governments also seemed happy to punish smokers; for example, in March 2000 the State of New York increased its own tax on cigarettes by an additional 55 cents, raising the current price of a pack to nearly $4. (By 2022, the tax had risen to $4.35 and the pack price to $12.85; prices in general increased by about 60 percent from 2000 to 2022.) Several economists have noted that the tobacco settlement was really a deal among the government, the tobacco companies, antitobacco campaigners, and (especially) lawyers *at the expense of* those who were hurt, the tobacco consumers. If so, and depending on how the states spend their receipts, the settlements represent an extraordinarily *regressive* transfer, from smokers, a group of taxpayers who are poorer and less well educated than the population at large, to lawyers and taxpayers in general. Yet one of the most remarkable features of the settlement was that it was supported by those who were opposed to taxes (it's not a tax but a penalty) as well as those who were opposed to taxing the poor (in this case, it's for their own good).

The National Governors Association provided details on how states planned to spend the money. Almost all states included a substantial health component (one of the stated goals of the settlement), sometimes aimed at reducing tobacco consumption, but often less specific—for example, the provision of health insurance coverage for children or prescription drug benefits for the elderly. The tobacco-growing states of Indiana, Maryland, North and South Carolina, Virginia, and West Virginia planned to use much of their money to compensate tobacco farmers. Others were more imaginative: Georgia planned to fund rural economic development, Michigan and Nevada planned to fund college scholarship programs, North Dakota planned to spend 45 percent of its funds on its water needs, and South Dakota's settlement was planned to help fund the conversion of South Dakota Public Television to digital broadcast technology. In many states, there are large provisions for education (teachers' salaries), while in others the money finds its way into the "budget stabilization fund" or general reserves or even, in the case of Connecticut, "tax relief to towns," presumably a reduction in property taxes. There is no evidence that any state has considered that, while it might be a good idea to increase the price of tobacco to discourage its use, some part of the receipts might be used to offset the decline in smokers' real incomes or to provide alternatives to smoking.

A group of health economists, including David Cutler and Joe Newhouse of Harvard and Jonathan Gruber of MIT (yes, the same), argued that the public perception is right, that the states' tobacco settlement is a good idea, even for smokers, because the benefits to smokers far outweigh the costs to them.[18] Although their calculations are complex, the main point is that, at $150,000 per year of life saved, the increase in price makes smokers better off, albeit against their will. The authors recognize and defend their rejection of the idea that people know what is best for them, and dismiss the idea that smokers are making rational choices for themselves. Even if it is true that people don't always know what is best for them, there is a long step from that to ceding their personal autonomy to a bunch of Harvard and MIT economists.

Some would argue that this represents a good case of economists belatedly recognizing that there is more merit in lay (not to mention psychologists') views than is traditionally recognized by the profession. Yet noneconomists are not very likely to approve of the way that lives are valued. The calculation involves the idea that people make rational choices between activities with different risks, exactly the sort of choice that is assumed *not* to apply to people's choices about tobacco. There is also the fearless use of the monetary arithmetic that calculates the improvement in economic efficiency by subtracting the value of deaths avoided from the amount paid in taxes.

In all this debate, only the tobacco lobby seems interested in defending smokers, a defense that is properly discounted. Yet surely there is much to be said for economists' once-standard belief: that people know what is good for them, that money and mortality are not the *only* determinants of welfare, and that smoking brings benefits to many. For people who have few other opportunities for enjoyment, a cigarette break can be a moment of pleasure in a difficult day. And there is little evidence that people are unaware of the risks. We are telling people no, stop it, though we will let you continue if you contribute to lowering our property taxes. If you live in the United States, if you are poor, poorly educated, and enjoy smoking, you must pay better-educated and more fortunate people for the privilege and be grateful to boot. Even if smokers are indeed making poor choices, paternalism is an assault on freedom that is deeply troubling.

I do not deny the existence of addiction or the difficulties of treating it. Some smokers may indeed welcome a price increase as an aid to quitting. Yet price increases do nothing to help those who cannot or do not quit, and revenue should fund treatment services, not reductions in property taxes. It would be good to believe that the eventual settlement of the opioid lawsuits will do better.

CHAPTER 3

POVERTY AT HOME AND POVERTY ABROAD

FOREIGN AID BEGAN after World War 2 and has evolved from its origins as help for the postwar reconstruction of European countries to today's focus on improving health and eliminating poverty around the globe. In the United States, it was often seen as useful in the fight against communism. As its purposes have changed, and after the fall of the Soviet Union, it has become more controversial, both in public debate and among economists. Most recently, the key issue is climate change, and how to integrate aid and climate policies.

In the beginning was the Marshall Plan in 1948, by which the United States gave around 5 percent of its national income over four years to aid in the postwar reconstruction of Europe, including West Germany, Britain, and France. A year later, President Truman proposed a continuing program of aid with the goals of "creating markets for the United States by reducing poverty and increasing production in developing countries" and of "diminishing the threat of communism by helping countries prosper under capitalism."[1] President Kennedy established the United States Agency for International Development

(USAID), which consolidated the Truman programs. Kennedy emphasized the inequality between the United States and the poor countries of the world, noting "our economic obligations as the wealthiest people in a world of largely poor people."[2] Today, USAID is an international humanitarian and develop- ment agency that focuses on poverty reduction, democracy, health, and development. Its current budget is less than 1 percent of total government spending, and about a quarter of that as a share of national income.

The World Bank is a multilateral agency owned and oper- ated by many countries. Founded in 1944, it originally made loans for reconstruction, but over time it has adopted an anti- poverty agenda. In the atrium of its headquarters in Washing- ton, DC, there is a large carving with the words, "Our dream is a world free of poverty." By tradition, the U.S. government ap- points the president of the World Bank and is its largest share- holder, with a little less than a quarter of the shares. The World Bank is therefore not an agency of the U.S. government, though it is difficult for the Bank to make major decisions without U.S. approval. China, whose total economy is larger than that of the United States once we adjust (as we should) for lower prices in China, has only around a quarter of the shares that the United States has.

The way that the Bank thinks about its mission is much in- fluenced by current views in Washington. In the early years, the Bank shared with many rich and poor countries an enthusiasm for government-formulated national plans. By the Reagan years, the Bank had moved toward the view that markets can work miracles if they are given a chance. More recently, its views have been and are influenced by the latest flavor of the month in the international development community, especially by the views of nongovernmental aid organizations, whether it is building

infrastructure, getting kids into school, getting prices right, fo-
cusing on poverty, improving governance, building equal
rights for women, or prioritizing health. The Bank, by its char-
ter, is prohibited from interfering in politics, even though, as
has eventually and belatedly become clear, politics is key. Development cannot take place without a contract between the
governed and the government, whereby the former pays taxes
and the latter delivers services. Although outside parties can
do little to help create or maintain such contracts, it is all too
easy for them to undermine them or prevent them from ever
coming into being.

There are now many other governmental and nongovernmental institutions that give development or humanitarian aid
both in the United States and abroad. Philanthropies, particularly the Bill and Melinda Gates Foundation, have come to play
a large role. The Gates Foundation declares that it is "guided by
the belief that every life has equal value," and says that "in developing countries, it focuses on improving people's health, and
giving them a chance to lift themselves out of hunger and extreme poverty."[3] In the United States, it focuses on education.

When asked in polls, large fractions of Americans say *less*
should be spent on foreign aid, though when asked, they grossly
overstate what is being spent. They are clearly not very well
informed about the topic, and the suggestion to cut is perhaps
no more than a preference for putting American interests ahead
of those of foreigners.

Economists have been much involved in thinking about international development and global poverty. The field of development economics grew up alongside postwar aid flows and
was boosted by the wave of newly independent countries
around the world, many of which were interested in advice

about postcolonial economic strategies. Many of today's senior economists spent time in those countries as advisers. The World Bank has a chief economist, a position that has been filled by many distinguished academics, including Nobel laureates Joe Stiglitz and Paul Romer, as well as by Larry Summers, who was later secretary of the Treasury. The U.S. Treasury has an undersecretary for international affairs, who oversees the administration's interests at the Bank and the International Monetary Fund (IMF), and that position too has been held by distinguished economists.

The first section in this chapter discusses how we should think about poverty in Africa, Asia, or elsewhere in the light of needs at home. This is not something I know the answer to, although I once thought that I did. It is a good topic to start with, because there is disagreement over the practical and philosophical issues, and because it lays a foundation for what we might do. My second topic takes us back to the early years of the first George W. Bush administration and to the ferment of views about aid coming from the administration and from competing voices in academia. The third section is about something that is often forgotten—it is not easy to help people in other countries from outside of those countries. It is not as simple as "just give them money" makes it sound. Finally, I revisit the question of poverty at home and poverty abroad, recounting a controversy during the Trump administration about whether anyone in America is as poor as poor people in Africa and Asia. Here again, measurement is key. Because the official poverty measurement system in the United States is flawed, and because politics gets in the way of repairs, the field is left open for charlatans and political hacks to claim legitimacy for their own numbers.

Rethinking Robin Hood

How should we think about poverty and deprivation at home when there is so much poverty and deprivation elsewhere in the world? Or vice versa. One guide is to think about for whom a little extra would do the greatest good, where the "whom" covers everyone in the world, no matter where or in what countries they live, and to recognize that those who are already better off have less urgent claims. This is a "cosmopolitan" view because the whole world is included. It is also a "prioritarian" view because it gives higher priority to those with less.[4] It is possible to be prioritarian without being cosmopolitan, giving priority to the worse off among our fellow citizens, and paying less or even no attention to those living in other countries. Or we could be cosmopolitan, ignoring country boundaries as being morally irrelevant, but reject prioritarianism in favor of some other ethical system.

Many ethicists are egalitarians, who believe that less inequality is better. Cosmopolitan egalitarians emphasize the moral importance of reducing extreme poverty. The great philosopher John Rawls argued that justice requires that political and economic arrangements be judged by their effects on the worst off, a strong version of prioritarianism. Rawls himself rejected the idea that the same criterion be applied globally, though other philosophers have done so, and argued that global justice does indeed require the elimination of the worst of global poverty.[5]

Cosmopolitan prioritarianism has worked well for many of us as a guide to our own thinking, or to our charitable donations, and it dominates the thinking of international aid organizations, such as the World Bank or USAID. Even so, I have come to believe that it needs to be seriously rethought for both ethical and practical reasons.

According to the World Bank's global count, the number of people living in extreme poverty has fallen by half in the last forty years, from over two billion to 650 million on the eve of the pandemic.[6] None of these millions live in the United States, a "fact" that has been challenged and that I will return to in the last section of this chapter. The reduction in extreme poverty happened despite world population growth and despite the long-term slowing of global economic growth, especially after the Financial Crisis in 2008. Yet the globalization that has helped so many poor people—in China, in India, or in Bangladesh—has also brought harm to some in rich countries, including the United States and Europe. For those of us who worried about global poverty and took a cosmopolitan and prioritarian perspective, these costs seemed acceptable because those who were losing were already so much wealthier (and healthier) than those who were gaining.

The cosmopolitan perspective led many (including me) to switch their charitable giving from home to abroad. A dollar sent to a poor country does more good because the recipients' needs are so much greater, and because the magic of the lower price level in poor countries doubles or triples the value of money on arrival at its destination. As any traveler will confirm, a dollar converted to rupees (pesos) buys more food or lodging in India (Mexico) than can be bought for a dollar at home. Giving at home, by contrast, is more expensive and, because it goes to those who are already relatively well off, does less good.

The worm that gnaws within this apple is our own shaky standing when we make these judgments. People like me are among the greatest beneficiaries of the globalized world, selling our services in markets that are larger and richer than anything our parents could have dreamed of. Most obviously, I was free to uproot myself from England and move to New Jersey. I am not exactly an impartial spectator. That people like me have benefited so much should at least alert us to the possibility that others might see it differently; globalization might seem less splendid to those who are not doing quite so well from it. And while I was once poor by my current standard of living, and poor enough to use much of my energy worrying about money, I was never close to the poverty that afflicts the poorest people in the world.

There are other troublesome facts. Less well-educated Americans have seen little or no improvement in their material circumstances for more than fifty years. For men without a four-year college degree, median real wages have trended downward since 1970. But are they not still much better off than the Asians working in the factories in Hanoi, Dhaka, Shenzhen, or Tijuana—factories that used to be in Ohio or Indiana? Most undoubtedly are, at least judged by material circumstances. But the bottom end of the American labor market is a brutal environment for many, and there are several million Americans— Black, white, and Hispanic—who live in households with per capita income of a few dollars a day and whose living standards are arguably as bad as or worse than those that the World Bank demarcates as destitute in India or Ethiopia.[7] The struggle to find shelter at low-income levels is much more difficult in the United States than in warmer places like India or Ethiopia. Beyond material living levels, the destruction of manufacturing employment in the United States has destroyed social and family life for many, making their poverty broader than material poverty.

America's prided equality of opportunity is less real than it used to be, if indeed it ever was real. Towns and cities that have lost their factories to globalization have also lost their taxes and find it hard to maintain the schools that are the escape routes for the next generation. It is much harder than it once was for people to move to more successful places because housing costs have risen greatly in the places that are flourishing. Elite schools court the elite to cover their costs, and court minorities to redress centuries of deprivation. All of this is worthy, yet it would be strange if there were not resentment among the white working class whose kids find no place in this new order.

Worse still is the rising tide of deaths of despair among Americans without a college degree—from suicide, alcohol abuse, and especially accidental overdoses of legal (prescription) and illegal drugs.[8] Overall death rates in the United States have been rising, and, even before the pandemic, adult life expectancy has fallen for ten years for those without a four-year college degree. We can legitimately argue about the measurement of material living standards, whether all sources of income are included in the data, how much the poorest spend, whether inflation is overstated and the rise in living standards understated, and whether schools are really that bad everywhere. But American deaths are hard to explain away—particularly the rising tide of suicides at a time when suicide rates are falling around the world.

There are also serious ethical objections to treating fellow citizens in the same way as we treat citizens of the world at large. Whether you chose to be an American or not, citizenship comes with a set of rights and responsibilities that we do not share with others in other countries. We must pay taxes and we are entitled to benefits. We can think about this as a mutual insurance scheme. If we are attacked from outside, we have a mutual responsibility to defend each other, a responsibility that, at least in recent years, has been disproportionately borne by those Americans who have benefited the least from globalization. Although most officers in the military have college degrees, that is true of few enlisted men and women.[9] National insurance arrangements—like Social Security or Medicare—can be thought of as a promise that we will not tolerate certain kinds of health or financial poverty for (at least some of) our fellow citizens.

None of this contradicts a genuine cosmopolitan perspective, in which we recognize obligations to everyone, but the obligations at home are different from those abroad.[10] But we cannot get the balance right if we count only material living standards, rank everyone in the world from high to low, and prioritize the latter. Doing so misses not only other components of wellbeing but also the rights and responsibilities that are part of being a citizen of one country and not another.

Many Americans, of course, were never cosmopolitans, and perhaps cosmopolitans who give priority to the materially poor are overrepresented among the elites, particularly academic elites or people who work in cosmopolitan organizations like the World Bank or the United Nations. If so, we need to better reconnect with the broader population in which we live and which supports us through their taxes, their work, and their willingness to serve.

Even if you are an unrepentant cosmopolitan prioritarian in theory, you cannot avoid the practical issues. Whatever your personal ethical system, there is no world government that could enforce a global prioritarian system; institutions such as the United Nations or the World Bank are much too weak to do so. If you try to help your fellow citizens at home, you are often close enough to see and judge the results, and if those you are helping don't like it, there is always the possibility of democratic feedback. Not so for aid spending in Chad or Sierra Leone, where remote donors cannot see what their aid is doing, so that cash spent is often the only measure of success. Failure is not a possibility as seen by the donors, even when awful things are happening to the recipients. "We" have no business telling "them" what they need in the absence of effective feedback.

Globalization has clearly benefited millions in India, Bangladesh, China, and other countries, and prioritarians can rejoice in that achievement, even if some of the benefits came at the expense of American workers. But the beneficiaries do not vote in American elections, while American workers do. National elections are not constructed to support global prioritarianism. And a populist administration, if one were ever elected, would have little or no interest in bettering the lives of the global poor. There is then a risk that successful global prioritarianism will destroy itself. For those who believe we owe something to the global poor, and I include myself, we need to do a better job of looking out for the interests of our fellow citizens before those wearing MAGA hats come for us with pitchforks.

Economists and Policymakers on Aid and Development

Paul H. O'Neill was secretary of the Treasury in 2001 and 2002 during the first George W. Bush administration. (This is not the same Paul O'Neill who was once an outstanding right fielder for the New York Yankees baseball team and is now a much-loved television commentator.) Paul H.'s career spanned both public and private sectors; he was CEO of Alcoa before going to the Treasury. He earned a BA from Fresno State in California, and he worked his way up within the government from a computer analyst to deputy director of the Office of Management and Budget in the mid-1970s. He was an economic conservative, with a strong belief in markets and in the ability of corporate America to solve almost any problem. He combined this with a concern for the poor, and especially for the health of

the poor. He was widely respected (though not by the hard-
liners in the Bush administration) for his attention to and success
in improving occupational health among workers at Alcoa, as
well as for health-related work in the community. His African
tour with Bono, the lead singer of U2 and aid activist, was not
out of character for him, though certainly unusual for a secretary
of the Treasury. O'Neill was also a man of impeccable manners,
courteous to a fault, and possessed of real intellectual curiosity;
he was a reader and liked to share, argue, and debate his views.

O'Neill came to Treasury determined to take a firm conservative line. There were to be no more bailouts of countries with
financial crises; the market was to be allowed to do its work.
International targets for development assistance in terms of
shares of GDP were anathema; instead, projects were to be
judged strictly by results and loans were to be replaced by grants
(because many were loans in name only given that they were
constantly rolled over). But while Treasury was still maintaining
its stance against increasing aid, the White House took a different line and announced substantial increases in funding for aid.
More battered still was O'Neill's policy on bailouts. When Brazil
encountered difficulties, O'Neill commented that the United
States was not going to lend money that would end up in Swiss
bank accounts. Not only did the expression of this view make
the crisis worse, but it made American assistance inevitable, if it
had not already been so. The Swiss bank is more than a sick joke. A
World Bank study in 2020 found that aid disbursements by the
Bank were associated with accumulations by elites in offshore
accounts, with around 10 percent siphoned off on average.[11]
The Bank initially refused to publish the results, and its then chief
economist, Pinelopi Goldberg, resigned and returned to Yale.

Two important books on globalization and development
were published by economists while O'Neill was at Treasury.

William Easterly's marvelous book, *The Elusive Quest for Growth: Economists' Adventures and Misadventures in the Tropics*, is an eminently readable (and often very funny) account of development failure interspersed with vivid and heartrending vignettes of poverty around the world.[12] The book is stronger on its analysis of what has not worked than in its prescriptions for what should be done ("incentives matter"), though, as I argue below, there is a strong case that "nothing" is indeed the right answer. Easterly also tries to explain to lay readers how economists solve causality puzzles using what they call "instruments." Indeed, he is so clear—and so funny—that alert readers are likely to learn (correctly) that such methods, much beloved by economists, are effective only as a smokescreen for statements of the form "You are not smart or well-trained enough to understand, so just trust me, I'm a scientist." Easterly was for many years leader of the macroeconomics group at the World Bank, but he later moved to New York University, supposedly because of the book. Perhaps not surprisingly, Easterly's documentation of the failures of development assistance proved irresistible to Paul O'Neill, who repeatedly used the book to justify his position against aid. "Have you read Bill Easterly's book?"

Another book in 2002 was Joe Stiglitz's diatribe against the IMF, with the excellent Freudian title, *Globalization and Its Discontents*.[13] Stiglitz's book was not widely admired by the economics profession at the time, though many of its arguments seem prescient now, particularly about the perils of unfettered capital movements and the benefits of globalization to Wall Street. Although a member of the Clinton administration as chairman of the Council of Economic Advisers, and later chief economist of the World Bank, Stiglitz targeted those who worked alongside him: Lawrence Summers, who was then at Treasury, and especially Stanley Fischer, long a top official at the IMF. Stiglitz's book became a kind of bible, not for the Treasury but for the antiglobalization movement, including many fringe elements on the far left, who cited it as support for the belief that globalization has increased world poverty and inequality. Endorsements from such groups, and the lack of solid numerical evidence, did not endear the book to the mainstream economics profession. Stiglitz's book provoked great resentment within the IMF, the villain of his analysis, which published an open letter of denunciation written by Ken Rogoff, a newcomer to the fund from Harvard and one of the world's leading international economists.[14]

The World Bank, which was far from entirely unified on the issues, responded by placing on its website the complete video of a session (originally intended as an off-the-record discussion of the issues raised in the book), which presents a more balanced picture.[15] Stiglitz's book was easy to attack; its self-righteous hindsight was grating, its attack on Stan Fischer's integrity was a mistake (and would have been so even if Fischer were not one of the most loved and respected members of the profession), and its facts were far from properly checked. All of which was unfortunate, because the obvious flaws have allowed his detractors to avoid the enormously important issues that he had unsurpassed authority to discuss: the governance of the IMF and the World Bank, whether the IMF acts in the interests of its member countries or of Wall Street, the desirability of unlimited capital movements, and the proper role at the IMF of the free-market fundamentalists who then largely controlled it. Stiglitz's critique, as well as those of others, has become more, not less, relevant over the two decades since and can take at least some of the credit for a very different IMF today.

Paul O'Neill's views (and openness to debate) led to his removal from office at the end of 2002. But the arguments on aid effectiveness went on, heating up into a war between Easterly, again, and Jeff Sachs of Columbia and the UN Millennium Project. Sachs's 2005 book, *The End of Poverty*, with a foreword by Bono, laid out his vision and plan for implementing his title.[16] Easterly reviewed the book for the *Washington Post*.[17] Easterly's review, which was sympathetic to the moral force of Sachs's concern and sensitive to his inspiring rhetoric, criticized him for unwarranted utopianism, for development planning reminiscent of the 1950s and '60s, for "mind-numbing technical jargon," and for believing that large-scale "big-push" programs by outsiders could fix poverty in other countries. This drew a vituperative, contemptuous, and ad hominem counterblast from Sachs, and a counter-counterblast from Easterly, which began, "At least he didn't mention my bald spot."[18]

Sachs's book is an extraordinary document. It is part autobiography, covering Sachs's previous successful and unsuccessful ("if only they had listened") attempts to help countries in crisis, and part a plan for elimination of world poverty that is both grandiose and detailed. It takes the reader back fifty years to the very beginnings of economists' thinking about development, when economists thought that a "big push" was needed to launch countries into sustained economic growth. Even so, and as is the case when listening to Sachs in person, it is hard not to be carried away by the imperative to do something. In the final, inspirational chapter, Sachs notes that while many people doubt that his vision can be implemented, that is also what they told Mahatma Gandhi, Nelson Mandela, and Martin Luther King.

This is all great circus. As Easterly makes fun of Sachs for associating with such distinguished (if recently minted) economists as Bono and Angelina Jolie, Sachs continually caricatures himself more effectively than can any of his critics. MTV showed a video, "The Diary of Angelina Jolie and Dr. Sachs in Africa," currently available on YouTube, that prompted speculation in the blogosphere that Sachs had better watch out, not only for Easterly but also for Brad Pitt, then Jolie's companion and later husband. On September 11, 2002, the National Cathedral in Washington held a day of reflection on global poverty, during which, between morning and afternoon worship, there was a free public lecture by "a prophet for the economic possibilities for the poor," Jeffrey Sachs.

The idea that foreign aid is of little use, or even pernicious, was long the preserve of the far right, who often appeared to care little about poverty, global or national. Easterly has opened up new space for the argument that it is possible to care while also believing that aid doesn't work. And while it is hard to judge for sure, my sense is that this idea has made real progress, at least in the United States. Nina Munk, in her splendid book about Jeff Sachs, *The Idealist: Jeffrey Sachs and the Quest to End Poverty*, tells the story about how she started out in admiration, having long looked for a worthy topic to write about, but, as she followed Sachs's trail in Africa, encountered aid-induced catastrophe after catastrophe on the ground; Sachs's much vaunted Millennium Villages Project (MVP), which was supposed to demonstrate the success of the big-push development idea, left a trail of destruction and unintended consequences.[19]

The MVP was Sachs's attempt to test the big-push idea that while one intervention at a time is unlikely to catapult a deeply impoverished African village into self-sustaining growth, that would not be true of a set of simultaneous interventions in health, infrastructure, education, and agriculture. This is not absurd. Using fertilizer to grow better mangoes does little good if there are no roads to transport them to markets, no healthy workers to tend the trees, and no courts to solve commercial disputes. The MVP, in fifteen villages in Africa, aimed to show that, with help across many areas, people could lift themselves out of poverty within five years. Munk's negative impressions are echoed by the more considered evaluations of the data. Claims by the project about infant mortality in the test villages were published in *The Lancet* and subsequently had to be retracted amid a storm of criticism, much to the embarrassment of the journal.[20] Perhaps not as bad as its 1998 publication of the paper on autism and vaccines, but bad enough.

Weak States, Poor Countries, and the Problem with Aid

In Scotland, I was brought up to think of police officers as my friends and to ask one for help if I needed it. Imagine my surprise, then, when, as a nineteen-year-old on my first visit to the United States, I was greeted by a stream of obscene insults when I approached a New York City cop who was directing traffic in Times Square and asked him for directions to the nearest post office. This was in the summer of 1965, and I had been fortunate to get a summer job working for a prominent British clothier that had the concession to sell aboard the Cunard liners *Queen Mary* and *Queen Elizabeth* as they plied their weekly runs between Southampton and New York. Part of my job was to mail the weekly receipts back to London, usually from the post office in Rockefeller Center, but it was July 4 and the post office was closed. In my embarrassment and confusion following the cop's abuse, I looked for an alternative. I managed to find stamps in a convenience store (not a service then available in Britain), and, in my triumph, I inserted the documents into a trash bin that I mistook for a mailbox. It was only on one of my later trips that I learned the difference and realized my error.

Europeans tend to feel more positive about their governments than do Americans, for whom the failures and unpopularity of their federal, state, and local politicians are a commonplace. Yet even American government works well compared with many of the governments in poor countries, and one of the most important but least appreciated consequences of foreign aid is that it can often make the dysfunction worse.

American federal, state, and local governments collect taxes and, in return, provide services without which Americans could not easily live their lives. Americans, like citizens of most rich countries, take for granted the legal and regulatory system, the public schools, health services and social security for the elderly, roads, defense and diplomacy, and a high level of government investment in research, particularly medical research. Certainly, not all these services are as good as they might be, nor are they held in equal regard by everyone; but most people pay their taxes, and if the way that money is spent offends some, a lively public debate ensues, and regular elections allow people to change government priorities. Or that is what happens when the system is working, as it often has in the past. Even during the pandemic, where there was much to criticize, there were great achievements, particularly the unprecedentedly rapid development of vaccines. State governments bypassed America's calamitously disorganized and fragmented healthcare system and distributed vaccines without its help in town halls, social centers, and mass vaccination centers.

All of this is so obvious that it hardly needs saying—at least for those of us who live in rich countries with effective governments. But much of the world's population does not. Many states in Africa and Asia lack the capacity to raise taxes or deliver services. The contract between government and governed—imperfect in rich countries—is often altogether absent in poor countries. The New York cop was little more than impolite and was providing an important service that I was ignorantly interrupting; in much of the world, police prey on the people they are supposed to protect, shaking them down for money or persecuting them on behalf of powerful patrons.

Even in a middle-income country like India, public schools and public clinics suffer from mass (unpunished) absenteeism. Private doctors give people what (they think) they want—injections, intravenous drips, and antibiotics—but the state does not regulate them, and many practitioners are unqualified. The state does not have the capacity to provide good healthcare on its own, nor does it have the capacity to adequately regulate private provision.

Throughout the developing world, children die because they are born in the wrong place—not from exotic, incurable diseases but from the commonplace childhood illnesses that we have known how to treat for almost a century. Without a state that can deliver routine maternal and child health services, or a reliable supply of clean water, these children continue to die. Likewise, without government capacity, regulation and enforcement do not work properly, so businesses find it difficult to operate. Without well-functioning civil courts, there is no guarantee that innovative entrepreneurs can claim the rewards of their ideas. Family businesses can provide their own loyalty and trust but face difficulties when they try to expand to the point where it is necessary to hire nonfamily members.

The absence of state capacity—of the services and protections that people in rich countries take for granted—is a major cause of poverty and deprivation around the world. Without effective states working with active and involved citizens, without public goods and state services and the taxes to pay for them, there is little chance for the growth that is needed to abolish global poverty.

Unfortunately, the world's rich countries often make things worse. Foreign aid—transfers from rich countries to poor countries—has much to its credit, particularly in terms of health, with many people alive today who would otherwise be dead. But foreign aid often undermines the development of local state capacity. This is most obvious in countries—many in Africa—where the government receives aid directly and aid flows are large relative to its expenditure (often more than half the total). Without external finance, governments must raise money locally, something that requires some kind of contract with taxpayers and their representatives, such as a parliament, in which the people provide money, and the government provides services like defense, education, or health. With donors supplying the cash, governments need no such contract and are not accountable to their citizens. If they are accountable to anyone, it is to the donors; but even this fails in practice, because the donors, under pressure from their own citizens (who rightly want to help the poor but have no way of seeing whether the aid is helping), need to disburse money just as much as poor-country governments need to receive it, often more so.

What about bypassing governments and giving aid directly to the poor? The immediate effects are likely to be better, especially in countries where little government-to-government aid reaches the poor. And it would take an astonishingly small sum of money—less than a dollar a day from each adult in the rich world—to bring everyone up to the World Bank's global extreme-poverty line.

Yet this is not a permanent solution. Poor people *need* government to lead better lives; taking government out of the loop might improve things in the short run, but it would leave unsolved the underlying problem. Poor countries cannot forever have their health services run from abroad. Aid undermines what poor people need most: an effective government that works with them for today and tomorrow.

One thing that we *can* do is to agitate for our own governments to stop doing the things that make it harder for poor countries to stop being poor. Reducing aid is one, especially in countries where aid is the overwhelming source of government funding, but so is limiting the arms trade, improving rich-country trade and subsidy policies that often discriminate against poor farmers, providing technical advice that is not tied to aid, and developing better drugs for diseases that do not affect rich people. We cannot help the poor by making their already-weak governments weaker still.

How American Poverty Became Fake News

During the administration of the incontinently mendacious President Trump, many of us worried about the integrity of the national statistical system. One place to look for cracks in the foundation was the administration's reporting of poverty. Here, it seems that the official poverty numbers produced by the Census Bureau were not compromised, though there was much mischief elsewhere, with a flurry of misinterpretations and misstatements from both inside and outside of the administration.

Commentators on the right often quote Ronald Reagan's 1986 claim that in Lyndon Johnson's 1964 War on Poverty, poverty had won. The claim, which is perennially used as a stick to beat welfare provision and to denigrate the effectiveness of government action, was clearly false between 1960 and the early 1970s, when poverty was in rapid decline, and has subsequently been true only because of flaws in the way that U.S. poverty is measured. Reasonably enough, poverty is calculated from the number of people whose incomes are below the official poverty line, and the line is regularly updated to take account of inflation. But what counts as income is a problem; only pretax income counts and payments from government programs are ignored, even when those payments are designed to relieve poverty. (In the 1960s, when the measure was designed, the poor didn't pay taxes or receive benefits, and changing the methods would have required a political consensus that has never existed, or at least the expenditure of political capital by an administration that cared more about poverty measurement than has any so far.) Food stamps are not counted, nor were the checks that were sent out during the pandemic to keep people afloat.

No matter how successful antipoverty cash transfer policies are at reducing want, their effects do not show up in the official counts. Statistical flaws always have the potential to turn into bad politics because they invite commentators to fix the flaws with prejudices, as Reagan did. The way poverty is measured means that the War on Poverty can never be won by sending money to the poor. This statistical stupidity, which the politics makes so hard to fix, is a constant source of mischief and misunderstanding.[21]

Trump's Council of Economic Advisers took the opposite view to Reagan's. According to them, the war was not lost, but won. In a report that extolled the virtues of work requirements, it reversed the standard conservative position by arguing that, thanks to the American safety net, the War on Poverty "is largely over and is a success."[22] Different argument, same conclusion. Reagan says that the government trying to help the poor just makes things worse. Trump says we don't need to worry about the poor because there aren't any. The Trump administration's trick was to lower the poverty line to the point where hardly anyone was beneath it. The argument was that the Consumer Price Index (CPI) is flawed and rises too quickly, by about 1 percent a year over the "truth," and so if we go back to the original poverty line and update using a more slowly growing CPI, the "corrected" current poverty line today is very much lower than the official line, and there is indeed hardly anyone beneath it.

Not everyone thinks poverty has been eradicated in America. At the invitation of the U.S. government, an invitation issued during the Obama administration but honored under Trump, the UN sent a special rapporteur on extreme poverty and human rights, Philip Alston, on a fact-finding mission to the United States. He reported on his findings to the UN Human Rights Council in June 2018.[23] The report makes for awful reading. It documents the extraordinary depths of poverty in parts of the United States, from people sleeping in tent camps on the streets of Los Angeles, to people whose yards are awash in untreated sewage because local authorities refuse to supply services, to the widespread use of fines and confiscations levied on poor people that many towns and cities are using to finance themselves. The War on Poverty has become a war on the poor.

I and many others think that, because its safety net is so full of holes, extreme poverty is more prevalent in the United States than in other rich countries. Welfare reforms that encouraged work were good for some of the poor but bad for the poorest, expanding inequality within the poor population and hurting the very worst off. Remarkable books by Kathryn Edin and Luke Shaefer, *$2 a Day: Living on Almost Nothing in America*, and by Matthew Desmond, *Evicted: Profit and Poverty in the American City*, have documented in detail the miseries of life at the bottom, and Edin and Shaefer argue that several million children in the United States are living on less than two dollars a day.

In an opinion piece published in the *New York Times* in January 2018, I (perhaps rashly, given the data difficulties) compared the fractions in poverty in the United States with those in other countries around the world. I used the World Bank's website PovcalNet,[24] which then allowed the user to specify a poverty line and to find the fraction of people living below that line in any country or all countries in the world. The website then estimated that 5.3 million people in the United States were living on less than the equivalent of the Bank's global poverty line of $1.90 per person per day. In my op-ed, I used $5.00 per person per day for rich countries to take account of both the higher prices in the United States and the need to buy more of things like clothes and housing in colder countries. According to my estimates from the Bank's site, using a $5.00 poverty line for rich countries and the roughly equivalent $1.90 for poor countries, there were more "globally poor" people in the United States than in Sierra Leone or Nepal, and the percentages of people in poverty in the United States and China were almost identical. The percentages of poor were much lower in European countries, where the safety net is much more comprehensive.

Not surprisingly, the calculations that I reported were widely denounced by both right and left. On the right, the Heritage Foundation produced a report arguing that there were only 250,000 globally poor people in the United States and arguing that poverty should be blamed on the "self-defeating and self-limiting behaviors" of the poor.[25] Which is where the close-up accounts of Edin, Shaefer, and Desmond are so valuable. I find it hard to reconcile the "no poverty" view with the horrors documented by them, including women selling their children's Social Security numbers to survive (the purchaser uses the numbers to cheat on their taxes by claiming they have children) or women with kids whose choices of places to live are so limited that they must sometimes choose between their children's safety or home-lessness. I find it hard to believe that people in such straits re-spond to the surveys on which the low estimates depend. It is also undoubtedly true that the data that the World Bank uses miss some of the income that poor people receive. But the same is true in other countries, and the World Bank is the only source for global poverty estimates that are even nominally comparable.

I was also denounced by the left, who hate the idea that any-one in the United States is as poor as the poorest in Africa or Asia; my critics here include many who believe in the cosmo-politan prioritarianism that I discussed above. But here, too, there is close-up evidence. The novelist and travel writer Paul Theroux, who has spent much of his life traveling and living in Africa, wrote about the American South in *Deep South: Four Seasons on Back Roads* and drew on that experience to write a piece for the *New York Times*.[26] He wrote about "towns in South Carolina, Alabama, Mississippi, and Arkansas that looked like towns in Zimbabwe, just as overlooked and beleaguered." He noted that the Clinton Foundation was trumpeting its "Partner-ship to save Africa's elephants" while doing nothing for desper-ate poverty in the Clintons' own state of Arkansas. I suspect that Theroux's comparisons between Africa and Arkansas would be convincing if we moved away from income-based measures and used Gordon Graham's persuasive notion of "im-poverishment." Graham's focus is not on money but on the quality of life itself, on cases where deprivation compromises one or more of the components of a good life, such as accom-plishments, experiences, and relationships.[27]

The UN report drew an angry rebuke from the U.S. ambas-sador to the UN, Nikki Haley, who claimed that "it is patently ridiculous for the United Nations to examine poverty in Amer-ica,"[28] and an official U.S. response saying that Alston got his numbers wrong.[29] But the only numbers that Alston used were the estimates of deep poverty provided by the U.S. Census Bureau—though in the general scuffle I was at one point blamed for those too. The administration's numbers were those that Heritage had calculated in its denunciation of me and that use my $5.00 poverty line, not the official line of about $20.00. And then, perhaps coincidentally and officially in response to the Human Rights Council's treatment of Israel, the administration pulled the United States out of the council, with the result that Haley did not attend the presentation of the report. Haley, like Trump's economists, noted that the Trump administration knows how to tackle deep poverty, which is to make people work to get their benefits. That, of course, is a legitimate political opinion, but replacing Census Bureau numbers with numbers from the Heritage Foundation—and there is evidence that agency officials tried to prevent it[30]—or arbitrarily but conveniently tinkering with the CPI is a step too far (not as bad as refusing to accept a legitimate election, but down the same road).

The elite presumption on the left is that increasing poverty in the United States is fine so long as it reduces poverty in China, even if they prefer not to put it so brutally. That is what cosmopolitan prioritarianism argues when welfare is taken to being material living standards. Theroux claims that this position provides a convenient ethical cover for corporate executives who are enriched in the process and who can signal their virtue by visiting Oxfam's tent in Davos (indulgences anyone?), by donating to reduce global poverty, or by leaving their fortunes to support that aim. Donating for poverty relief in the places in the United States where the jobs were being lost (Arkansas anyone?) would be altogether too uncomfortable and would certainly draw attention to those corporate behaviors that were contributing to that domestic poverty.

CHAPTER 4

THE POLITICS OF NUMBERS

FIXING THE PRICE?

WHEN ASKED WHY he liked to teach accounting, my late colleague Uwe Reinhardt explained that "in a democracy, you need accountability and accounting is one of the surest ways to ensure that." The dictum applies both to corporate accounting, which aims to keep firms honest, and to national accounting, which aims to keep governments honest. This chapter is about one particularly sensitive government measure, the Consumer Price Index (CPI).

The CPI is a measure of the average level of consumer prices, and inflation is measured by how rapidly the CPI is rising. It is one of the most closely watched numbers produced by the U.S. government. Inflation is one of the targets for policymakers at the Federal Reserve. High inflation brings misery to many, and, as is the case as I write in 2022, the failure to control it is taken as an indicator of failure by the president and his administration. The CPI is also used to update, or "index," millions of contracts by both private individuals and the government, from wage contracts, to divorce settlements, to pensions and Social Security payments. More than 69 million Americans receive

Social Security checks every month; those checks, typically between $2,000 and $4,000, are updated every year to keep up with inflation, as measured by changes in the CPI. The official U.S. poverty line, first established in the 1960s, is updated using the CPI. If the CPI is mismeasured, too many poor people will be counted as poor if it is overstated, and too few if it is understated.

When national statisticians publish numbers that politicians dislike—and politicians really hate inflation—there is always a temptation to blame the messenger. In a few countries there have been threats of dismissal or even jail time.[1] More often, the response is to challenge the methods behind the accounting, either directly or through proxies in the media or in academia.

Such challenges could easily be dealt with if there were a bright line between the facts, on the one hand, and the politics, on the other, but it is not so simple. The construction of official statistics rests on assumptions and implicit understandings of how the world works, so that, even if we drill down into the minutiae of data construction, there are always choices that someone must make. Those choices must be and are shaped by conceptions of the ideal to which the measure approximates. Different people have different ideas of what the "perfect" price index is, and those ideals are sometimes shaped by philosophical and political positions. One deep division in price index calculation is whether the price index should simply be an average of prices—with things people spend more on getting more weight—or whether the statisticians should be more ambitious and aim to calculate a "cost-of-living" index. The two concepts are often close or even identical, but not always so.

As we will see, statistical agencies are held to account for their work, and politicians do not hesitate to demand methodological changes that will yield more "desirable" numbers. This can seem reprehensible, as in cooking the books, but is not always so. Agencies can get things wrong, and mistakes may not be politically neutral. So, even when there is no error, it can pay off for politicians to claim that there is one and try to reshape the numbers to suit them. Sometimes academic economists can step in and help resolve controversies. Sometimes, as we will see, they can make them worse.

The first section is about a controversy from the mid-1990s whose consequences are still with us today, not only for measuring inflation but also for measuring poverty. Indeed, as political polarization has sharpened, we have almost reached the state where the right and the left choose different measures of inflation. And because prices and inflation are so important in seeing and interpreting the economy, being able to choose one's own index allows the right and the left to live in different worlds—one that is economically successful, and one not.

Conservative Corrections

The CPI is calculated and published by the Bureau of Labor Statistics (BLS). Only a handful of experts understand the details of how it is calculated, and their work rarely makes it into the public eye. Not so in 1996, when an angry controversy erupted. Several groups played key roles in the debate, including government economists, academic economists, and (largely conservative) elected officials. Collecting prices, averaging them, and publishing the results might seem like a dry, technical task. Yet here, as in all government statistics, politics is always present. *Statistics* are the numbers of the *state*, and politics determines not only what and why but every detail of how they are collected.

The story begins with the Federal Reserve, whose research suggested that the CPI, as estimated by the BLS, was growing too quickly. In part, they argued, this was because the CPI does not make sufficient allowance for what economists call substitution bias. When not all prices rise at the same rate, people will tend to move their spending away from the more expensive items and toward the less expensive. This moderates somewhat the effect of rising prices on the cost of living. Because the CPI is based on calculating the cost of a fixed bundle of goods and services, this cost-moderating substitution is missed. This critique does not say that the CPI is wrong as a measure of average prices, just that, if we are interested in the cost of living, then an average of prices is not enough. A cost-of-living index is not the same thing as an "average of prices" index.

More important, according to the Fed's critique, was the failure of the BLS to allow for improvements in the quality of goods and services over time. To give a simple example: suppose that a new and better gasoline were invented that allows motorists to drive twice as far on each gallon of gas. If the price at the pump doesn't change, the cost of driving is reduced by half, and that reduction from the quality improvement should be taken into account when we calculate an overall price index. In this case, the quality improvement is exactly equivalent to a larger quantity and there is an easy fix—just include *half* the price in the index. However, as we will see, most quality improvements are not like this. Calculating the cost of *living* is much more difficult than calculating the cost of *driving*.

Because so much federal entitlement spending—including Social Security—is indexed to the CPI, Fed Chairman Alan Greenspan's endorsement of the critique in January 1995 was quickly seized upon by lawmakers. If the BLS could be persuaded to decrease the rate of growth of the CPI, large amounts of projected government spending would never materialize, and no politician could be held responsible for cutting benefits for powerful constituents, such as elderly Americans. About a third of the federal budget is linked to the CPI, and Greenspan calculated that a 1 percent per year reduction in the rate of growth of the index applied to indexed programs would lower the federal budget deficit by $55 billion in the five years after 1995. Some politicians hate entitlement spending anyway—or at least they hate the taxes that finance it—and here was a way of reducing it that could be defended as a mere technical fix.

Then Speaker of the House Newt Gingrich quickly threatened that if the BLS didn't "fix" the CPI, he would abolish the agency. According to Gingrich, "We have a handful of bureaucrats who, all professional economists agree, have an error in their calculations. If they can't get it right in the next 30 days or so, we zero them out, we transfer the responsibility to either the Federal Reserve or the Treasury and tell them to get it right."[2] It is no accident that Gingrich is seen as one of the founders of today's adversarial politics.

Instead of zeroing out the offending bureaucrats, the Senate Finance Committee appointed a committee of experts to consider the issue. The Advisory Commission to Study the Consumer Price Index contained some of America's most distinguished and well-known economists. It was chaired by Michael Boskin of Stanford University (previously the chairman of President G. H. W. Bush's Council of Economic Advisers) and included Ellen Durenberger of IBM, Robert Gordon of Northwestern University, and Zvi Griliches and Dale Jorgenson, both from Harvard. The commission's report confirmed Greenspan's analysis, estimating that the CPI growth had an upward bias of around 1.5 percent in recent years, and projected that there would be a bias of about 1.0 percent a year in future years if no corrections were made.[3] As in the Fed's analysis, only a minor fraction of the bias was attributed to failure to allow for substitution from more expensive goods and services to cheaper ones. The commission argued that new goods were brought into the index too slowly; despite their dubious importance to the debate, a great deal of fun (and embarrassment) was had with the failure of the BLS to add cell phones to their basket quickly enough, though, in the mid-1990s, cellphones were rare except for business use and *business* use is not included in the *consumer* price index. Jerry Hausman of MIT estimated that General Mills' introduction of a new brand of cereal, Apple Cinnamon Cheerios, was worth $60 million a year to consumers and that the total cereals' component of the CPI was overstated by perhaps 20 percent.[4] It is fair to say that Hausman's calculations—though a bravura feat of statistical legerdemain—failed to convince many that his assumptions made sense or, more precisely, that his estimate did not owe more to his assumptions than to his data.[5]

The commission's main conclusion was that most of the bias came from the failure of the BLS to capture enough of the ongoing improvements in the quality of goods and services.

The question of how to measure quality is unsettled to this day, but the political urgency of "fixing" the CPI was removed after President Clinton and the Republican majority agreed on a plan to balance the budget without the aid of any revisions to the CPI, revisions that, like any other downward modification to Social Security or to Medicare, were opposed by the powerful lobbies for the elderly as well as by a majority of both Republicans and Democrats in the House of Representatives.

Meanwhile, the economists in the BLS, ably led by two excellent individuals, the commissioner Katharine Abraham and the chief of price index research Brent Moulton, conducted a sterling counteroffensive to the commission's arguments.[6] In the eyes of this observer, the BLS won a clear victory on points. The agency already makes very substantial (and careful) corrections for quality—whenever it has a solid basis for doing so. Little of this was acknowledged by the commission.[7] It is instructive to compare the BLS analysis with that of the commission, which was willing to assume large quality effects— usually described (with an unconsciously well-chosen adjective) as "conservative"—for groups of commodities in which there is neither a solid estimate of quality effects nor literature or previous research of any kind.

Here is just one example from the commission's report: "Regarding house furnishings other than appliances and video-audio products, there is no available research to provide guidance. The available range of furniture, draperies, etc., allows consumers to substitute among products, fabrics, and outlets along dimensions that are not captured by the CPI. There have been many new products in this area, including furniture and fabrics that are much less susceptible to damage by stains and children's accidents than was previously possible. This category also includes soap and cleaning products, where substantial progress has been made. We view a bias rate of 0.33 percent per year, or 10 percent over the past 30 years, as conservative."[8] The word "conservative" in this sense and with a similar lack of evidential support is used ten times in the report, including for healthcare and cable TV.

Economists understand a great deal about price indexes and know quite a lot about substitution; in particular, there are well-worked-out and well-understood methods for making corrections, though the application of these to specific sub-populations (such as Social Security recipients, who are older and spend their money differently) is difficult and controversial.

But there is less solid work on the measurement of changes in quality or even on what quality means. There are simple but very special cases—like the gasoline example, where better gas is the same as more gas. There are also studies for specific commodities such as computers and automobiles, where we can collect data on what they do (e.g., faster computation, higher miles per gallon, or fewer deaths) and make a correction, which the BLS does when it can. There are more complicated issues with items like healthcare, whose contribution to health, although clearly considerable, has never been pinned down despite decades of research. If we count *all* reductions in mortality as coming from healthcare, it is cheap at (even its very high) price, but that is clearly wrong because it ignores the effects of lower smoking rates, better nutrition, and better sanitation.[9] And even for the part that comes from healthcare, it would be inappropriate to reduce pensions for the elderly, because the healthcare system is enabling them to live longer on the strange logic that healthcare is not *really* as expensive as it appears to be. The Boskin Commission did not actually recommend doing so, but it cites both increases in life expectancy and falling crime rates—neither of which is included in the CPI—as reasons why elderly Americans are being overcompensated by the use of the CPI to index their payments.

I am not arguing here that the Boskin Commission's estimates of quality improvements are wrong, and I understand that the absence of evidence is not the same as evidence of absence. And as one commission member argued, perhaps a squishy number is better than a firm number that is wrong. Like the commission, I believe that there have been improvements in many goods and services: I am old enough to remember when there were no ATMs and we had to line up inside banks to wait for a teller, and I should (almost) certainly prefer to be treated in a hospital of 2022 than a hospital of 1970. Though if hip replacements are twice as good as twenty years ago, I would still resist being told that I needed only one hip replaced when both were damaged, or being told by my insurance company that it would pay only half the bill.

Better healthcare is not like better gasoline. You can no longer get the 1970 healthcare at 1970 prices, even if you wanted to, nor can you choose to discard from 2022 healthcare the improvements that are not worth the cost. Nor is it true, as the commission assumed, that the cost of living is the same as the price level; the cost of living in the winter is higher in Minnesota than it is in Miami, even if all prices are the same in both places. So perhaps the original sin here was that the BLS, along with the economics profession at large, agreed to measure the cost of living when the best it could reasonably hope for was to measure the price level. And that decision was itself the result of decades of academic work on cost-of-living indexes beginning with A. A. Konüs, who did some of the key work in Russia in the 1920s. Much later, I, too, contributed to that work and once endorsed the cost-of-living approach,[10] but as a result of this controversy I came to change my mind.

If an agency like the BLS were to make the sort of arbitrary corrections that were suggested by the commission, there is nothing to prevent it from making other arbitrary but politically convenient corrections. There is a long history of governments trying to interfere with their statistical offices' calculation of CPIs—Argentina around 2010 was only one example.

In the end, all data construction has an irreducible political element. But it is precisely because of this that our statistical systems must be able to defend the theoretical and evidentiary bases of their methods. If we are honest, economists do not currently know how to account for most kinds of quality change, and so we are a long way from being able to present methods that would prove persuasive in a full democratic debate. Then Secretary of the Treasury Robert Rubin noted that there are many experts on price indexes; thus, "Congress, in acting, would have to reflect a broad-based agreement among these experts about changes in the CPI that would cause it to better reflect inflation."[11]

The 1996 controversy, in my view, was essentially an attempt to cook the books in a way that would reduce the cost of entitlement spending, and we are fortunate that our statisticians held the line. If the Fed's research had shown that the CPI was *underestimating* inflation, there would have been no commission and no recommendations, at least not with a Republican majority in Congress. But a statistical adjustment that might lead to a reduction in entitlement spending is catnip to those who would like to see entitlements reduced for other reasons.

Boskin's "corrections" are still frequently used by commentators on the right. A common and simple version is to deduct one percent a year from the rate of inflation as measured by the CPI. If prices have indeed not risen as fast as officially documented, then real living standards have risen by more than what the official statistics show, by 10 percent more over a decade, and by 64 percent more over fifty years. Poverty has fallen much more rapidly than the statistics show (see the discussion at the end of the last chapter). With the correction, the well-documented stagnation of working-class real wages since the early 1970s becomes a statistical illusion. It is true that these wages cannot buy any more goods and services now than they could then, but, according to the argument, we are ignoring the quality improvements that are making them better off. Nor is it obvious that having better goods and services is equivalent to having more of the same goods and services; drapes that are more fire-resistant still must cover my windows, and if I need both of my hips replaced, I need *both* of them replaced, not just one, however effective or advanced is the one that gets replaced. It is not just that the commission pulled its corrections out of the air, but that those kinds of corrections often make no sense.

Prices and Places

One of the first things Europeans confront when they come to America is just how enormous the country is, an enormity that is somehow enhanced by the fact that, after many hours in a plane, you get off and discover that almost everything looks the same as where you got on, something that is rarely true in Europe. There may be mountains, palm trees, or a temperature difference that tells you something has changed, but one thing that you will not find is any difference in the CPI.

The CPI tells us about differences in the price level compared with last year or a decade ago, but it does not tell us about the difference in prices between Maine and Texas. Many federal statistics and programs are keyed to the CPI but not to local prices. The federal poverty line is the same everywhere, independent of the local cost of living, even though it costs a great deal more to live and spend in Manhattan, New York, population 1.6 million, than in Manhattan, Kansas, population 54,100, let alone Manhattan, Montana, population 2,086 (not counting the millions of trout in the nearby Gallatin River).

In 1995, when a panel of the National Academy of Sciences considered how poverty ought to be measured, one of its recommendations was that the poverty line should be adjusted for differences in the costs of living in different places, something that was then impossible, because the statistical system did not produce such price indexes. Contrast this with Europe, where

Eurostat, the European Statistical Agency, regularly calculates average price levels for member countries. Those prices are used to calculate real living standards in different countries, which are the basis for transfers from richer to poorer countries within the European Union.

In the absence of better data, the panel recommended constructing local price indexes using house prices and ignoring differences in other prices from place to place—though these other prices together make up a larger share of what people spend. A box of cornflakes or a pair of Nike sneakers costs much the same everywhere, which is not true for housing.

There had long been some reluctance, including from the BLS, to calculating geographical price indexes. One head of the agency worried about political pressure from legislators to alter price indexes in their favor, to entitle their constituents to greater federal benefits, just as the census counts—which are used for drawing boundaries of congressional districts—have always been politically contested and are often mired in the courts. Having Newt Gingrich threaten to close the agency over the national CPI was bad enough, but CPIs for each state would be fifty times worse, though not all governors are as aggressive as Gingrich, but then there are mayors, and more. Whether for this or other reasons, no policy change or new data collection took place for many years. There are private-sector price indexes— used to compensate employees for (usually) temporary visits away from home such as business trips—but those are not keyed to the spending patterns of the general population. Visitors spend a lot more on hotels and restaurants than do locals.

Change came through a combination of analysis, personality, and the passage of time. The late Rebecca Blank, an economist who, as a professor at Northwestern, had been a member of the National Academy's poverty panel, was appointed to the

Department of Commerce by President Obama, finally becoming acting secretary of Commerce before returning to academia as the chancellor of the University of Wisconsin–Madison. Since the Bureau of the Census is part of the Commerce Department, Blank could help support the unfinished agenda of improving the poverty measure. Census, under the leadership of David Johnson, had developed a "Supplemental" Poverty Measure largely based on the recommendations of the National Academy report. Incorporated into this new measure—which is *not* the official poverty measure—are price indexes that vary from place to place and are constructed using differences in rents for housing. The measure makes other, even more important corrections, particularly adjusting income to include benefits received and to exclude taxes paid.

Today it is at last possible to capture spatial differences in prices beyond those in the cost of shelter. Another arm of Commerce, the Bureau of Economic Analysis (BEA)—which is responsible for the National Accounts—has created what it calls regional price parities, price indexes that capture all consumer price differences, not just those in rents for housing. These are constructed in the same way as "purchasing power parities," price indexes that are used to compare price levels between countries. Purchasing power parities (PPPs) have a long and distinguished history in economic measurement and are best known through the Penn World Table, first created in 1976 by Alan Heston, Irving Kravis, and Robert Summers at the University of Pennsylvania. The PPP program was later adopted by the United Nations and is currently hosted by the World Bank, though the Penn World Table itself has moved to Groningen in the Netherlands.

The regional price parities (RPPs) use the data collected by the BLS for the CPI, but because they are indexes designed to compare many places at once, they are constructed in a different way. With these "multilateral" indexes, we need to ensure that if our measured price level in Minneapolis is 1.0 percent higher than in Los Angeles, and if the price level in Los Angeles is 1.0 percent higher than in Albuquerque, then the price level in Minneapolis must be 2.0 percent, or more precisely 2.01 percent—1.01 times 1.01 is 1.0201—higher than in Albuquerque. The BLS, by some accounts, was not comfortable constructing such statistical exotica, though it supported the work at the BEA, which employed Bettina Aten (who had worked with Alan Heston on recent versions of the Penn World Table), who put together a team to produce the new indexes.

The 2012 RPPs showed big differences across space. Hawaii and New York were the states with the highest price levels, and Arkansas and Mississippi the lowest; New York State's price level in 2012 was 36 percent higher than Mississippi's. The metropolitan statistical area of New York, Newark, and Jersey City was nearly 50 percent more expensive than the metropolitan statistical area of Rome, Georgia. When we compare across cities, if city income is twice as high, prices are about one-third higher, and although housing rents showed the largest differences across places, there were notable differences in the prices of other goods. Gas is one. In early 2022, the motoring organization AAA reported that gas prices varied from $2.87 in Oklahoma to $4.66 in California. Wages vary from place to place, so the prices of wage-based services—restaurants, hairdressers, healthcare—vary with them. And the variation in home rentals is not really about the cost of constructing a home but about the value of the land underneath it, and land costs affect many other local items, such as retail space and hotels.

These numbers tell us about the average level of prices in different places, but they are far from complete as indicators of the cost of living in different places. That is because they do not recognize that to attain the same living standard in different places sometimes requires different kinds of goods and services, and so there can be differences in the cost of living even between places where all of the prices are exactly the same. People in Milwaukee need to buy more winter fuel than do people in New York, and there are many rural areas where it is hard to live and work without a car. The cost of living does indeed depend on prices, but it depends on other things too, like climate or the availability of public transportation.

Do people feel less well-off in places where prices are higher? Perhaps not if they can move away from high prices to lower ones, though that could hardly happen overnight. I have used Gallup data on how people rate their lives in different places, and it is indeed true that life evaluations are higher where the RPPs are lower. As we would expect, household incomes have a big effect on wellbeing, but if we look at prices and incomes together, it is *real* income that matters (real income is defined as how much your income can buy given the local price level). Real income is a better indicator of wellbeing than money income, and the RPPs do a good job of picking up the difference. This makes sense, but it ducks the question of why people live where they live, and if one place is generally happier than another— college towns tend to be happy places, for example—why don't people move there? Spatial mobility in the United States has slowed, with many fewer people moving in recent years than once was the case, in part because house prices have become unaffordable in many of the most attractive cities. We need to be careful not to assume that people can costlessly move from one place to another.

What about income inequality? Are real incomes more equally distributed than money incomes, given that prices are high where incomes are high? The answer is yes, but the difference is small. The big differences in income between people are *within* places—between poor and rich people in New York, or in Miami—not *between* places. But that is not to say that differences in real income between different places are unimportant; inequality between flourishing and languishing cities is an important issue in its own right.

The Supplemental Poverty Measure has never been adopted as *the* official poverty line, and indeed, its greater complexity might make it difficult to use for testing for individual eligibility for benefits, for example. The official poverty measure, with all its flaws—including the failure to take local prices into account and, much worse, its neglect of taxes paid and government benefits received—continues to be used, something that is unlikely to change any time soon. Even so, the new measure is widely used in analysis including in official documents. It was used to assess the effects of the Great Recession and of government response to the pandemic, where it gave an account that was superior to that of the official measure—not because of spatial price indexes but because the official measure ignored the safety net's supplementing people's incomes after the crisis.

A bad measure can survive for a long time even when its deficiencies are well understood, though perhaps the two most recent crises—the Great Recession and the pandemic—have helped make those deficiencies more starkly and widely apparent. It may even help create the political momentum that will eventually lead to change.

Government statistics are inevitably political because they are used to measure how policies are working out, and policies are frequently contested. Beyond that, the concept of "objective facts" is unhelpful, whether about prices, poverty, or most anything else. The decisions that go into construction of statistics are often political too, even at levels that might seem to be entirely technical. Recognizing this is not to cast doubt on statistics but is a prerequisite for understanding them. Beyond that, the democratic debate around the numbers of the state is both necessary and proper. If no one pays attention to or questions a statistic, it is likely to be neither important nor even necessary.

CHAPTER 5

MONETARY INEQUALITY

ACCORDING TO THE 2022 *Forbes* list, Elon Musk had $219 billion and Jeff Bezos $177 billion. The median American household had a net worth of $121,700, about one-thousandth of the net worth of Bill Gates, who was number three on the *Forbes* list. The top 10 percent of incomes in the United States account for nearly half of all income, compared with only 14 percent for the bottom half of incomes. Numbers like these illustrate the extent of monetary (or material) inequality in the United States, the vast differences between rich and poor and between the rich and the rest. Many people hate such inequalities in and of themselves and see them as symptoms, or even causes, of what ails the country. They argue that today's huge inequalities of income and wealth are unjust, that no one needs or deserves to be as rich as the richest, and that democracy is not compatible with such inequalities.

Others worry less or not at all. These include some economists and some philosophers; one common argument is that, if everyone has enough, so that there is no poverty, high incomes and high wealth are not of moral concern.[1] Beyond that, great wealth sometimes comes from innovation—Musk, Bezos, and Gates are all examples, as are most of America's richest people—and their innovation has benefited us all. Perhaps those innovations would not have happened without the prospect of immense wealth. Or perhaps they would.

This chapter is about inequalities in money or in material wellbeing and how economists, politicians, and the public write and think about them.

There is another kind of inequality that is not about money but about how people relate to one another in society, particularly about differences in status. Such inequalities include differences in opportunities between men and women, between people of different racial and ethnic groups, between urban and rural Americans, between those with different sexual orientations, or between those with a college degree and those without. Material and relational inequality are related to each other, but they are not the same. For example, extreme material inequalities are likely to compromise relational inequality, if there are landowners and serfs or if money owns politics so those without wealth have little say in how the country is run. People living in different countries who have different amounts of wealth but do not know or communicate with one another are unequal, but there is no relational inequality. I will turn to relational inequalities in the next chapter.

The first section of this chapter contrasts thinking on inequality on either side of the Atlantic: in Cambridge, England, where I grew up as an economist and where inequality was at the forefront of thinking and discussion, and in Chicago, where worrying about inequality was seen as unhelpful or even counterproductive. I then move on to what happened here in the United States and how the topic moved from the wings of public debate to center stage. Finally, I try to summarize my own current thinking about material inequality, why it can be either good or bad, and how it might best be dealt with.

Inequality in Chicago, and Inequality in Cambridge

Many people today have lost faith in capitalism, as well as any faith or trust they had in economists, who are seen as its apologists. Did economics take a wrong turn? Did those of us who do *not* subscribe to neoliberalism or to Chicago economics à la Milton Friedman let ourselves be pushed too far in the direction of trusting the market? Would the world have been a better place if Cambridge had had more influence, and Chicago less? By Cambridge, of course, I mean Cambridge, England.

When I first became an economist in Cambridge fifty years ago, philosophers talked to economists, and the economics of inequality, of justice, and of wellbeing was talked about, taught, and taken seriously. Harvard philosopher John Rawls's 1971 *Theory of Justice* was much discussed, and Amartya Sen, Anthony Atkinson, and James Mirrlees, all then in Cambridge, thought and wrote about justice and its relationship to income inequality. Amartya Sen, as a first-year undergraduate in Calcutta, had been inspired by Kenneth Arrow's *Social Choice and Individual Values*, a single copy of which appeared in the Das Gupta bookshop, whose proprietor allowed Sen and his friend Sukhamoy Chakravarty to borrow it for a few days.[2] In Cambridge, Sen wrote about how societies should organize themselves, about relative and absolute poverty, and about utilitarianism and its alternatives.

Mirrlees solved (one version of) the problem of how much inequality we *ought* to have. In his version of the story, people are egalitarians and ideally would like a society in which everyone gets the same real income. Even so, they understand that if they push too hard for equality through taxes and redistribution, people will work less and produce less so that the total amount to go around will fall. What comes out of his work is an income tax system that makes the best possible trade-off between the key players in the drama: equality, on the one hand, and incentives, on the other.[3] This was the work for which Mirrlees, who was a friend and fellow Scot, received the Nobel Prize in 1996.

Mirrlees also thought about how to "correct" market prices to account for the different effects of prices on rich and poor, an idea that was directed to policy in poor countries, many of which, newly independent, were looking for advice from economists.[4] In these brave new worlds, freed of colonialism, everything seemed possible, even equitable policymaking. For a while, until they were sandbagged by the reality of politics in poor countries, these ideas were incorporated into a manual that was used by the World Bank for evaluating projects for possible lending.[5]

Atkinson spent his life studying and writing about poverty and inequality. He explained something that is close to the heart of this book, that measurement neither can be nor ought ever to be freed of values (or politics). Inequality is in the eye of the beholder, and so, at one extreme, there *is* no inequality for those who do not care about it, while at the other extreme, those who care most about the least fortunate will see inequality everywhere. How you measure inequality tells us a great deal about how you feel about it.[6]

Sen, Mirrlees, and Arrow all won Nobel Prizes. Atkinson deserved one but did not win one, perhaps because he died too soon; he was still alive in 2015 when I was honored, and nothing would have given me more pleasure than to share the prize with him.

Meanwhile, in the United States, in another hothouse for Nobel Prizes, Chicago economics was following a line that was diametrically opposed. No one should ever doubt the intellectual contributions of Milton Friedman, George Stigler, James

Buchanan, and Robert Lucas to economics and political economy, or those of Ronald Coase and Richard Posner to law and
economics. Only Posner has yet to win a Nobel. Yet it is hard to
imagine a body of work more antithetical to worrying about
inequality.

Even if you were to worry about inequality, it would be best
if you just kept quiet and lived with it, or at least that was the
Chicago view. Regulation, taxation, or political action is unlikely to help. Politicians, after all, are just like everyone else,
looking after their own interests. Cures for inequality through
politics are often, perhaps always, worse than the disease itself.
Despite enacting progressive taxes and benefits that favor the
less well-off, governments can and often do make inequality
worse, by enacting laws that help the rich fleece the poor or by
protecting their cronies or favored industries or professions.
Government regulators can be "captured" by the firms they are
charged with regulating, which is like asking the fox to guard
the henhouse. In a country where government is more responsive to the needs of those who finance it than to its constituents,
this is what we would expect. For someone like me, brought up
in Cambridge in the shadow of Keynes, these were unfamiliar
but clearly important ideas. This is not an endorsement; I recognize the importance of the arguments but am far from convinced that government can never do good.

At its worst, Chicago economics makes money the sole measure of wellbeing, inequality doesn't matter, and efficiency is
the only thing that counts. The only injustice is to make the
economy less efficient than it might be, and, since redistribution
inevitably has losses attached—"deadweight loss" is the term of
art—then redistribution in the name of justice is inherently
unjust. The influence of Coase and Posner on the law has increasingly brought this kind of thinking into the courts.

When I first came to the United States, I remember being roundly chided for my "unprofessionalism" for trying to take equity into account in my calculations. In the spirit of Mirrlees and Atkinson, I was working on designing a tax system that would raise money for the state—for example, through taxes on goods—but would protect the budgets of the least well off. "A totally uninteresting social problem" was one of the kinder comments, and perhaps if I was going to talk at their university, I could talk about something else. This was the other side of my own earlier reaction to reading George Stigler's 1959 argument that "the professional study of economics makes one politically conservative."[7] When I read that in Cambridge, I had thought it must be a typo. Surely no one could believe such a thing and I had never met a conservative economist and didn't know that there were any. In Cambridge in the 1960s, Fabian socialists were as far right as it was possible to go.

The belief that Stigler was correct, that economics is inherently conservative, is widely held today among economists, their critics, and the public. Right-wing and pro-business foundations have for many years funded "judicial education programs" in which judges are brought to luxurious resorts and taught economics without overt political bias, in the (most likely correct) belief that understanding markets will make them more sympathetic to business interests and will purge any "unprofessionalism" about fairness. A friend of mine, a conservative economist and deeply religious man, is fond of saying that "fair" is a four-letter word that should be expunged from economics. As Americans turn against the excesses of American capitalism, they can be forgiven for turning against economics too.

The influence of Chicago economics and of Friedman's own arguments remains widespread today. Friedman dismissed much of inequality as natural; some people like to work hard and get rich, while others prefer to enjoy their leisure. Some like to save and build up fortunes for their heirs, while others are more concerned with their own immediate enjoyment. Any attempt to diminish this sort of inequality would penalize virtue and reward vice. He believed in equality of opportunity, yet stridently opposed the estate tax as "a bad tax" that "taxes virtue" and "encourages wasteful spending." In 2017, 727 economists endorsed that argument, including three Nobel laureates besides Friedman, signing on to an earlier letter by Friedman himself.[8] Many economists oppose a wealth tax on the same grounds, believing that it would encourage vice and discourage virtue. Friedman liked tax competition between countries and supported tax havens, because they put a brake on governments' ability to tax. And he repeatedly argued that attempts to limit inequality of outcomes would not only stifle freedom but, in the end, result in even more inequality. Left to themselves, free markets would produce both freedom and equality.

It doesn't seem to have worked out that way.

Instead, we got a world in which the Sackler family paid themselves more than $14 billion while igniting and promoting an opioid epidemic that has killed hundreds of thousands of Americans. Johnson & Johnson, the makers of Band-Aid and Baby Powder, grew opium poppies in Tasmania to fuel the opioid epidemic while the American military was bombing the Taliban's heroin supply in Helmand province. Private equity firms discovered they could make money by buying up ambulance services and staffing hospital emergency rooms with their own physicians who charge "surprise" fees to patients even when their insurance includes the hospital.[9] Surprise fees in emergency rooms (and operating theaters) were eliminated beginning in January 2022, but surprise bills for ambulance services continue. If you need an ambulance, you are not in the best position to find the best service or to bargain over prices; instead, you are helpless and the perfect victim for a predator.

Private equity firms continue to buy up failing firms, and with judicial permission—perhaps from judges who have been to economics school—they strip out the contractual health benefits and pensions of the workers and sell the remnant as a going concern. The physical assets are restored to efficiency, and workers' losses are sacrificed to the greater "justice" of the efficient market.[10] None of this is to deny the legitimate role of private equity, which is to buy up poorly managed firms and restore them to profitability. But this works when markets are competitive, which is not the case for hospitals, ambulances, or even jails, where private equity is active. Nor does it work when private equity buys up a large fraction of outlets in a particular place, creating a local monopoly.

The excesses are not abnormalities but are exactly how we would expect unregulated markets to work, especially when capital has the law and politics on its side. Monopolies can charge a high price when consumers (once known as patients) do not react or when they move to another provider, and thus an unconscious roadside casualty is the perfect victim. In retrospect it is not so surprising that free markets, or at least free markets with a government that permits and encourages rent seeking by the rich, should produce not equality but an extractive elite that predates on the population at large. Utopian rhetoric about freedom has led to an unjust social dystopia, not for the first time. Free markets with rent seekers are not the same as *competitive* markets; indeed, they are often exactly the opposite.

One especially troubling example is the military. This is one of the best examples in Binyamin Applebaum's critical examination of the economics profession.[11] Applebaum tells how

Friedman and his ex-pupil Walter Oi waged an ultimately successful campaign, despite the wishes of the generals, to replace
the military draft with volunteers. It is unclear how much of
Nixon's acquiescence was due to Friedman's undoubtedly extraordinary powers of persuasion, and how much to Nixon's
using the arguments as a prop for something he wanted to do
on other grounds. Either way, this was the achievement of
which Friedman himself was reputably most proud, bringing
the market to the military, something that I suspect most
economists still favor. But is it really a good idea to draw our
military from those with less education and fewer opportunities? In 2015, only 8 percent of enlisted troops had a bachelor's
degree, compared with 84 percent of officers.[12] In an America
where those without a college degree are suffering and are
increasingly suspicious of democracy, we may have to rely
on the military to help preserve it. There is evidence, too,
that inequality in the population, by undermining solidar-
ity, can spill over into the military and compromise battlefield
success.[13]

The inequality between the less educated and the well educated in America is widening, and the material differences are
spilling over into relational inequalities. Anne Case and I have
documented divergences between the groups in wages, in labor
force participation, in marriage, in social isolation, in pain, in
suicides, in drug deaths, and in alcoholism.[14] The less educated
are being asked to fight for an educated elite, who choose
whom, when, and where to fight. They are fighting so that the
children of the elite, the children of those who run private equity funds, do not have to serve. We have lost the social con-
nectedness to and the respect for others who are different from
us that came when all kinds of people served together. One of
our greatest economists, Robert Solow, left his undergraduate

studies at Harvard in 1941 and enlisted in the army as a private. It is both moving and instructive to listen to him talk about how his experience in the army, working with a wide range of Americans whom he would never otherwise have met, was one of the best and most important periods in his life.[15] His experience provides an antidote to the polarization and lack of mutual understanding that characterize America today. Solow is a Cambridge (Massachusetts) economist who fought against the Chicago view in his writings throughout his long career.

As of the time of writing, the repercussions of the 2020 election, and of the insurrection of January 6, 2021, are far from settled. Although several dozen (mostly ex-) military personnel have so far been charged, we can be grateful that there was no mass uprising of the enlisted men and women, most of whom come from the places that most fervently support Trump.

Chicago economics gave us a healthy respect for markets, as well as a previously underdeveloped skepticism about the idea that government can do better, but it left economists with too little regard for the defects of markets and what they can and cannot do. Not everything should be traded. The profession bought too far into the idea that money is everything and that everything can be measured in money. Philosophers have never accepted that money is the sole measure of good, or that only individuals matter and society does not, and economists have spent too little time reading and listening to them.

America Reawakens to Inequality

For many years, income inequality was little discussed in the United States, among academics, politicians, the media, or the public at large. The emergence of inequality as a front-line issue is quite recent, and it is good to understand why.

I have already noted how surprised I was as an immigrant by the lack of public concern and debate on inequality. Yet there was some interest. My Princeton colleague Alan Blinder (later the vice chairman of the Federal Reserve), who is my age, wrote his PhD thesis on income inequality and its effect on spending patterns. He found no such effect, mostly because inequality changed so little from the 1950s to the mid-1970s; in Henry J. Aaron's famous phrase, studying income inequality was like watching the grass grow.[16]

In politics, too, at that time, income inequality had little traction. Americans were not interested in or disturbed by stories of "fat cats," a staple of the tabloid press in Britain. Instead, they rather approved of them and wished feline obesity on themselves. Attempts by Democratic politicians to talk about inequality or redistribution were dismissed as "class warfare" by the representatives of the wealthy. Americans, we were told, believed in the American Dream, that anyone could get rich if they tried hard enough. It was equality of opportunity that was important, not equality of outcomes, and America, so the story went, was the land of equal opportunity.

Starting in the mid-1970s, the data began to show that income inequality was rising, and the politics began to change with the data. The rise in income inequality after 1975 was apparent even in routine household survey data from the agencies in Washington, but documenting the huge rise in the very top incomes had to await the seminal work by Piketty and Saez in 2003, who looked not at the surveys of randomly selected households but at the income tax records.[17] Although the very highest American incomes are very high indeed, there are few who are so fortunate, and there is little chance of them showing up in the usual surveys of a few tens of thousands of people. The

Internal Revenue Service, by contrast, catches everyone, or at least all of us who obey the law.

Piketty and Saez discovered that the share of total income going to those with the highest incomes (the famous top 1 percent) followed a long U-shape in the century after the income tax was introduced in 1913. It was high at the beginning—after the Gilded Age at the end of the nineteenth century—but fell through the two world wars, reaching its lowest level after World War 2. Nothing much happened through to the 1970s (the age of watching the grass grow), but the share of top incomes then began an inexorable surge, eventually reaching its original heights—today's new Gilded Age.

The documentation of the growth of top incomes inspired examination of other aspects of inequality, such as stagnant median wages and the effects of globalization and automation—China and robots—on those in the middle of the income distribution. The grass had turned into a forest of beanstalks.

In 2013, President Obama talked about "the defining challenge of our time" posed by "dangerous and growing income inequality and lack of upward mobility."[18] Alan Krueger, chairman of the Council of Economic Advisers in 2012, made a highly publicized speech (based on work by the economist Miles Corak) in which he showed that countries with high income inequality (like the United States) were also those with the least equality of opportunity. This gives the lie to what we were always told—that income inequality didn't matter in the land of abundant opportunity. To the contrary, income inequality seems to get in the way of opportunity. It is easy to see why this might be the case if the rich hoard the best opportunities for themselves and their children. Of course, there are other interpretations of what is going on in these data, including that low mobility is itself a cause of high inequality, but the previous absence of debate had now turned into a lively controversy.

The press began to provide a regular diet of commentary on inequality. The *New York Times* ran a series called "The Great Divide," with Joe Stiglitz contributing regular pieces on the baleful effects of inequality. The *Wall Street Journal* led the counterattack. Economists are split. In 1998, well into the beanstalk era, Martin Feldstein commented that "income inequality is not a problem in need of remedy."[19] It is possible to question the data—for example, by arguing that it is spending that matters, not income, and inequality of spending has not risen as much as inequality of income. But we have no data on spending among the very rich, apart from stories of the launch of Bezos's gargantuan yacht requiring the destruction of a famous bridge in Rotterdam, or the competition for rides on the spaceships owned by Bezos, Musk, and Branson. In any case, income provides more benefits than just the spending that it supports.

One might ask whether the exclusion of taxes and transfers, or government spending on healthcare, is not exaggerating inequality (yes) or reversing the trend (no). Though it would be ironic indeed if the rising cost of medical care were used to argue that the least well-off are doing OK. The cost of health insurance is grossly inflated by anticompetitive practices and lobbying by the healthcare industry and could be provided at a fraction of the cost, as is the case in other countries. As a result, the value of the benefits to workers who receive them is much less than their cost. Britain has much lower income inequality than does the United States, and it would be lower still if the costs of the National Health Service were divided up and added to individual incomes. Single-payer national health insurance is a great leveler and helps keep inequality down because we all share the risks of ill health and do not allow the unequal burdens of sickness to turn into inequalities in earnings or wealth.

The economist Greg Mankiw, who for many years taught the basic economics course at Harvard (EC10—also the license plate on his car) has long been a vocal defender of inequality and of the social value of the high salaries "earned" on Wall Street and paid to CEOs (or that CEOs paid themselves). He was brave enough to defend the apparently indefensible—the tax break granted to private equity firms that allows them to treat partners' incomes as capital gains, which are subject to lower tax rates.[20] When I talked at the libertarian Cato Institute in Washington and questioned whether the mass popular grief at the demise of Steve Jobs of Apple would be replicated after the deaths of prominent bankers, I was told by a member of the audience that the public does not understand the social importance of what bankers do. I think that what bankers do, and what they can get away with, became very clear during and after the Financial Crisis.

There are many parallels with the original Gilded Age. The extreme inequality a century ago affected politics, sometimes to diminish inequality and sometimes to reinforce it. In her joint biography of Presidents Taft and (Teddy) Roosevelt, Doris Kearns Goodwin writes about TR's "trust busting," attempts to rein in the illegitimate market power of the giant trusts in banking, oil, and railways; TR saw the trusts as accumulating great wealth in a way that prevented competition and that immiserated a substantial share of the population.[21]

Closer to (my) home is Woodrow Wilson's reaction to inequality, documented in Scott Berg's biography.[22] While president of Princeton, Wilson was outraged by the fact that the college was effectively owned by the wealthy: Wilson's predecessor, Patton, liked to claim that he was running the finest country club in America and noted that "Princeton is a rich man's college and that rich men frequently do not come to college to study." Wilson attempted to democratize the university and to make people study but was defeated by the alumni and by his board of trustees, on which the "rich men" were well represented. Two years after his resignation, he was elected president of the United States, where he succeeded in putting into law a number of anti-inequality measures, including reductions in tariffs, the creation of the Federal Reserve (to protect the country from the bankers during financial crises), and the introduction of the income tax on a permanent basis, which incidentally made it possible for first Simon Kuznets and then Piketty and Saez to document top income inequality. Whether these policies would have reduced inequality is something that we will never know; the (First) World War (a name coined by Wilson) swept all before it.

Wilson challenged wealth and income inequality but not racial inequality. He grew up in the South, and far from dismantling discrimination in Washington, he extended and reinforced it. In a second rebuke by Princeton, a century later, his name was removed from its school of public and international affairs. Ousted then for challenging material inequality, ousted now for accepting and creating racial inequality.

How Inequality Works, and How to Tame It

Inequality is a favorite villain in stories of what is wrong with America, including the recent rise of populism, and even the insurrection of January 6, 2021. But just what is it about inequality that is a problem, and what role does it play in inhibiting or encouraging growth or in undermining democracy? Does inequality kill, say, by driving people to suicide or to "deaths of despair"? Is inequality like global warming or air pollution, something that is bad for all of us? And if so, what is the best way to reduce it?

These are questions I am often asked. But truth be told, none is helpful, answerable, or even well posed. If inequality is a *cause* of economic, political, and social processes, it is also a *consequence*. Some of these social processes are good, some are bad, and some are very bad indeed. Only by sorting the good from the bad (and the very bad) can we understand inequality and what to do about it. And if we are to make things better, we must identify the harmful processes and rein them in, not simply reduce income inequality by a more progressive tax system, even if that might be part of the solution.

Inequality is not always unfair; and it is unfairness more than inequality that is currently disaffecting many Americans. When people see the economy and politics as rigged against them, populism and even violence can seem warranted. America was founded by those who hated the unfairness of being taxed without representation, and many Americans today feel they are being held back but have no control of a government that they see as rigged against them. And if the election of 2020 did not offer the long-delayed relief, then to hell with it.

Most do not object to innovators getting rich by introducing products or services that benefit everyone, though most also think these individuals should pay their taxes. Some of the greatest inequalities in today's world trace back to the industrial and health revolutions that began around 1750. Originally, these improvements benefited just a few countries in northwest Europe. Since then, they have spread and have bettered the lives of billions of people around the world. This progress had losers as well as winners. In Britain, as industrialists got rich, handloom weavers were impoverished, and many made their livings in intolerable conditions in cities. Beyond that, some accounts of the Industrial Revolution argue that progress in the leading countries could not have been sustained without harm to poorer countries, especially colonies and dependencies.[23] Whatever the balance of causes, good and bad, the gaps be-tween the leading and following countries have never gone away. The inequalities stemming from these advances, within and between countries, came with progress itself, which rarely comes to everyone equally, even when it does not hurt those who are left out.

The richest people in America today made their fortunes from Big Tech, from Amazon, Microsoft, Google, Facebook, Tesla, and Apple. Others, like the Waltons of Walmart or Mi-chael Bloomberg, pioneered new and better ways of doing things: inventory management from Walmart and financial in-formation and software from Bloomberg. In the Gilded Age a century ago, fortunes were made in oil, steel, and railroads, all innovations in their day. Then and now, the wealth seemed like a just reward for the benefits that came to society in general, *at least initially*. The problems come later, when the innovators stop innovating and turn from benefactors into robber barons, from "makers" into "takers." They may use their position and wealth to block the next generation of innovators, including by per-suading (or financing) government to enact rules to help them.

This is one of the ways that capitalism works. Egged on by the prospect of fabulous riches and working to develop new applications of some general-purpose technology—computers, the internet—new entrepreneurs build innovative and im-mensely profitable firms. The wave of creative destruction sweeps away many existing firms, which are still riding the last wave. The new firms, once they have achieved a dominant posi-tion, have little incentive to innovate; they can instead opt for a

quiet life and use their wealth to frustrate threats to their position by buying up young competitors before they are a threat,
by aggressive patenting, or by lobbying efforts.[24] In 2021, Meta
(Facebook) spent more than $20 million on lobbying, seventh
overall, and more than any other individual firm, as opposed to
associations of firms. Two places below comes Amazon, with
Alphabet (Google) not far behind.[25] In its early days, Google
had no presence in Washington at all.

Inequality is good if it comes from socially beneficial innovation, and if it is true that innovators need the incentives, then we
should be careful not to kill the goose that lays the golden eggs.
About this, there is much dispute. Would Elon Musk have built
Tesla or Jeff Bezos built Amazon even if it were clear in advance
that most of the wealth that would be created would go to the
government? People have different views. But no one disagrees
about something quite different, that inequality created by *theft*
is a bad thing, whether it is officially sanctioned or not.

When firms or associations of firms—for example, PHARMA,
the National Association of Realtors, U.S. Chamber of Commerce,
or the American Hospital Association—press the government
for special favors, their relatively rich executives and shareholders are effectively stealing from everyone else. In some countries,
government is less concerned with protecting its citizens or
promoting equality than with co-conspiring with business and
interest groups to extract resources from them. The police are
working with the bandits.

Wealthy minorities often block public provision of entitlement-
like pensions or of healthcare because they do not want to pay
taxes for them and do not need them for themselves or their
families. Pharma companies lobby for extended patent protection to keep prices high, and wealthy partners in private equity
firms lobby to preserve the tax breaks for their incomes by

labeling them as capital gains. Banks lobby for rules that allow them to keep profits but share their losses. The American Medical Association restricts the number of places in medical schools and stops foreign doctors from working in the United States, both of which keep doctors' salaries higher than they would be in a competitive market. Credit card companies are allowed, by the Supreme Court no less, to prevent retailers from giving discounts to people who pay cash, so that less well-off people who do not use cards are paying for the free air tickets and other benefits that credit card companies provide to their members. States have made it illegal for anyone other than dealers to sell automobiles, so manufacturers cannot sell direct. And so on.

If this kind of lobbying and granting of special favors could be restricted—and campaign finance reform would help— inequality would be reduced, even without changes in taxes.

National income per head in the United States has more than doubled in real terms in the past fifty years, growing on average at 1.8 percent a year between 1971 and 2021. But if we look at real wages in the middle of the distribution, they have stagnated since 1970. And if we look at the real wages of men without a college degree, they are *lower* now than fifty years ago. Why has this growing general prosperity not been shared among working people?

One account blames impersonal and unstoppable processes like globalization and technical change, which have devalued low-skill labor and favored the well educated. Another account is more sinister: that stagnation for most is the direct result of rising incomes and wealth at the top. In this account, the rich are getting richer at the expense of everyone else. Rising financialization of the economy is a case in point; banks, hedge funds, and other financial institutions have become larger, accounting for around a fifth of the economy, compared with a tenth after

World War 2, yet there has been no clear gain in the efficiency of capital allocation. More immediately, if monopoly and monopsony have become more common as industries have become more concentrated, prices are higher and wages are lower than they ought to be, and money is being transferred from workers and consumers to managers and to the owners of capital.

Although globalization and technological change—China and robots—have disrupted traditional work arrangements, economists like to emphasize that both globalization and technical change are potentially beneficial *given the right policies*, policies that would compensate the losers. But we did not have the right policies, largely because politics was more beholden to those who had benefited and who would have had to pay the compensation. Then Texas senator Phil Gramm argued that such compensation policies are the sort of thing that socialist countries do, and that even they were trying to stop doing them. Even without compensation, jobs that were destroyed used to be replaced by other, often better, jobs, albeit in other places. For reasons that we don't fully understand, perhaps that Americans are now less willing to move—and there has indeed been a marked reduction in mobility—the process of destruction and replacement has become slower and more painful.

Wages are being held down by other faulty social arrangements. One is the disastrous effects of healthcare financing on wages and jobs. Most working Americans' health insurance is provided by their employers, money that would otherwise be available for wages. In this system, workers' wages are essentially paying for profits and high salaries in the medical industry, as well as for a much larger healthcare system than we need. Every year, the United States *wastes* a trillion dollars—about $8,000 per family—more than other rich countries on excessive healthcare costs and has worse health outcomes than nearly all of them. Any one of several European financing alternatives could recoup those funds, but adopting any of them would trigger the fierce resistance of those profiting from the status quo. A single-payer system, like campaign finance reform, would be good in and of itself, and it would reduce pretax inequality.

A similar argument applies to the increasing market consolidation in many sectors of the economy. As a result of hospital mergers, for example, hospital prices have risen rapidly, but hospital wages have not, despite a decades-long shortage of nurses. Telephones that used to be cheaper in the United States than in Europe are now more expensive.[26] Increasing market concentration can also slow productivity growth; it is easier to reap profits through rent seeking and monopolization than through innovation and investment. Better antitrust enforcement, like single-payer healthcare and campaign finance reform, would help the economy work better *and* help reduce inequality.

I could list many similar improvements that would do the same: an increase in the minimum wage, banning noncompete clauses or compulsory arbitration in low-skill occupations, repealing antiunion laws, weakening the growing pro-business bias of the courts, and perhaps—though many economists would disagree—a reduction in immigration. In 2021, 13.6 percent of the U.S. population was born abroad, compared with 4.7 percent in 1970. The Gilded Age a century ago was the last time that the foreign-born share of the American population was as high as it is today. Many working-class Americans believe that their wages would be higher if there were fewer immigrants and that today's high level of foreign-born population is buoying up inequality, just as it did in the original Gilded Age. Most studies by economists find no such effect, but not everyone is convinced that the studies are correct.

With the right policies, there is a chance that capitalist democracy can work better for everyone, not just for the wealthy. We do not need to abolish capitalism or selectively nationalize the means of production. But we do need to put the power of competition back in the service of the middle and working classes. There are terrible risks ahead if we continue to run an economy that is organized to let a minority prey upon the majority. Taxing those who prosper is good and is certainly part of what needs to be done. But stopping the predation is the key.

CHAPTER 6

INEQUALITIES BEYOND MONEY

VAST INEQUALITIES in wealth and income are disturbing and often unjust, but they pale in comparison to the injustices experienced by people who are treated differently because of ethically irrelevant characteristics such as race, ethnicity, or gender. When society refuses to assign dignity and respect to some of its members, not everyone is a full citizen. We can (and do) argue about whether billionaires should be allowed or whether their wealth benefits the rest of us. But there can be no justification for Jim Crow.

Wealth itself can bring its own tyranny if money is required for full citizenship. Democracy doesn't work if money captures the legislature, leaving those without wealth with no say, or if some offices (for example, in politics) are open only to those with money or those who are supported by money. Or if good healthcare is available only to the rich. But there are other forms of discrimination and inequality that do not depend on money. The stories in this chapter are examples of these inequalities.

The first is about noncitizen immigrants, a status that was my own for thirty years. For many, like me, being a landed immigrant is a transition state toward citizenship, but until that goal is achieved, immigrants are not full members of society and run the risk of being what Michael Walzer calls "live-in servants."[1] The second section is about race in America, about the gaps in health between Black people and white people, gaps that have existed for as long as we have had data. I explore the links between income inequality, on the one hand, and racial inequality, on the other. The third section is about climate change and what we owe to future generations; here the inequality is between us and them. Finally, I turn to the vexed question of meritocracy; I always saw myself as one of Britain's first generation of meritocrats and once thought that the implementation of the idea would open up a better new world. That idea doesn't look quite so good today.

Immigrants in America

For noncitizens, even those who are in the country legally, their status is often a source of anxiety. Donald Trump demonized and insulted immigrants from the beginning of his first campaign, and his administration implemented sometimes brutal anti-immigration policies. He attempted to bar visitors from Muslim or terror-prone countries, which, as I noted in chapter 1, would have excluded many distinguished scientists and writers who brought their talents to enrich the United States.

Yet there is a strand in right-wing politics that sees mass immigration after 1965 as a great disaster. More immigrants came to the United States after 1965 than ever before, and, according to Trump's anti-immigrant supporters, not only did they help immiserate the white working class, but they were different from the previous immigrants (most of whom were European) and so changed the nature of the country and undermined its original liberal constitution.[2] In comparison with helping reverse such a catastrophe, who could worry about separating parents from their children or putting kids in cages?

Trump was by no means the first president to maltreat immigrants. To his eternal shame, between 1942 and 1945, Franklin D. Roosevelt interned more than a hundred thousand people of Japanese descent, including many American citizens. One of those was Walter Oi, born in Los Angeles in 1929, the economist whom we met in the last chapter and who argued for bringing the market to the military. Half a century later, after the barbarities of 9/11, several anti-immigrant policies were enacted. Under the USA PATRIOT Act of October 2001, the U.S. authorities could detain indefinitely, without trial and without acknowledgment, anyone suspected of terrorism who was not an American citizen, including the 20 million or so people who were then long-term, taxpaying, legal residents of the United States.

Economics departments in the United States have for some years been heavily populated by non-Americans. In my own department at Princeton, half of the faculty in 2001 were born outside the United States, and of the younger (untenured) faculty, more than three-quarters were born abroad. Most of our graduate students were born outside the United States, and the last time I taught one of the introductory graduate courses, the pre-class chat in the classroom was often in Mandarin. Under the terms of the PATRIOT Act, universities, as well as other employers, could be ordered to open their personnel files (or books, records, papers, or documents) on noncitizens to the FBI on request; not only were universities not required to seek the target's permission, but they were legally bound not to disclose to anyone, including the target, that they had been asked or had provided information. Such measures, as well as the suspension of habeas corpus for noncitizens, were widely supported among Americans, at least at the time. Protests were dismissed as helping the enemy, and George W. Bush's then attorney general John Ashcroft liked to say that terrorists deserve no protection. To many immigrants, that sounded a lot like immigrants deserve no protection.

The Trump administration tried but was eventually defeated in its attempt to add a citizenship question to the 2020 census. Other large official surveys provide good local information on the geography of citizenship, and many believed that the only purpose of the question was to allow the Immigration and Customs Enforcement agency to target or even round up individuals, as had been the case for Japanese Americans in World War 2. The question would certainly have intimidated noncitizens from responding to the census, which would reduce the representation and federal funding of the areas in which they live. All in the aid of repairing the Constitution.

In part because of such attitudes, I have never given up my British citizenship and did not become an American citizen until 2012, in part because, until Obama became president, I was less than enthusiastic about swearing allegiance to the United States and its leadership. But as the years passed, it seemed perverse not to acknowledge that my home was here, as were the homes of my children and grandchildren, who had built their own lives in Chicago and New York.

While I never suffered under the PATRIOT Act, being a noncitizen can be unpleasant. One boorish immigration officer took a dislike to me as I reentered the United States from Canada and used a magic marker to deface my green card to ensure that I could never use it again; an immigrant without a green card is effectively criminalized. Its loss turned my life into a bureaucratic hell that lasted for more than a year. There were endless waits to be seen in rooms where no telephones or even books were allowed. In one waiting room at a Newark airport, an officer ordered a weeping supplicant to go back to Miami. "But they told me in Miami I had to come here." "Not my problem, go back to Miami." Another, in an open room in front of dozens of people, loudly and aggressively asked a man when he had last had homosexual intercourse. As President Obama wrote in his autobiography, immigrants "are always afraid that the life you'd worked so hard to build might be upended in an instant."[3] Even after my own near upending, I was deterred from applying by the impossible requirement that I document every trip abroad for the past thirty years. I eventually realized that, at least for the earlier trips, their records were no better than mine. And Anne found my old passports in the basement.

Once I decided to apply for citizenship, the agency that I'd dreaded and seen as a persecutor became my friend. The boors turned polite, the thugs into angels. The bureaucracy could not have been more helpful—it seems that votes count after all—and I even qualified for a special old-age dispensation that required me to answer correctly only 12 out of 20 possible questions (instead of 60 out of 100), many of which had the same answer. (What is the capital of America? Who was the first president? Who famously crossed the Delaware?) As a final hurdle, with no chance to prepare, on the day of the ceremony I was asked by an officer at the door whether, in the two weeks since I had passed the test, I had worked as a prostitute (homosexual or heterosexual was not specified). My late colleague Uwe Reinhardt claimed to have answered, "I have long looked for something in that line of work, but so far without success." At the ceremony, the immigration official who welcomed the new Americans began by telling us that voting was not an important part of citizenship, something that I already knew to be false. I resisted the urge to raise my hand at question time.

That I delayed my citizenship for so long is a good measure of the ambivalence that runs through this book.

Health, Healthcare, Segregation, and Race

It is often claimed that America, unlike Britain, is a classless society, but that Britain's class-based inequalities are mirrored by racial and ethnic inequalities in America.

Black Americans experience a wide range of disadvantages relative to whites, and the disparities go beyond but also contribute to overall income inequality. In late 2022, median earnings for Black men were 19 percent lower than median earnings for white men.[4] In 2020, 39 percent of white men were managers or professionals, whereas only 29 percent of Black men were. (Sixty percent of Asian men were managers or professionals.[5]) In the 2020 poverty statistics, 19.5 percent of Black households were in poverty, as opposed to 8.2 percent of (non-Hispanic) white households.[6] The median net worth of white families is nearly *eight times* that of Black households, $180,200 versus $24,100,[7] a stunning difference that is playing an important part in today's discussion of reparations. Test scores for reading and mathematics are substantially lower for Black people than for white people.[8] In 2020, the birth rate for unmarried women was 27.6 per 100,000 for white non-Hispanics and 54.9 per 100,000 for Black non-Hispanics.[9] Black people are around five times more likely than white people to be murdered, and five times more likely to be murderers.[10] In 2019, according to the Department of Justice, 1.1 percent of the Black population was in state or federal prison, compared with 0.2 percent of the white population.[11]

None of these racial inequalities inspires more discomfort than differences in health and longevity between Black people and white people. Life expectancy at birth in 2020 was seven years less for Black men than for white men (68.0 to 75.0 years) and 4.5 years less for Black women (75.7 to 80.2 years).[12] These gaps had widened in 2020 because of the pandemic, with Black people losing 2.9 years and white people "only" 1.2 years. Immigration turns out to be strongly selective on health because sicker people do not or cannot migrate, and perhaps because so many Hispanics are immigrants or the children of immigrants, Hispanics, like immigrants in general, live longer than whites. This positive gap was almost eliminated during the pandemic, which hurt both Hispanic and Black people more than white people.

Many who are tolerant of economic inequalities find these health differences to be unacceptable. For example, the George H. W. Bush administration, which certainly did not make reduction in *economic* inequalities a priority, made minority health a focus of research within the Department of Health and Human Services, establishing a center in 1990 that eventually led in 2010 to the Institute on Minority Health and Health Disparities as a full-fledged institute of the National Institutes of Health.

One account of racial health disparities assigns at least some of the blame to healthcare, a view that was documented in the 2003 report *Unequal Treatment*, prepared by a panel of the Institute of Medicine of the U.S. National Academies of Sciences.[13] According to the report, physicians, who are largely white, discriminate against minorities through outright racism or through statistical discrimination based on the different patterns of disease among patients in the different groups, a process that *Unequal Treatment* refers to as "bias, stereotyping, and uncertainty." There is evidence that physicians treat some conditions less seriously among Black patients—pain being one example, which paradoxically may have spared these patients from the overprescription of opioids in the late 1990s and early 2000s. How your pain is treated in America has always depended on who you are, what historian Keith Wailoo calls the "politics of pain."[14] The report notes that Black people are less likely to receive (desirable) preventive care, or cardiovascular bypass grafts, while they are more likely than whites to experience such (hugely undesirable) treatments as lower-limb amputation or double bilateral orchiectomy (google it, if you must). Once upon a time, according to Wailoo, the medical system even believed that Black people were immune from cancer, which was thought to be a white woman's disease.[15]

These health inequalities can be linked to income inequality through several stories. An obvious account is that people with more money get better healthcare, especially in the United States, where money plays such a large role in access, so that in places or at times when wealth and income gaps are particularly large, so will gaps in health be particularly large. Such gaps will exist for anything that is bought with money—not just healthcare but housing, food, gym memberships, and so on. But there is another, more intriguing mechanism that has long been argued by the British epidemiologist and activist Richard Wilkinson and Katie Pickett.[16] According to this view, inequality is a kind of social poison, like air pollution, that makes *everyone* sick, rich and poor alike. In the "obvious account" above, in which money affects health, *inequalities* in income and wealth drive *inequalities* in health; in Wilkinson's view, *inequalities* in income drive *levels* of health. It is not just the sick and poor who are hurt by income inequalities; even Musk, Bezos, and Gates would live longer if America were not quite so unequal.

Wilkinson has a nice evolutionary argument. Human beings spent nearly all their evolutionary history in tribes of hunter-gatherers whose members walked a dozen miles or more each day and ate mostly fruits and vegetables with almost no fat or sugar, just what your doctor tells you to do. But most hunter-gatherer bands were relentlessly egalitarian, sharing everything, and that too is something that our bodies evolved to expect.[17] So once you have become a vegan and upped your gym attendance, you should think about moving to a state or town where incomes are more equally distributed.

Material inequalities are different from other, relational, inequalities, such as inequalities in health, but it would come as no surprise if the two phenomena were linked. And indeed, if we compare states in the United States with more and less income inequality, the more unequal states will have lower life expectancy than will the less unequal states. Or they once did. The relationship was strong in the 1980s and 1990s but began to dissolve around 2000 and, according to my calculations, had almost entirely vanished by 2018. Contrary to simple versions of the story, the states with the largest increases in income inequality in the past forty years, such as New York, California, and Connecticut, have been the states with the largest increase in life expectancy.

That inequality makes us sick is a great story and would provide a powerful argument for reining in income inequality, but I do not believe that it is true. Instead, the patterns of inequality and health across the United States are mostly driven by race and by policies associated with race. Back in 1980, the most unequal states were in the South, with Mississippi the champion. At that time, more than a third of Mississippi's population was Black, as it is today. Black Americans have both lower incomes and lower life expectancies than white Americans; thus, states with a large Black population had (and still have) high income inequality and low average life expectancy. Conversely, the states with the highest life expectancy in 1980 were northern plains states, such as Minnesota, Iowa, Utah, and North Dakota, where the fractions of the population who were Black were very low: 1.3 percent, 1.4 percent, 0.6 percent, and 0.4 percent, respectively. Beyond that, the history of racism in the United States has meant, and still means, that public provision of health, education, and welfare is low in states with large Black populations. Put crudely, white majorities in some states do not like to pay taxes to support people who do not look like them. The patterns across American states are the domestic version of the pattern between the United States and European countries; America does not have a European welfare state because of its history of race and racism.[18] Both in the United States (in comparison with Europe) and in the American South (in comparison with the rest of the country), the low level of health and welfare provision hurts everyone, Black and white alike. Racism, not income inequality, is the pollution that harms everyone's health.

High income inequality and poor health persist in the American South to this day. But there have been changes elsewhere. Finance and big tech have become sources of income inequality, especially in New York, Connecticut, New Jersey, and California. At the same time, those are the states where health has improved the most, as their state governments pursue policies that promote health and welfare. Cigarette taxes are only the most obvious example of such policies; New York State levies $4.35 a pack, while Mississippi levies only $1.04. By 2019, we had states that are both very healthy and very unequal.[19]

Black people and white people typically live apart in the United States, a legacy of redlining and of systemic racism. But people seek physicians and hospitals in their communities, and so there are essentially different sets of physicians and hospitals for Blacks and for whites. A group led by Peter Bach at Sloan-Kettering Cancer Center, publishing in the *New England Journal of Medicine*, found that the doctors who treat Black patients rarely see white patients.[20] Work by Amitabh Chandra and Jonathan Skinner documents the granular geographical structure of healthcare and shows that both white patients and Black patients do worse in hospitals that treat more Black patients.[21] These findings hold for Medicare patients, whose age entitles them to almost free treatment at the point of healthcare. The Sloan-Kettering study shows that the doctors who predominantly treat Black patients are less well qualified and are less likely to have access to the resources needed for advanced treatment.

These findings tell us that if healthcare is an important determinant of health, as it certainly is in at least some circumstances, there is more to racial difference than differential treatment by white doctors. Such a result is also consistent with the fact that some racial and ethnic groups, such as Hispanics and Asians, have longer life expectancy than whites. Both studies are unsupportive of the case that is sometimes made for a "matched" healthcare system, in which patients are treated by doctors of the same racial or ethnic group. But what is truly appalling is that the United States has a healthcare system that is run on something close to apartheid lines, with separate but very much unequal facilities for Black people and white people. The racial segregation of American cities supports this arrangement, and so areas where the population is largely Black are served by less sophisticated healthcare, less well-trained physicians, and less well-funded hospitals. These poorer facilities hurt the health of everyone who lives in those areas, white and Black alike.

Income inequality across cities and states is not a basic determinant of health, and its correlation with mortality is a consequence of deeper processes of racial segregation and inequality in America.

Racial differences in health have been diminishing for some years now, at least until the pandemic, which is good news, though it would be better news still if one cause of the shrinking gap were not the worsening health of whites. Beyond that, the educational gap that I have already discussed is increasingly affecting racial differences. For both Black people and white people, mortality rates for those with a college degree have been falling, but not so for those without a degree. Whether people do or do not have a degree, Black mortality rates are, as always, higher than white mortality rates. But Black and white mortality rates for those with a degree are much closer to each other than they used to be, just as are Black and white mortality rates for those without a college degree. Two decades ago, Black mortality rates were not very different between those with a college degree and those without, but that is no longer the case. Educational inequalities in health are becoming more important relative to racial inequalities in health.[22]

Inequality between Generations

It is perhaps not immediately obvious that climate policy is about inequality. Yet preventing global warming is about doing costly things now—like switching to electric cars or using renewable energy or implementing mitigation measures to protect low-lying cities—that will make those of us who are alive now worse off so as to benefit our children and grandchildren. Leaving an unlivable planet to unborn generations would be an act of great selfishness. Yet those unborn generations might be much richer than we are, just as we are richer than our ancestors, and they might have access to technologies that we can only dream of, in which case we might not want to inflict too much pain on ourselves to benefit our much richer descendants. Of course, there is great uncertainty about all of this, but one fundamental question is how we ought to distribute resources between the current and future generations. It's them or us.

If you live long enough, some of the people you have known forever—or at least since college—become famous and make important contributions to world affairs. My friend Nick Stern and I were undergraduates together at Cambridge in England. We both became economists and have stayed friends, including getting to know each other very well during an interminable cricket match in Bangalore in India. While the circling vultures threatened to attack the players, who were moving so slowly as to tempt the hungry birds, there was nothing for us to do except chat and become friends. Stern had a second distinguished career as a public servant, culminating in the publication in 2006 of *The Stern Review on the Economics of Climate Change*, a report commissioned by the British government.[23] The different reactions to the *Review* on the two sides of the Atlantic reveal much about different transatlantic attitudes to inequality and to the extent that we should allow markets to deal with it.

When it was first published, the report sparked enormous debate in Britain and in much of the rest of the world but drew less attention in the United States. Although Stern was besieged by paparazzi lurking in the bushes of his Wimbledon house, courted by heads of state and national academies around the world, decorated by universities with honorary degrees, and made a lord—Baron Stern of Brentford—the report had limited press in the United States. The *New York Times* contained two brief factual reports at the time of publication, an editorial, and occasional discussions in the non-news sections; the *Wall Street Journal*, predictably, was hostile. Interest in the topic has of course greatly risen in the intervening years, and the Biden administration is taking action, most notably in the Inflation Reduction Act of 2022, which, in spite of its name, is mostly about the climate.

Climate change raises difficult issues of how to project the future, of how to trade off costs and benefits, and of ethics, all of which are typically treated differently by American and British economists. In 2007, the *Journal of Economic Literature* (published by the American Economic Association) had two exceptionally fine reviews of the *Stern Review*: one by William Nordhaus of Yale, who won the Nobel Prize for his climate work in 2018, and one by the late Marty Weitzman of Harvard. They focus, as have many other commentators, on the central role of discounting, which is the extent to which future benefits and costs are down-weighted relative to today's benefits and costs. If the future is heavily discounted, what happens to future generations doesn't count for much today. At a discount rate of 1 percent, $100 a year from now is worth $99 today, which is perhaps not much of a reduction, but $100 a year a century from now is currently worth only $37. At 3 percent, the numbers are $97 and $5. Higher discount rates mean that future generations count for very little, and we need pay little attention to inequality between them and us.

The *Stern Review* uses a discount rate that is close to zero. The argument is one of equity, that all people should be treated equally, in this case, no matter when they happen to be born, a date that is of no moral significance. Indeed, the only reason to discount at all is that there is some chance of planetary extinction—if the earth is hit by a large comet or we blow ourselves up—in which case sacrifice today would be pointless;

we don't care about the future when there is none. *Stern's* choice of a low discount rate means that the avoidance of future harm, even very far in the future, is worth substantial sacrifices now. According to much of the American discussion, *Stern's* discount rates cannot be correct because *market* rates of discount, the interest rates that we see on stocks and bonds, are (usually) much larger than zero. In a related version of the same argument, the *Stern* discounting rates cannot be right because we do not observe the rates of national saving that would happen if people really cared so much about their descendants.

Both Nordhaus and Weitzman[24] express their discomfort with *Stern's* taking an explicit ethical position on what the current generation owes to those yet unborn, on the grounds that Stern has no right to impose his ethical position on others. Both Nordhaus and Weitzman believe that a close to zero rate, while perhaps defensible in theory, is typically defended only by British economists and philosophers, a comment that is clearly not meant to be taken as any recognition of the superiority of British thinking. Indeed, Nordhaus refers to "Government House" ethics, in which a ruling elite runs a society whose members' preferences are ignored, and suggests that Stern is "stoking the dying embers of the British Empire."[25] Back to Bangalore, where the British, some of whose players already appeared to be dead, (eventually) lost.

Certainly, the paternalism of any such ethical judgment is a concern, and it is right to demand a democratic discussion and determination of the ethics of climate policy. But a judgment needs to be made on some basis, and Weitzman, Nordhaus, and others argue that we can find at least some of the relevant evidence in markets, revealed by, as Weitzman writes "preferences for present over future utility that people seem to exhibit in their everyday savings and investment behavior."[26] Even if the markets do not reveal *everything* that we need to know about the present and the future, whatever ethical choices we make need to be consistent with market behavior that reveals how ordinary people think about these matters. *Stern's* choices about the ethical parameters are wrong, according to Nordhaus and Weitzman, because market rates are higher than those with which he works.

An even clearer statement of hostility is made by the mostly American (and all non-British) economists (Tom Schelling, Bob Fogel, Douglass North, Vernon Smith, Nancy Stokey, Jagdish Bhagwati, Justin Lin, and Bruno Frey, four of whom won Nobel Prizes) who signed on to the 2004 "Copenhagen Consensus" statement that climate change was not important relative to the world's other problems.[27] At the interest rates commonly prevailing in the bond market—and the group used a rate of 5 percent, which Stokey, in her account of the process, defends as "a reasonable figure, falling within the range of various market interest rates"—climate change is not a serious problem. At 5 percent, the $100 a century from now is worth only 60 cents today, and we should postpone serious action while we accumulate funds to deal with it and hope that irreversible discontinuities do not doom us in the meantime. Yet an irreversible discontinuity of some sort is surely quite likely; there is nothing that indicates that the effects of climate change will be a smooth process, which makes waiting an extremely dangerous recommendation.

If zero discounting (with perhaps a touch of paternalism) is the British vice, the refusal to consider ethical questions directly but leave them to the market is surely the American vice. How do the preferences of unborn generations get expressed in the bond market? If our generation is spending too much and saving too little, does that mean that it is ethically acceptable for our views to be the only ones that count even if our children and grandchildren would think differently? Do we really want to discriminate across people by their date of birth? And do we really think that saving rates, whether by individuals or governments, are the results of considered judgment, even over their own lives, let alone over those of their unknown descendants who will live as far in the future as King George III and George Washington lived in the past? Do we think that markets will do better by future generations than they do with income distribution today? Do we believe that the prices and wages that markets throw up are *just*? Or that what people earn reflects their moral worth?

Whatever it is that is generating market behavior, it is not the outcome of an infinitely farsighted "representative" individual whose market and ethical behaviors are perfectly aligned, and who we can use as some sort of infallible guide to our own decisions and policies. According to some stories, the government will do this for us, correcting our collective missteps, but is it conceivable that this will be done by Congresses and administrations whose favorite sport is kicking problems down the road?

A failure to discount the future, if it is a vice, is a minor one. Relying on markets to teach us ethics is much worse. And as for the British Empire, I should be surprised if Stern has much affection for it. It was the British who transported his father to the other end of the empire, placing him in internment in Australia during World War 2 because he was a Jewish refugee from Germany, and thus an enemy alien.

My fellow economists will berate me for the simplifications that I have made in the arguments about discounting. But that points to another issue, which is that economics is not doing enough to think and write about climate change. As of 2019, "the *Quarterly Journal of Economics*, which is currently the most-cited journal in the field of economics, had never published an article on climate change.[28]" Other leading journals have done little better. Professional economists have every incentive to work on topics that are covered in our most important journals, even at the expense of neglecting the most urgent problem facing the world today. Economists, along with physical scientists, sociologists, and behavioral scientists, have much to contribute to thinking about and shaping the policies that might save us.

Meritocracy and Inequality

For my generation in Britain, born immediately after World War 2, passing exams was our route to opportunity, and meritocracy was the system that distinguished our age from earlier ages of unearned privilege and inequality. It made sense economically that the people who had good jobs were qualified to do them. It made sense ethically because we thought that privilege should be open to all and earned, not inherited. I have no nostalgia for the old system, but on meritocracy itself, it is no longer easy to be so enthusiastic. The elimination of the old inequalities has brought new and different inequalities.

In Britain, the Butler Education Act of 1944 made it possible to go to a university without money. Education helped us develop skills and reach positions that had been closed to our parents. My father started life in the Yorkshire coal mines, with only a primary education. He somehow managed to help me win a scholarship to Fettes—a private school in Edinburgh—(exam number one), so that by the time I won a scholarship to Cambridge (exam number two), it was expected of me to pass exams to get ahead; it was the normal thing to do. Other young people came directly from state schools, public schools in

American parlance, though only about 7 percent of my birth cohort went to a university. Only one in ten of the students at Cambridge were women.

The culture of the old Cambridge was often difficult for the new meritocrats. The historian Tony Judt, who went to King's College, Cambridge, in the mid-1960s from a state school in south London, tells how one mother in his community could not explain to people on her street where her boy had gone; Borstal—prison for young offenders—was the only convincing answer she could come up with.[29] A young mathematics don at King's regularly telephoned his parents in Walsall—a working-class manufacturing town near Birmingham—and was just as regularly told by the apologetic switchboard operator that the lines to *Warsaw* were busy. A summer research assistant was told he would have to wait for his wages until Michaelmas—a medieval festival celebrated in September and which Cambridge still used to organize its calendar—and when he asked when that was and what he should do to get by in the meantime, he was told that he would simply have to sell some securities.

When I had to help grade the scholarship exam for Cambridge entry, I was proud of our open and meritocratic procedures; we did not know the names or the candidates or whence they came, and we were proud of our questions, which tried to select those who could "think like an economist," something that could not be learned by accumulating facts without an understanding of how they fit in or hung together. When the names were revealed, we were distressed but should not have been surprised that the top scorers all came from the same private school. Our attempts to build a meritocracy had been subverted by money; a recent star graduate in economics at Cambridge had been recruited by the school, and he knew exactly what to do to give the parents their money's worth.

That the beneficiaries of the old system would guard their privilege was something we expected, but we did not expect that the meritocrats themselves would soon become the guardians. That we ourselves, who hated privilege so much, would so quickly learn to be its enablers.

In the United States, as in Britain, universities worked to broaden their intake to smart kids of all backgrounds, including women, Jews, and Blacks, using their endowments to support need-blind admission and emphasizing academic merit at the expense of other characteristics such as sports and, particularly, family background. James Bryant Conant, president of Harvard in the 1940s, was a key figure in the transition. He used the Scholastic Aptitude Test (SAT) to admit more students on the basis of academic merit, not only social background. He and many others saw these test scores as great levelers, opening opportunities to all.

The broadening often brought fury from the alumni of top colleges, who saw their children being excluded to make room for people who looked very different from them (though they did like the fact that their daughters could now follow them). In the decades since, the composition of the professions has changed, with class-based privilege replaced by talent in medicine, in law, in banking, and in commerce. The new people were cleverer than those they replaced, which seemed like a good idea, as indeed it is. It's good to have a surgeon who has studied anatomy, an architect who can design a building that doesn't collapse, a lawyer who knows law, and a pilot who can fly a plane.

The newly empowered talent set about making money, at which they were extremely successful, especially in a globalizing and technically changing world, and they opened ever-growing gaps between themselves and those who had not passed the exams. The philosopher Michael Sandel notes that the winners attribute their success to their own merit—it's a meritocracy after all—and have little sympathy for those who have not succeeded, who had their chance and blew it.[30] They come to believe that they know what is good for the less talented, that their technocratic skills replace the need for democracy. Those who make the most money—legitimately or not—get to start philanthropic foundations that try to shape others' behavior. Those who failed the exams, the "demeritocracy," may come to doubt their own merit or may believe that the system is rigged against them.

This sort of meritocracy has given us something that is far from an egalitarian democracy. It may even be less stable than a society based on hereditary privilege, at least in the days when people knew and accepted their place. When I was a child in Scotland, in school and in church, we would sing the lines from Mrs. Alexander's hymn for little children: "The rich man in his castle / The poor man at his gate / God made them high and lowly / And ordered their estate."

Those who missed out on being bankers or corporate executives could be persuaded to believe for a while that the huge salaries of others were in the public interest, helping everyone by creating jobs, paying taxes, and inventing marvelous and sometimes life-changing goods and services. There is a superficial plausibility to "trickle-down" arguments. But the financial crash of 2008 pulled back the curtain and revealed the depths of the scam; the bankers walked away with enormous riches while many others lost their jobs and their homes. I am probably hoping in vain that the trickle-down arguments were dealt a mortal blow. In October 2022, the ephemeral British government under Liz Truss certainly seemed to believe them.

With high income inequality, every test becomes a high-stakes test, whether making tenure, becoming partner, placing at a top hospital, or, most of all, getting your kids into a top university.[31] Cheating pays off in an unequal meritocracy, and the more unequal it is, the more it pays off. It is almost irresistible when everyone seems to be doing it. We recently saw the exposure of the college cheating scandal, where parents paid sums ranging from tens to hundreds of thousands of dollars to gain admission for their children to desirable colleges by faking exam results or bribing sports coaches, who are allowed to admit a few students every year. Yale was one of the universities involved, as was the University of Southern California, where (full disclosure) I have had a visiting position (but not on the sports coaching staff).

Top American schools still make "legacy" admissions, kids whose parents are alumni, and the system plays an important part in the financing of the schools, building commitment and inheritances. But many outsiders have difficulty drawing an ethical distinction between the alumni parents and the parents who bribed the coaches, though the latter now face time in jail. Sandel in his *Tyranny of Merit* argues that after weeding out those who clearly cannot cope with the syllabus, elite universities should select randomly from the remainder.[32] A side benefit would be the elimination of the social engineering by university officials who wield enormous power but face little accountability. Only half of American adults think that colleges are having a positive effect on the country; 59 percent of Republicans think they are having a *negative* effect.[33]

When experts overreach, we get what Bill Easterly has aptly called "the tyranny of experts," and expertise gets devalued along with the experts.[34] Some argue that economists have been among the worst offenders. To an angry underclass, science is spurious, and lies and facts have equal credibility. What *is* true is that opportunity restricted to talent is no more equal than opportunity restricted by class or by wealth. But the clever ones know how to turn themselves into a permanent elite that functions much like the old one, although, in the new dispensation, those excluded are led to blame not the accident of their birth or their parents' failure to get rich but what they are told is their own lack of talent.

CHAPTER 7

RETIREMENT, PENSIONS, AND THE STOCK MARKET

Introduction: Pensions and Inequality

Talking about pensions tends to put people to sleep, young people at least. The young can't believe that they will ever need a pension and are reluctant to think about the tedious choices that they will need to make. I remember Bristol University asking me in 1975 when I was twenty-nine years old to decide about my pension, due to start being paid in 2011, a date that then seemed about as immediate as Ragnarök. Today, in 2022, I am in happy receipt of that pension and am grateful, if not to my younger self, to the administrators, unions, and politicians who made me take care of it. If the young go to sleep at the mention of pensions, the elderly sometimes lie awake worrying about them.

For most of human history, people worked for as long as they were able, and when they could no longer work, they were taken care of by their families. We are not hardwired to plan our pensions, because they were not necessary. Even for those who tried, there were formidable difficulties. In many cultures, people who have wealth are expected to share with their

kinfolk, especially those in need. Sharing makes mutual insurance work and can replace a pension, but it can make it hard for
individuals to save if they want to. Building a nest egg takes a
long time, and, even over the past few centuries, few countries
have seen long enough periods of political and economic stability to ensure that savings in youth and midlife would be available in old age and not be destroyed by inflation, by wars, or by
theft. For those of us born after 1945, long periods of peace and
economic stability can seem like the norm. In truth, such pro-
longed periods have been historically uncommon.

Economists, like others, are divided on whether pension
provision should be a personal or a social decision or, if some
of both, in what proportions. The political right is usually in
favor of individual provision, letting people choose for themselves, while the left favors a large element of communal provision that then involves an element of compulsion. Should social
pensions be supported from the wealth that today's pensioners
built up when they were young, or by taxes on those who are
currently working and who thereby support the elderly? If the
latter, will national savings be reduced, and if so, will that diminish investment, limit economic growth, and penalize future
generations? What happens if people stop having kids or sud-
denly have more kids, so that there is either no one to pay for
today's elderly or a large baby boom generation waiting to get
old and stretch the resources of their kids and grandkids, or of
other people's kids and grandkids.

Whether pensions are social or individual has profound implications for inequality, an aspect that is not discussed as much
as it should be. Here is an analogy. Imagine a fleet of small boats
whose position depends on waves and wind. Over time, the individual boats will drift apart, depending on their shape and size,
on the weather in their immediate vicinity, and on the skill of

their pilots. However, if the boats are connected to one another, or each to a central mother ship by a long and flexible line, the fleet will stay together, with shocks to each boat absorbed by the whole fleet. The fleet will still move around and may finish up far from its starting point, but the boats remain together. This is the social insurance story. The argument against it is that the most skilled pilots are limited by the fact that they are tethered to the group. They share in the mutual insurance but might have done better by themselves. Their experience as successful loners might even be subsequently useful for other members of the fleet, even if they are no longer a part of it.

There is a parallel story for health insurance. Collective health insurance, as in a single-payer scheme, does not eliminate the luck of the draw, in which some get sick, some stay healthy, or some live longer than others, but the pooling of the costs, or the communal provision of health and disability benefits, reduces the effects of health on wealth. That some get sick while others stay healthy tends to widen wealth disparities, through potential loss of earnings or medical costs, but less so when there is collective insurance. Of course, collective insurance also reduces the incentives of individuals to save against misfortune.

Looming over all of this is the stock market, with its often impressive and tempting returns, and sometimes spectacular risks. Who should bear the risks of pensions? Ordinary people? Their employers? Or perhaps the state on behalf of everyone? In the United States, as in other countries, pensions that once were promised and guaranteed by employers have been replaced by pensions that may be paid for (in part) by employers but are invested by employees, who bear the risk if the market crashes and get the proceeds if it booms. The old schemes were not riskless, because there was always the chance that employers would not be able to meet their pension obligations—as in legacy airlines or in defunct coalmining companies. Worse still, firms had an incentive to declare themselves bankrupt to shed their pension obligations. There have been several notorious cases of private equity financiers buying bankrupt firms and restoring them to profitability by persuading judges to default on pension obligations. Evan Osnos, in his book *Wildland,* gives an excellent account of this from coalmining in West Virginia,[1] but this is only one of many such cases.

There is no political or economic consensus on these issues, and views—especially political views—have changed as administrations have come and gone. The numbers are huge; the Organisation for Economic Co-operation and Development estimates that the total value of pension funds in the United States in 2019 was almost one and a half times national income.[2] That stock of pension wealth is part of the total capital stock owned by Americans, and it is that stock of capital that is the basis for future output and income. It is not just pensioners who must care about pension wealth but everyone who expects to work and earn in the future. Pensions are one way in which each generation passes on national wealth to the next. Decisions about pensions by people, employers, and government can have huge consequences for all of us.

The stories in this chapter are about pensions in one form or another, how pensions affect economists, and how economists have affected pension policy.

Star Wars and the Wrinklies

When George W. Bush cut taxes in 2001, the administration was not shy about it. Those of us who were sufficiently well heeled to have paid enough tax received our rebate checks in the fall, the first installment of a multiyear tax cut. We received an advance letter from the Internal Revenue Service telling us to expect it and prominently featuring President Bush as our benefactor. Meanwhile, the economy slowed in the wake of the end of the dot-com bubble, the tax rebates reduced federal inflows, and the huge federal surplus all but vanished, a surplus that only a few months earlier had stretched as far as the eye could see. That left only the surplus from Social Security, which, in the way that the accounts are done, is included in the current federal budget.

The tax cuts were only one of President Bush's election promises in 2000; among the others were increased spending on the military, particularly the construction of a missile defense system (Star Wars), the preservation of Social Security, and the provision of prescription drug benefits for the elderly (the "wrinklies" of my title—then youth slang for the elderly). This last item is an expensive benefit because the cost of drugs has become a larger share of healthcare costs, a trend that has accelerated subsequently, partly for technological reasons and partly because of the effects of providing the pharmaceutical manufacturers with the unlimited money machine that federal prescription drug benefits has given them. By 2022, the benefits totaled $111 billion, about 15 percent of net Medicare outlays, and are expected to double to $224 billion by 2031. Until 2001, big pharma had not pushed for those benefits, fearing that their audacity might trigger price control (their worst nightmare), but as their lobbying strength increased, they decided to shoot for the moon: prescription drug benefit without price control.[3] And indeed, the subsequent legislation prohibited Medicare from negotiating on prices. By 2020, pharma companies had three lobbyists in Washington for each member of Congress. (The prohibition on price negotiation was partly repealed in 2022.)

But even the government cannot have everything it wants, and the immediate clash in 2001 was between the military and the elderly. All of this was before 9/11 changed the administration's priorities.

Secretary of Defense Rumsfeld, recommissioned from the museum of cold warriors, and before he was later diverted to adventures in Iraq and Afghanistan, was determined to begin construction of the missile shield and to expand other areas of military expenditure. The budget for all this was to come out of the available funds that were otherwise earmarked for Social Security. No doubt, there would be widespread benefits from the missile shield, should it ever be built, though I suspect that pensioners would not value them enough to make up for cuts in their pensions. My then colleague Paul Krugman sardonically proposed that the problem should be solved by consolidating the Pentagon with the pension program, thus presumably creating a new catchall Department of Security. Others have noted that the U.S. federal government is essentially an insurance system with an army.

There was also activity on the Social Security front itself. President Bush set up a high-level bipartisan commission to make recommendations for reform, cochaired by former senator Daniel Patrick Moynihan and then CEO of AOL Time Warner Richard Parsons. Its members, including economists John Cogan, Estelle James, Olivia Mitchell, and Thomas Saving, were selected from those known to support another campaign pledge, the creation of personal retirement accounts. (Cogan and Saving were publicly declared Republicans, James and Mitchell Democrats.) The commission immediately encountered one of the central difficulties of creating personal retirement accounts: if today's workers put their retirement savings into their own personal accounts, that money is no longer available to pay for the long-promised benefits of today's retirees. The young are paying into their own pensions and can hardly be expected to pay for the currently elderly too. Not to mention that people might invest their pension funds unwisely or unluckily. All of this would have been easier in the presence of the budget surplus that had been dissipated by the tax cuts.

The commission's report, whose terms of reference required commission members to recommend some form of personal accounts, proposed three possible schemes and suggested there be a discussion period of at least a year before legislation be enacted.[4] That legislation never came, but as I will recount below, President Bush returned to the issue in his second term. Even so, as of 2023, there are no personal retirement accounts available within Social Security.

Back in 2001, behavior was changing in ways that might have made it easier to enact reforms, at least in the long run. One helpful adjustment for Social Security would be to increase retirement ages so that any increase in life expectancy is shared between work and retirement. (That was in the days when life expectancy could be reliably expected to increase from year to year.) Increasing the retirement age is generally opposed by unions, many of whose members do not think of work as a positive part of their lives, and who regard retirement in their sixties as an important part of the promise of Social Security.

Closer to (my) home, retirement in American academia perhaps provides a preview. When the baby boom generation started going to college in the late sixties, a generation of professors was hired to teach them, and they passed through the transition from work to retirement well ahead of the baby boomers themselves. When Congress passed the Age Discrimination Act in 1986, outlawing compulsory retirement, colleges and universities were granted an exemption allowing them to retain

compulsory retirement at age seventy until 1994. This exemption was based on the argument that compulsory retirement was
necessary to make space for young faculty, especially women
and minorities. Based in part on a study that showed that the
removal of compulsory retirement would have little effect on
actual retirements[5]—the last thing that a professor wants to do
is to go on teaching when there is no need—the exemption was
allowed to expire.

But it turns out that the projections—including a similar one by
the National Academy of Sciences[6]—were wrong, and professors
stayed on in large numbers. An analysis by Orley Ashenfelter
and David Card showed that before the change, essentially
all professors reaching their seventieth birthdays retired,
while, afterward, only 30 percent did so.[7] As a result, while only
10 percent of the seventy-year-old faculty used to still be at work
at age seventy-two (there were some states in which mandatory
retirement was always prohibited), 50 percent of them did so
once they could.

One young academic friend was stunned to discover that the
chair of his tenure review committee was someone he had long
supposed to have departed not only the university but also the
world. At some universities, administrators have actively tried
to promote the retirement of older faculty, with flexible part-
time bridging arrangements and some supplementation of pension funds for those whose salaries (or investment decisions)
have left them unable to depart in comfort. Ashenfelter and
Card find that professors in private research universities are a
good deal less likely to retire than those in institutions where
teaching loads are relatively high, as are professors with higher
salaries or lower pension accumulations.[8] Interestingly, a high
salary relative to others in your own institution discourages retirement, even conditional on wealth and absolute salary;

power and status are pleasurable in themselves and vanish at retirement. They report no effect of missile defense on the probability of retirement.

That so many professors have no wish to retire may simply indicate that we have easy lives and that teaching a few classes is not like running a company, let alone like working in a low-level job. If so, a good solution to national pension provision would be to make all jobs as pleasant and fulfilling as those of college professors.

At the Pension Office

Over the past fifty years, there has been a huge change in the way that Americans earn and receive their pensions.[9] In the old days, most employees who had pensions had "defined benefit" pensions. This is just what it sounds like: the amount and timing of the pension are set in advance, or according to agreed rules (for example, in relation to final salary). Payments are guaranteed by the employer or, if the employer goes out of business, by a government entity, the Pension Benefit Guaranty Corporation, which covers at least part of the obligation. The pensions are paid for by employer and employee contributions during the employee's working life. In the private sector, defined benefit pensions have now largely been replaced by "defined contribution" pensions, where, as before, the employer and the employee make contributions during the employee's working years, but the money is invested and the employee gets the proceeds after retirement, in the form of a monthly payment.

Many university professors, including me, are in a defined contribution scheme. Such an arrangement presents an aging professor with a huge disincentive to retire, and as we have seen, universities, like other employers, cannot force retirement. Even for those of us who have an adequate accumulation, the idea of going from a large monthly paycheck to a precisely nothing paycheck is a terrifying one. A defined benefit scheme (usually) has a downward step, not a precipice. Many academics are well paid, but the world is a tough place, and many friends of my age have grown-up children whose financial futures are far from ensured and who depend on their parents' support, now and in the future. Many who would be delighted to quit the classroom with a pension are unwilling to do so with zero salary replacement.

A dean at Princeton once told me that he spent most of his time on three tasks: trying to hire minorities, trying to find jobs for the spouses of potential new hires, and trying to persuade people to retire. He and his assistants had long stalked a recalcitrant eighty-five-year-old, explaining to him (very loudly and with much repetition) the contents of the retirement document, only to see their prey drop the pen from his shaking hand and declare, "Damn it, I'm going to shoot for ninety."

I decided early in October 2015 that I would sign the retirement papers before the deadline of my seventieth birthday and take an incentive bonus of half a year's salary. The decision would have been easier had I anticipated the phone call from Stockholm that came four days later, but Anne and I had decided, not without trepidation, that we had enough for the future. Anne had no intention of retiring any time soon, and we were fortunate not to have dependents in need. At the same time, my calculations included claiming both my British and American state benefits, which required encounters with the pension administrations of both countries. How these dealings are conducted is a feature of state safety nets that is almost as important as the financial rules themselves.

No one looks forward to dealing with bureaucracies. I had always been fortunate in Britain and am of an age, born in the first days of the welfare state, that saw the government as my friend. It still proved to be so, more than half a century later. The online forms were not easy; much that was demanded seemed not to apply, and, as usual, there was insufficient space to explain just why. But I did the best I could and pressed the submit button. I received some snail mail and even managed to mediate an implausibly successful interchange between the American tax authorities and the British pension system. There were two phone calls to officials, who I imagined as kindly and boundlessly competent middle-aged aunts wearing cardigans and drinking tea, who knew exactly what they were doing. Soon, I was the happy recipient of two modest but welcome monthly checks from Britain, both defined benefit, one from the Universities Superannuation System, and one from the state. They appear in my bank account with neither fuss nor bother.

Not so with my application to the American Social Security Administration, though it promised an easy all-online experience. All went well at first, but my joint citizenship must have raised a flag, and I was told to come into one of the Social Security Administration centers. I should have been just as pleased to be told to report to the nearby state prison. When I got there, bearing my internet-issued appointment, I was seen quickly by a not very friendly employee behind very thick glass. I presented the number the system had given me but was told that the computer had no record of it or of me. I was told to wait to be seen in an inner sanctum and settled down and tried not to think of Dickens or Kafka. I was surrounded by unhappy supplicants, mostly African American or Hispanic, some with physical or mental disabilities, and a good many in distress. People had lost documents, had been cut off from support, and were battling not very responsive or helpful officials whose own powers were clearly limited. It was hard to know which group to sympathize with more.

Perhaps I had read too much Dickens and Kafka, for I was quite soon ushered through a security check into another office, without glass barriers this time, and quizzed by a young woman with a presumably more powerful or better-connected computer. "What will your income be this year?" she asked. Given the Social Security rules, this should not have been relevant, but it was hardly the place to argue the point. Nobel Prizes are treated as ordinary income, and then there was my half-year retirement bonus as well as Anne's and my regular full-year salaries (I was not retiring until the following July), some speaking fees, and a little consultancy income, so when I named the preposterous amount—including the prize money—I thought that the game was up. Millionaires go home. My interrogator did not react but left her desk for a minute or two, and on her return she told me that what I earned was irrelevant and asked which bank should receive the payments.

As I got up to leave, one of her colleagues stood and asked if it was true that I had won a Nobel Prize. Yes, I said. "Wonderful," he said, beaming and shaking my hand, and as he and all his coworkers crowded around, he said, "We've never had a Nobel Prize winner in this office before."

Pensions and the Stock Market

When I moved to Princeton from Britain in 1983, I started contributing toward my pension. Given that I would not retire from teaching until 2016, I had more than thirty years to build a fund. Princeton made contributions and I made contributions out of my salary. How much I would have to spend in retirement would depend on my portfolio choices and on how the stock market performed. This was quite different from the pension arrangement I had left behind in England, where there were no investment choices to make, and where my retirement income, which was indexed for inflation, depended on my last salary and on my years of service. I had been promoted young, so compared with someone promoted just before retirement, I contributed more over my working life but received the same pension afterward. But I have no complaints, and I have received a nontrivial sum from it every month for the past decade.

Most American academics working in private universities have pensions like my Princeton one, but many in public universities, notably the very large University of California system, have arrangements more like my British one. The choice reflects deep philosophical and political differences; California and Britain take a collective responsibility and the investment is done centrally, with the proceeds disbursed in a way that reflects the individual's service and not his or her individual prowess or luck in the stock market. This approach is more like "to each according to their need" (or perhaps "to each according to their deserts," given that the amount depends on university service) and less like "to each according to their luck in the casino." In the individual approach, the results depend on individual choice and on the market, and the individual takes the risks. Of course, there is no way of eliminating investment risks—someone must take the risk—and the success of the collective approach depends on the central investment authority doing well. This has not been the case in Britain in recent years, with much agony and dispute, including strike action by university teachers. Conservatives, who are deeply suspicious of government, also worry about the irresistibility of collective funds to predation by politicians, even well-meaning politicians who are rarely short of pet schemes to make the world a better place given only a ready supply of other people's money.

Like many young people, I gave little thought to events that were many years ahead. But I was soon filled with delight rather than with fear. When I started at Princeton, the Dow Jones Industrial Average stood at 1,200, having not long passed 1,000. When the Dow broke 7,000 in 1997, it had seen a 16 percent annual growth rate, about 13 percent a year in inflation-corrected terms. By the spring of 2022, the annual growth rate since 1983 had been 9 percent nominal and more than 6 percent corrected for inflation. Like other stockholders, we did very well during the pandemic, at least until Putin invaded Ukraine. House prices in many parts of the United States were almost stagnant in the 1990s, so that the stock market portion of their pensions replaced housing equity as the engine of enrichment for professors.

Academics are not the only middle-class Americans with a personal interest in the stock market. American corporations have systematically replaced their once-standard defined benefit pension schemes with defined contribution and employee-directed plans. As a result, many white-collar workers were given an immediate and transparent interest in events on Wall Street. For the many Americans whose first experience of the market was a defined contribution plan in the 1980s and '90s, the stock market has been a fairy godmother. So long as the market boomed, corporations and politicians could also cash in. Governor Christine Whitman of New Jersey, elected in 1994 on a promise to reduce state income taxes, did so by using the stock market gains on the (defined benefit and at that time overfunded) pension funds of state employees. Her success (very temporarily) made her one of the rising stars of the Republican Party—until the Republican Party in the Northeast, along with other moderate Republicans, went virtually extinct.

As the stock market and private pensions boomed, the federal pension system, Social Security, was running out of money. When that happens, experts convene and try to figure out what to do. According to a 1997 report of an Advisory Council on Social Security chaired by Edward Gramlich of the University of Michigan, payments to beneficiaries were estimated to exceed pay-as-you-go contributions within twenty-five years, with exhaustion of the fund a decade later in 2032. Contrary to popular perception, the problem was not the aging of the baby boomers moving into retirement, an event that had been anticipated for many years. The problems were more mundane, particularly the reduction in contributions from slower than expected growth in employment and earnings. The system could be made solvent for the next seventy-five years if the current Social Security payroll tax were raised from the current 12.4 percent to 14.6 percent, a solution that was about as likely as universal health insurance, gun control, or the abolition of the death penalty. Indeed, the rate remains at 12.4 percent in 2023. Instead, the council recommended that social insurance turn to the same fairy godmother as private insurance, investing a part of Social Security on Wall Street.

The issues of how to do this and the extent to which it should be done left the council hopelessly fractured. The smallest faction (the chairman and one supporter) adopted a middle-of-the-road position, while the two other larger groups embraced the extremes. One group—largely union representatives but also an ex-commissioner of the Social Security Administration and the chairman of TIAA/CREF (now just TIAA), the fund that holds my Princeton pension—regarded the stock market with deep suspicion, saw the current Social Security Administration as a great success, and proposed solving the financial shortfall partly by the government investing current surpluses in the market and partly by increasing taxes in 2045! Everyone can vote for that.

If this proposal is a caricature of the sort of irresponsible and time-inconsistent planning that opponents of Social Security have always charged it with, the views of the opposite group were a similarly extreme endorsement of the ability of individuals to use the market to plan their own retirements. They recommended that up to a half of Social Security contributions be invested in personal saving accounts under individual control—privatization—without controls on the selection of assets, and with people allowed to withdraw all their investments in a lump sum at the date of retirement should they choose to do so. The late eminent economist James Tobin referred to this as a "madhouse" in which stock and bond salesmen compete "for every old geezer's Social Security fund."[10] One group emphasized the high mean returns in the market, while the other emphasized the risks, which were highly variable, both across time and across people.

As I recounted above, President George W. Bush appointed a committee of his own in 2001, whose recommendations for private accounts went nowhere. In 2005, buoyed by his reelection, Bush tried to use the political capital of being legitimately elected without the intervention of the Supreme Court to set off down the privatization road once more, but the Democrats' capture of both houses in 2006 brought that effort to a halt. Later still, the Financial Crisis in 2007 and the drop in the Dow by almost a half by early 2009 tarnished the reputation of the fairy godmother, and for a while there was little talk of privatization. And indeed, even today, when the stock market reached its all-time high during COVID-19, none of Social Security is invested in the market. The system limps on, always under the threat of financial exhaustion, though the date of calamity remains firmly in the future and has been pushed back by modest increases in the age at which Social Security payments can begin, the age that Social Security deems the age of retirement.

What about the professors? Back in the 1980s, professors were not allowed full control over the choice of assets in their retirement portfolios; they could choose only between stocks and bonds and could allocate only new deposits, not the accumulation. As part of the general societal move toward individualism and belief in markets, this kind of paternalism went out of fashion. Academics are now presented with a much larger menu, including such recent exotica as green funds, as well as plain, old-fashioned cash, so that we can play the market. For professors who distrust the stock market (but not of course economists!), they can invest for retirement using Treasury Bills, an option that John Shoven of Stanford once compared to trying to travel from New York to Los Angeles on the subway. When Richard Thaler, of later "nudge" fame, tried to find out how people chose their allocation, many recollected that they had chosen the default, despite there being none, and when pressed, they recalled that they had asked the administrator who had handed them the forms when they were first hired. The administrator, in turn, mostly told new entrants what other people had done. In this haphazard manner, millions of dollars in pensions were gained or lost.

This situation can be likened to not just a casino but a casino where the players are blindfolded and are advised on what to bet by the waiters bringing the drinks. Still, some go home happy. That is what casinos do; even if everyone has the same when they enter, that is far from the case when they leave.

By giving the faculty such freedom of choice, Princeton and other participating universities have lost the assurance that their faculty will be secure in their old age, an assurance that was surely one of the reasons for the universities' participation and for the restriction on the range of investments that were allowed. Such restrictions provided a halfway house between defined benefit pensions, where individuals had no control, and unrestricted defined contribution pensions, in which individualism triumphs. There once was no risk that the doorways of Nassau

Hall would become shelters for homeless elderly Nobel laureates, whose caution had led them to believe that cash was the
"safe" asset for long-term investment or who believed that fairy
godmothers always smile.

But perhaps that would not be a problem, either in the university or in the country. Judging by the Advisory Council's
report, many Americans believe that their incomes and their
stock market successes (or failures) are the result of their own
efforts and are available to everyone. Those who are successful
in the market owe little to those who are not. Ayn Rand strikes
again. The distributional battleground between left and right
had moved away from the old, static questions of tax progres-
sivity and toward more dynamic issues, particularly insurance
and the extent to which the lucky bear responsibility for the
unlucky. Along the way, there has been a massive shift in who
bears risk, from corporations and investment managers to individuals, many of whom are neither skilled in risk management
nor adequately protected if they get it wrong. The shift from
collective to individual risk management that has taken place
since 1975 is a recipe for dividing people into winners and losers
and for widening inequality.[11]

Suns and Moons: After the Financial Crisis

There is a sexist joke about two women sitting on a park bench
in the moonlight in Dallas:

> "Which do you think is closer," muses one, "the moon or
>   Houston?"
> "Duh."
> "What do you mean, duh?"
> "Duh, can you see Houston from here?"

Less than 10 percent of Americans reported being able to "see" any reduction in unemployment as a result of President Obama's 2009 stimulus, the American Recovery and Reinvestment Act, which was spending more than $800 billion to offset the crash.[12] The idea that such spending would reduce unemployment traces back to the work of Keynes in the 1930s and was (and is) supported by a very large majority of, though not all, economists. As the government spends the money, new jobs are created or old jobs are brought back, and incomes are higher than they would have been without the stimulus.

Not so, according to many Republican candidates who were then running for senior office, often successfully, on platforms that promised to cure unemployment by *eliminating* the deficit in Washington. Let's put out the fire by turning off the water. More seriously, many people believe that what applies to families—where, at least eventually, you must tailor your spending to your income—applies to governments too. This belief was widely held during the Great Depression in the 1930s and remains so today, even though it is wrong. Its attraction comes, no doubt, from its homely and apparently simple analogy. But governments do not run out of money in the way that people do—they can print more money if they need it, and there is little risk of inflation when the economy is running below capacity. Reducing government spending in a slump is like reducing imports of food during a famine.

For those of us brought up on Keynesian economics, we had long thought that the antideficit dragon had long been slain. We can perhaps blame the dismal state of much of American education for such ignorance, but it is hard not to blame economists, whose internal divisions and failure to develop an agreed-upon narrative have failed to set any limits on the public debate about cause and effect in macroeconomics. Perhaps not—we would hardly blame astrophysicists for the relative positions of Houston, Dallas, and the moon. Yet astrophysicists are surely in closer agreement on the structure of the solar system than are economists on the structure of the economy.

Economics is like Darwinian evolution, where people's beliefs are well predicted by their political ideology; it is not fanciful to imagine state governments and school boards in Texas or Florida legislating against the teaching of Keynesian economics, even before they get to thinking about the relative positions of Houston and the moon or about critical race theory. While I am not naive enough to suppose that economics has a core scientific content that can be separated from politics, an outsider might wonder just what we have all been doing for the past eighty years. The profession has not done well in building a consensus about fundamental macroeconomic questions such as stimulating growth or maintaining full employment, even within itself, so it is perhaps not surprising that we have not persuaded the lay population.

Universities were hurt in the Financial Crisis of 2008, but they did not suffer to the degree that many Americans thought they deserved. At a time when unemployment was high, there was (and still is) a good deal of irritation over the lifetime employment guarantee granted by tenure and a lack of understanding as to why a bunch of academics, with short work hours and high salaries—and a notable inability to predict or to handle a financial crisis—should somehow be exempt from the insecurities experienced by others. The irritation is not mollified by the cost of university education rising much faster than the price level, or by the stock of student-loan debt having grown larger than credit card debt. Tenured professors are about as popular as bankers. A recent newspaper article about disaffected white voters in Virginia reported on "umbrage at what they consider condescension from outsiders" and "bemoan 'Ph.D. pollution' from the big local university, Virginia Tech."[13]

Universities made substantial cuts after the crisis, especially in support staff, not because the support staff were particularly to blame but because, without tenure or unions, they were easily fired. Especially outside the top universities, costs were reduced by accelerating the gradual replacement of tenured faculty by "adjuncts," who have no tenure, heavy teaching loads, no research time, and low salaries. By some estimates, more than two-thirds of university teaching is now done by non-tenure-track adjuncts.

Universities are now much more exposed to market fluctuations than in the past. They took most of the twentieth century to move out of bonds and into equities, but only twenty years beyond that to adopt the more aggressive investment strategies that were pioneered at Yale, including private equity, venture capital, hedge funds, and commodities. From 1986 to the eve of the Financial Crisis, their collective endowments exploded, from under $50 billion to more than $350 billion, with a brief interruption from 2000 to 2003. Even the 45 percent reduction in the S&P 500 from May 2008 to March 2009, if reflected in university endowments, would have eliminated only the previous two years' returns so that, even *after* the crisis, the search for "absolute return" paid off handsomely.

Perhaps, with such portfolio gains, universities would have been well placed to ride out a financial storm. After all, just why *was* Harvard sitting on $37 billion in June 2008? Or, say, $25 billion after the crisis? Administrators seem more concerned to use the university to protect the endowment than to use the endowment to protect the university. Ben Bernanke, when still at Princeton, complained that the administration's only concern was to make the endowment "as big as the sun," even bigger than the moon. (Bernanke used to claim that chairing Princeton's economics department was more difficult than chairing the Federal Reserve, but that was before the crash. Even after the crash, he believed that the most difficult public service of his life was chairing the school board in Montgomery, the town outside of Princeton where he lived.)

While it is not clear what administrators *should* do in the face of financial fluctuations, it would seem reasonable for endowments to be run down further after a crash, not rebuilt. But universities typically use spending formulas that are a percentage (say 5 percent) of their endowments averaged over the past several years. These rules were conservative on the way up, but as markets soared in the early 2000s, they nevertheless generated large new expenditures—for example, on the creation of new programs on currently fashionable topics, some of which are of low inherent value but are hard to eliminate once established. As a result, even though universities were still much richer after the crash than they were only a few years before, the spending rules could not be maintained without cuts, and administrators (and trustees) have typically been unwilling to allow more than temporary increases in the spending rule. Spending out of shrunken endowments means that the share of endowment being spent is too high by the usual rules, something that has terrified many administrators. According to a study by Jeff Brown and his colleagues, the typical behavior was to *cut* the spending rate to try to rebuild the endowment, turning it into a millstone, not a life preserver.[14] Universities cut the sizes of their incoming classes, reduced financial aid, and cut everything *except* the number of administrators. Some also borrowed very large sums to deal with the liquidity crises induced by their private equity and venture capital activities, a possibility that appears to have been entirely unanticipated.

Outside the academic gates of Princeton is the state of New Jersey, which, like most other states, had acute problems of its own. Most American states are constitutionally required to balance their budgets, and so they had no option in the crisis but to fire employees as their revenues decreased. For a while, the stimulus from Washington provided temporary help. Desperate for cash, states, like the universities, sought "absolute return" through alternative investments, particularly for the pension funds that support the (still mostly defined benefit) pensions of their retired workers.

Many state pensions are protected by constitutional guarantees that make them almost impossible to modify (and many state workers are not covered by Social Security, and so they have no other source of pension income), and some—although by no means all—states were clearly going to be unable to meet their obligations. When there was almost nothing left, a high-stakes poker game (shooting the moon?) offered the only chance of solvency, albeit a slim one—so states, like universities, invested their pension funds in ever-riskier investments.

The Financial Crisis changed all this. States that could at one time use the profits from their pension funds to cut taxes were at risk of running out of money to pay pensions that they were constitutionally bound to provide, at least until the state treasurers won the poker game. The Financial Crisis made it almost impossible for states to repair these problems in a prudent way, and politicians, even more than individuals, have enormous incentives to avoid pain now at the expense of much greater pain later. Illinois made its federally required contribution to its pension fund in one year by borrowing the funds from the pension fund itself. In 2010, the State of New Jersey was sued by the Securities and Exchange Commission for securities fraud for lying about the solvency of its pension fund, and other states also came under investigation.

Princeton and Harvard are not going bankrupt any time soon, and their employees were "safely"—at least from the universities' perspective—bearing the risk of their own pensions. Of course, with interest rates held near zero during the pandemic, and the stock market at new records, at least temporarily, our pension accumulations are doing much better than any of us dreamed. And the state pension funds have recovered too, some through sharply increased contributions over the past decade, and some, once again, from the fairy godmother and her (presumably temporary) largesse.

There is no painless or risk-free solution to providing and funding pensions. People are often myopic, and politicians very much so—political lives are shorter than people's lives. The stock market is often irresistible, but it is folly to tie the fates of ordinary people to its fluctuations. There is no fairy godmother. While there is certainly scope for people to share in the growing wealth of the economy, pensions need to be collectively managed so that unscrupulous but relatively well-informed politicians and managers are not able to shift risk to poorly informed individuals whose material wellbeing in retirement is often barely adequate. More recently, bitcoin has become the new tempting mirage, with even greater risks than the stock market. Egged on by the industry,[15] and despite warnings from the Biden administration,[16] the Fairfax Virginia County Retirement System invested in bitcoin in 2022.[17]

Movers and Shakers:
Letters from Baby Boomers in the Bathroom

The links between economic research and economic policy are slow and unpredictable, when they exist at all. Few doubt that academic ideas have important long-term effects or that economists working in Washington help shape the immediate debate. But it is unusual to find examples where changes in the law can be traced to specific pieces of academic research not only without a delay of many years but even before the results have been published. Yet that is what happened in the spring of 1996.

The economics profession in the United States is impressively open. Economists can become full professors at major universities when still in their twenties, and the rewards for such success come not only in academic status but also in cash. Competition from business schools generated continuing real growth in the salaries of academic economists, even for those not in finance. An initially high salary, a long career, and a friendly stock market can generate very large accumulations. To take a high-end, but by no means impossible, example, a sixty-year-old senior professor of economics, earning $200,000 a year in 1998, whose salary has grown at 5 percent real per annum, who has been a professor for thirty-five years, whose institution has always contributed 12 percent of his salary, and who has invested the proceeds in the S&P 500, would have a pension fund of around $2.3 million in 1998 prices, $4.0 million in 2022 prices. The same trends would give the young twenty-five-year-old superstar more than $24 million at 1998 prices ($41.35 million in 2022 prices) in her pension fund by age sixty. These amounts have yet to be taxed, but they are large enough to trigger then-existing exotic taxes that had originally been designed to apply only to the truly wealthy.

The effects of the "excess accumulation" and "excess distribution" taxes were brought to the attention of the profession, policymakers, and the public in a November 1996 working paper by John Shoven of Stanford and David Wise of Harvard.[18] These taxes were designed to prevent pension schemes from being used as tax shelters by the rich and were imposed in the Tax

Reform Act of 1986, one of whose general concerns was to dismantle abusive tax shelters. The effects were to undo many of the benefits of tax-free accumulation within a pension fund, particularly after death, when the funds are passed through an estate. The "excess" taxes were levied on top of state and federal income and estate taxes, so that if someone on the verge of retirement were unfortunate enough to die and had enough put away to trigger the tax, the heirs could easily inherit less than ten cents on the dollar, or if they had the further misfortune to live (and die) in New York, only a quarter of one cent on the dollar. Nor did you have to be super rich to trigger the taxes; compound interest works sufficient magic for someone of even modest means who persistently saves over a long working life.

Shoven and Wise's paper attracted an enormous amount of attention, not only among tax accountants and estate planners but in the general press. There was widespread outrage that middle-class baby boomers, whose only vice was thrift, should face confiscatory "success" taxes just because they'd had the foresight to put their money in the stock market. This is the same argument that Milton Friedman had long used to support the abolition of estate taxes.

In the summer of 1997, when Shoven and Wise presented their work at a conference at a golf resort in Arizona whose house-sized hotel rooms are disguised as giant boulders in the Sonora desert, with saguaro cacti standing guard all around, the thoughtful housekeeping details included the provision of reading material in each bathroom, including *Worth* magazine. The magazine's cover article warned the resort's golfers and gourmets (and economists) of the imminent threat to their wealth. *Esquire* magazine bemoaned the fate of what it called "America's new 'underrich'—wealthy enough to boast seven-digit estates, but not enough to afford the estate planning that the real rich have enjoyed for generations"—and urged its readers to "take pencil in hand, write a couple of blunt letters, and send them to Senator Bill Roth and Representative Bill Archer, the chief tax legislators in Congress. Tell them you want these levies repealed, like, yesterday."[19]

If not yesterday, at least tomorrow, and the "excess" taxes were repealed as part of the Taxpayer Relief Act of 1997, which "scored" the repeal as a revenue increase, citing the incentive to make withdrawals and pay the deferred tax. The voices of well-heeled baby boomers are rarely ignored in Washington, even if their complaints are written in pencil on toilet paper. For good measure, the 1997 budget also effectively abolished capital gains tax on the sale of owner-occupied homes. Until then, such gains could be rolled over but (subject to a limited exemption) were ultimately taxed; once again, it is hard not to see the preoccupations of the baby boom generation, whose time to pay capital gains taxes on their homes was coming close. In such an environment, it is much harder to deal with the really big issues, like funding Social Security and, especially, Medicare. But no matter, so long as the "underrich" are taken care of.

Economists Working Together on Pensions and Social Security

Economists often share a secret sympathy with those non-economists, journalists, and policymakers who accuse us of being more concerned with efficiency than equity, and more likely to respond to the needs of the rich than those of the poor. We are also accused of being overpaid, overspecialized, and overformal, as well as being obsessed with methodology, with theory (not fact), and with the "sophisticated" analysis of unreliable data. It was not an outsider but a former editor of one of our leading technical journals, *Econometrica*, the late

Hugo Sonnenschein, who wondered whether it might not be time to split that journal into its constituent parts: *Esoterica* and *Trivia*.

Viewed from outside the United States, American economics is often seen as something worse than irrelevant. Joan Robinson, Cambridge professor and friend and pupil of Keynes's, used to like to accuse neoclassical economists of being apologists for capitalism, and it is not hard to find examples where the label fits. But there are counterexamples, and here is one.

Twenty years ago, I attended the third-annual Social Security Day at the National Bureau of Economic Research (NBER). The Bureau is a nonpartisan research organization in Cambridge, Massachusetts, just along the street from Harvard on the road to MIT, that acts as an umbrella for a large collection of research projects and workshops. Each year, it organizes a "Summer Institute," an overlapping festival of workshops in almost all areas of applied economics. Social Security Day is a one-day workshop held during the Institute and was organized by the late Martin Feldstein, then a long-serving president of the NBER and very much responsible for its modern shape. (The NBER was also responsible for the conference in Arizona described in the last section.)

As we have seen, the U.S. Social Security system is in perpetual need of reform. Many different schemes are discussed, including raising the retirement age, partially replacing the current pay-as-you-go system with a set of individual accounts, and investing part of the Social Security trust fund in the stock market, as well as some combination of raising taxes and reducing benefits. Each of these options makes some people better off and some people worse off, and all involve serious political risk. There are sharp political divides. Conservatives, like Feldstein was, tend to favor market-based solutions that reduce the role of government, arguing for individual saving accounts, with the government providing no more than a backup safety net. Many conservatives have a deep, and often well-founded, concern that politicians will interfere in the investment of a trust fund and that it will be difficult to construct institutions to prevent such legalized theft. They also point to the historical record, which shows that over periods of any reasonable length, the stock market has outperformed other investments.

Those more skeptical of market solutions worry about the increasing inequality that inevitably comes with individuals making their own investments, some of which do better than others. They also like the mutual insurance that comes from a shared system and worry about the administrative costs and possible abuses by the financial sector of millions of individual accounts. Several times friends have come to me to ask about investment advisers who ask for 1 percent of the portfolio each year to manage the fund. They are usually surprised and even skeptical when I note that thirty years at 3 percent is only 75 percent of thirty years at 4 percent, and thus the adviser is reducing their final wealth by a quarter.

The most remarkable feature of the Social Security Day that I attended was the ability of economists of different political positions and, perhaps even more divisively, of different academic specialties to work together and pool their skills. Feldstein himself took strong public positions in favor of individual accounts, and much of his academic work tends to support that avenue of reform. But this did not prevent the NBER from doing its job under his direction, which was to provide a forum for broad discussion. Nor did it prevent Feldstein from exposing his arguments to the fiercest professional criticism and questioning—one memorable question from Stanford economist Robert Hall was, If the stock market has such great rates of return, why shouldn't we finance *all* of government from the profits of issuing government bonds and putting the proceeds into the market?—or using his vast personal knowledge of economic theory, data, and policymaking to benefit others' work. Feldstein had been the head of the Council of Economic Advisers in the Reagan administration until his principled arguments against federal deficits ran afoul of the voodoo economics of Reagan's other advisers.

On the opposite side of the privatization argument, the subsequent Nobel laureate Peter Diamond has long been an effective public voice drawing attention to the distributional consequences of possible reforms and to the effects of apparently small administrative costs on the ultimate accumulations in individual accounts. Diamond's fundamental work in macroeconomics provides part of the framework within which almost all serious discussion of Social Security rests.

Both Feldstein and Diamond are economists who focus on public finance (the field is nowadays called public economics), and perhaps the largest fraction of the group could be similarly classified. But there were also health economists, demographers, and actuaries—a great deal hinges on projections of life expectancy and on the relationship between mortality and income. Finance specialists from economics departments and business schools were there to discuss portfolio allocation, risk sharing, the costs of being in the market, and the possibilities for portfolio management. Macroeconomists and general equilibrium theorists traded the (infinitely many) fine points of thinking about equity between generations; microeconomists and welfare economists reminded us about incentives, moral hazard, and the powerlessness of the unborn; and political economists and game theorists worried about the political viability of economically attractive solutions. Applied economists argued about the determinants of saving, of mortality, and of portfolio choice, and there were empirical results from big data.

We saw some of the first fruits of the new Bureau of the Census centers for data analysis, behind whose firewalls it was becoming possible to merge survey data with government administrative records. There were economists from economics departments, from business schools, from law schools, from schools of public health, and from government and international agencies. Much of the material was technical, and there was no lack of mathematical economics or of econometrics, close enough to the frontiers to please an editor of *Econometrica*. Indeed, many would have thought the discussion esoteric, perhaps even many economists. Yet this workshop was the opposite of trivial, presenting clear, serious, and relevant thinking, with a harvest of important insights about the many sides of a truly complex issue. There are times when economists need make no apology for their profession.

CHAPTER 8

ECONOMISTS AT WORK

LIKE OTHER professionals, academic economists have their own organizations and ways of working. Although economists are frequently in the press, most people do not see what we do each day, what our work involves, how much we get paid, whether we are working toward the general social good or are just a bunch of unprincipled charlatans on a get-rich-quick bonanza. Given the many critics who argue that economists are in part responsible for the dismal state of politics and society in the United States and the world, it is worth exploring just what we do. That is my aim here. The chapter is not intended as an exculpatory document, just a clear-eyed look at my own profession. In chapter 11, the finale, I will try to come to some sort of verdict on the current state of the profession, its strengths, its weaknesses, its good deeds, and its sins. The current chapter is more in the way of discovery.

I start with two of economics' most prominent professional societies: the American Economic Association and its British equivalent, the Royal Economic Society. Both were founded in the late nineteenth century, and both were thought of by their founders as progressive organizations that would use economics to improve the social good.

Economics societies frequently hold conferences, and the second section looks at two: the largest of all, the annual meeting of the American Economic Association, and a small conference I attended almost half a century ago that was something of a watershed for me. It helped me understand the direction of the profession in the mid-1970s, as well as the fault lines between the old and the new.

I then turn to economics journals. The journals are where economists' research and discoveries see the light of day and where the cumulative total of economists' thinking is stored. Selection into journals builds careers but also plays a big role in building the received body of economic thought. If that selection is done poorly, both the profession and its subject matter can come off the rails. Journals matter, and not just to economists.

I then describe some of the topics of inquiry for economists; the idea that economics is about supply and demand, prices, markets, and money remains true but captures only a fraction of today's range of topics. Here I focus on economists' work on health. I then turn to money, where, rather than look at economists' research on money, I look at how economists make money, not only through their often very high salaries but also in ways that have sometimes got them into trouble.

I conclude the chapter on a more positive note, specific rather than general, with brief portraits of four very different economists linked only by the fact that they died within a few months of one another. They had only economics in common, and I offer their portraits to those who have perhaps never known an economist or who believe one of the many distorted impressions in the media. Stereotypes aside, economists, even academic economists, sometimes lead interesting lives.

The American Economic Association
and the Royal Economic Society

Like other clubs for like-minded individuals, economists' societies organize conferences where economists can meet and talk,
try out new ideas, congratulate or disparage one another, and
give each other prizes. They publish journals that stimulate cre-
ativity and give economists a place where they can validate their
work and their careers, and they decide what is good economics
and what is bad economics. They can decide who is in the mainstream and who is outside of it. They are both inclusive and
exclusive; excluding those outside the mainstream creates safe
space for insiders. This is necessary if the profession is to make
progress without being constantly challenged to answer foundational questions that may have little relationship to what is
currently being done. But it is dangerous for the same reasons,
because the neglect of foundational questions may bring down
the whole edifice. And indeed, there are certainly areas where
large groups of economists work on topics of zero ultimate interest because they throw up interesting problems and puzzles.

When I was president of the American Economic Association (AEA) in 2010, I was curious to compare the association
with its counterpart in my native Britain, the Royal Economic
Society. I had long imagined that the British society was much
older than its American sister, just as the Royal Society, founded
in 1660, predates the U.S. National Academy of Sciences by two
centuries. Not so. The AEA was organized in 1885 in Saratoga,
New York, predating by five years the founding of the Royal Economic Society, as the British Economic Association, in 1890.

The journal of the Royal Economic Society, the *Economic
Journal*, started publication in 1891, twenty years before the first
issue of the *American Economic Review*. The first issue of the

Economic Journal opens with a statement of purpose by the editor, Francis Ysidro Edgeworth, proclaiming that the "difficulties of Socialism will be dealt with in the first number, and the difficulties of Individualism in the second."[1] Which pretty much covers the field. The issue continues with an account of the founding meeting, attended by (among others) Edwin Cannan, Edgeworth, Robert Giffen (later Sir Robert Giffen), John Neville Keynes, Professor Alfred Marshall and his wife Mary, and George Bernard Shaw. Cannan, whose name is the least familiar to economists today, was an economic historian and demographer who argued that Malthus was wrong. Robert Giffen, a Scottish economist and statistician, is remembered today for the "Giffen good," a perhaps mythical commodity whose demand *rises* with its price—a phenomenon described in Alfred Marshall's famous *Principles of Economics.*

Marshall's work was, and remains, immensely influential; he and John Maynard Keynes, son of John Neville, and a longtime editor of the *Economic Journal,* are the two towering figures of Cambridge economics. Recent accounts suggest that Marshall borrowed extensively from and relied profoundly on Mary Marshall, née Mary Paley. She was part of the first group of women to study economics at Cambridge; she excelled in her examinations but never received a degree, in part because of fierce opposition (including by her husband, who had initially encouraged her) to women getting Cambridge degrees. Her own book, *The Economics of Industry,* was absorbed into his work, and although he always decried it, some have claimed the original was superior to the later, joint version. According to Austin Robinson, "Mary Marshall was enslaved to forty years of self-denying servitude to Alfred: the 'fool-ometer' by which he measured the popular intelligibility of his writing, the organizer of his materials, the breakwater between himself and the irritations of life."[2] According to Robinson, Maynard Keynes asked, "Why did Alfred make a slave of this woman, and not a colleague?"[3] This sentiment resonates with many women economists today.[4]

George Bernard Shaw needs no introduction, though some may be surprised by his hanging out with economists. He was an active member of the Fabian Society and a regular attendee at British Association meetings; he was a eugenicist, as were John Maynard Keynes and many "progressives" of the time on both sides of the Atlantic (more on this below).

The first issue of the *American Economic Review* opens with a paper on irrigation by Katharine Coman of Wellesley College, who lived in what was then referred to as a Boston marriage with Katharine Lee Bates, a Wellesley colleague and songwriter, best remembered as the author of the much-loved anthem "America the Beautiful." The AEA effectively began publishing in 1886, with its *Publications of the American Economic Association*, the first issue of which contains an account (written by Richard Ely) of its founding and its platform, which, bolder and more progressive than the British equivalent, declares in its first item that "the doctrine of *laissez-faire* is unsafe in politics and unsound in morals."[5] Early supporters included John Bates Clark, Woodrow Wilson, and Francis Walker, a Union army general (a rank he attained at age twenty-four). Walker was the inaugural president of the AEA, as well as superintendent of the 1870 census, president of MIT, superintendent of Indian Affairs, and president of the American Statistical Association.

Like much else in American history, the establishment of the AEA was tied to what was happening in religion. Richard Ely came from a family of strict Presbyterians, but he rejected the doctrine of predestination and became an Episcopalian; he believed that both predestination and laissez-faire did not leave enough space for individual and social improvement. He was one of the leading lay spokesmen for the Social Gospel movement, and his book *An Introduction to Political Economy* was accompanied by his *Social Aspect of Christianity*; both are about economics and Christianity. He taught for many years at the University of Wisconsin, but his employment was unsuccessfully challenged by a member of the Board of Regents on the grounds that he supported strikes and advocated socialism. The AEA's policy of bringing economics to the aid of Christianity explains why 23 of its 181 original members were Protestant ministers.[6]

Francis Walker was a fierce opponent of the United States' accepting more of what he perceived as low-quality immigrants; the 1880s saw the peak of mass migration to the United States. By the turn of the century, more than 14 percent of the population was foreign born, only a little higher than the proportion today, and the immigrants whom Walker saw as low quality were increasingly from southern and eastern Europe rather than from the historically dominant areas of northern and western Europe.[7] Today, the "new" immigrants are from Latin America and Asia, and in today's new Gilded Age, as was true in the original, many see immigrants as hurting the "legacy" population of European stock. The Walker Medal, instituted in 1947 and awarded every five years, was the premier award of the AEA but was awarded only five times before being discontinued after the Nobel Prize in Economics was instituted in 1969. As the number of economists has expanded, there have been suggestions that we need more medals and that the Walker Medal might be revived, though Walker's views on immigration and race—his views on Native Americans were even more extreme than his views on immigrants—would certainly disqualify the use of his name for any kind of honor or award today. The contemporary equivalent would be for the AEA to award a Donald

Trump prize, though I have no doubt that even that would have its takers.

The progressive era in the United States had many achievements to its credit, including the establishment of the federal income tax, the creation of the Federal Reserve System, the enfranchisement of women, and the strengthening of democracy by abolishing the right of state governments to appoint U.S. senators. It was also responsible for Prohibition, then seen as a measure to protect women. These—though perhaps not Prohibition—would also be classified as progressive in today's usage. The deeper philosophy underlying progressive ideas in both the United States and Britain was that social science, both statistics and economics, could and should be used for social control and improvement. One aim was to limit inequality, at least within the white native-born population. Which was one reason why the progressives were so hostile to laissez-faire.

The progressive movement's endorsement of eugenics through selective breeding, immigration control, and even compulsory sterilization of the feeble-minded or criminals was part of the creed and, at the time, was part of mainstream thought on both the right and the left.[8] The ideas also have contemporary echoes among those who advocate for population control as a remedy for global poverty, a movement that is weaker today than it once was, but far from dead.[9] Many today would revive population control as a part of the climate agenda.

The economic eugenicists had a distinctive view of the minimum wage that was very different from the views discussed earlier in this book. Like today's opponents, they agreed that a high minimum wage would create unemployment but thought this would be a *good* thing because it would protect American workers—immigrants of earlier generations—against what they saw as the inferior races and ethnic groups who would be prepared to work for less. In this way, a minimum wage was an instrument of immigration and population control, protecting white workers against the "inferior" immigrant races of "Latins, Slavs, Asiatics, and Hebrews." The words are those of Edward Ross, another founding member of the AEA, and another of its early presidents.[10]

Today's AEA takes great pains to dissociate itself from the views of its founders. Starting in 1962, the keynote lecture at its annual meetings was called the Richard T. Ely Lecture; it and the President's Lecture are the two high points of the meeting. In 2020, a committee appointed by Janet Yellen (now secretary of the Treasury) and including Lisa Cook (one of President Biden's appointees to the Federal Reserve Board) recommended that the keynote lecture be renamed. (In the 2022 program it was titled the "Distinguished Lecture" but with Richard T. Ely's name in brackets, presumably to help elderly economists recognize and locate it.) The committee noted that although Ely "made positive contributions to economic thought, he also wrote approvingly of slavery and eugenics, inveighed against immigrants, and favored segregation." His writings "express views inconsistent with the AEA's code of professional conduct."[11] The code was adopted in 2018, sixty-five years after Ely's death. One of Ely's most famous pupils was Woodrow Wilson, whose views on income inequality (good) and race (bad) I discussed in an earlier chapter, and whose reputation met a fate at Princeton similar to that of his teacher at the AEA.

Conferences

Economists go to conferences. I have already mentioned the granddaddy of them all, the annual meetings of the AEA. Before the pandemic, as many as 12,500 people went to these January meetings. Not all were there to listen to presentations, because the gathering also served as a job market, where departments from all over the world rented suites to interview prospective junior faculty. To allow people to move quickly between presentations and interviews, the AEA needed to find a group of adjacent hotels with meeting rooms and interview suites, and such configurations exist in only a few American cities: Chicago (not so great in January), New Orleans, San Francisco, Atlanta, San Diego, New York, and Boston. There must also be a large supply of cheap rooms for the graduate students looking for jobs. Las Vegas, where rooms are subsidized to encourage gambling, would seem like an ideal location, but the meetings are held over weekends, when rooms are expensive.

The annual meeting is at worst a chore, and at best a chance to meet old friends and ex-students and to hear new ideas.

The COVID-19 pandemic forced the meetings online for two years and showed that virtual interviews worked well; thus, the scientific and job-market features of the meetings are likely to be separate in the future, and the meetings smaller. This is a good example of an adaptation for the better that could have been made before the pandemic, albeit with costly coordination, but once forced by an external event, it will become a permanent part of how things are done.

There are hundreds, perhaps thousands, of smaller economics conferences scattered around the world. In the summer of 1972, when I was a junior researcher in Cambridge, I went with a few colleagues to the meeting of the Econometric Society in Budapest. We were intrigued to visit a communist country and were charmed by the Hungarian capital, but much less so by the presentations at the conference. We were applied economists, who used econometric tools, but the conference seemed to be almost entirely about abstract mathematical theory; in retrospect, we likely did not know enough to find presentations that interested us. With the arrogance of youth, a group of us—including Mervyn King (now Lord King and ex-governor of the Bank of England) and Hashem Pesaran, an impressive and irrepressibly argumentative Iranian econometrician (now at the University of Southern California)—decided that we could do better on our own and would start up a new society for applied economics. This might well have happened in a bar but, in fact, took place in the beautiful Gerbeaud Café in Vörösmarty Square; fifty years later, I remember more about its menu than the program of the conference.

Hashem did indeed establish a new society, the International Association for Applied Econometrics. The rest of us thought we would begin by organizing a conference. Our mentor, Richard Stone, wisely suggested that, instead of a new society, we make use of an existing economic society, the International Economic Association (IEA), whose bread and butter was then supporting small conferences. Stone agreed to be the organizer, and in 1976 we held a conference in Urbino, Italy, on econometric contributions to public policy. Stone knew economists from all over Europe and the United States, many of whom agreed to come. The International Economic Association is not an association of *economists* but an association of *national economic societies*, which meant that there were several economists from communist countries, including Hungarians and Russians (the latter of whom were not then routinely allowed "out" and at the conference were more notable for their Hawaiian shirts than for their contributions to the discussion).

The combination of youth and age at the Urbino conference was full of potential conflict, though age was only one of the fault lines. In retrospect, the participants encapsulated what was happening in economics as the subject changed. *We*—the then young—were brash, mathematically well-tooled, international (or more accurately Anglo-American) in outlook, and confident that the future was ours, while *they* were senior European economists with high status within their countries, more literary and legal than mathematical, who thought that *we* were arrogant ruffians who should not be questioning their elders and (much) betters. Even the American contingent had its divisions. My longtime coauthor John Muellbauer talked about the U.S. consumer price index (CPI) and how the fact that it was weighted by total expenditure to which the rich contributed more than the poor meant that the CPI itself was not *democratic* but *plutocratic*—rather like the American economy in general. One American participant demanded that the minutes of the meeting (which did not exist) be expunged of such socialist talk.

The Europeans balked at what I now see as an early version of the infamous Anglo-American seminar style in economics, where questions are asked during presentations, not at the end, and where necessary clarification often shades into harassment or, even worse, a demonstration that the interrupter is smarter than the speaker. There was much less of this in Urbino than there is in American economics departments today, and the Europeans were perhaps oversensitive to *any* questioning. Even so, some were genuinely upset. Austin Robinson, an ex-president of the International Economic Association and a longtime attendee at its conferences, pulled me aside during a break to tell me that if I did not "call off" my American friends, the meeting would disintegrate.

Not that the Europeans did not have claws of their own. The great French economist Edmond Malinvaud bestrode the new and old economics with grace and distinction and had almost single-handedly kept modern economics alive in France for decades. I am still recovering from being assigned his econometrics text as an undergraduate in 1966; its 769 pages were then available only in French.

A young American economist, considerably less talented in fact than in his own assessment, talked about his many achievements in settling a key question in economics, ending with the modest admission that, despite his accomplishments, there were a few important questions remaining. Malinvaud, affecting a much more pronounced French accent than usual, ended his response by noting that he had no doubt that, given the presenter's extraordinary talents, he would surely come up with answers very soon. The chastened young man spent the subsequent days trying to discover from the rest of us whether he had been complimented or insulted by the great man, hoping against hope, and reality, that it was the former.

Economists' aggressive seminar style has recently come in for serious criticism from another direction, which is its nonneutral treatment of women. Like the Europeans in Urbino, women are less interested in display than are men and are much less likely to let ego trump politeness or their interest in listening. Which tends to cause them to be ill-treated in seminars. Recent empirical analysis has shown that "women presenters are asked more questions and the questions asked of women are more likely to be patronizing or hostile."[12] Some economics organizations are paying attention and trying to set codes of conduct for seminars. There is some resistance from those who believe that robust questioning is often needed during talks to find out what presenters have done; economists' talks are not carefully written literary presentations—as in history, for example—and it is sometimes necessary to probe deeply to find out what is going on. But there is no reason for the excess displays of testosterone. If we can do better, it will be one more example where the increasing presence of women has improved the profession.

Economics Journals: How They Work
and What They Do

Economics journals are where economists publish their re-search, and they shape what economists do and what they think. "Publish or perish" applies to economics as elsewhere in academia, making journals the gatekeepers for deciding who succeeds and who fails. There are no restrictions on who can submit their work, but the top journals are highly selective, and *what* they select not only makes and breaks careers but powerfully shapes the content and direction of economics. It is a dangerous strategy for a young economist, no matter how talented, to work on a topic that is not familiar to the journals. Young researchers in graduate school sort into "fields"—macroeconomics, labor, or health, for example—and their advisers and the concerns of the field shape their work and provide a path to good jobs. There was very little of this in Britain when I was starting out, and it is sometimes held against me that I do not have a proper field: What sort of economist is he, anyway?

When I talk to economists who do not live in the United States, one of the complaints that I hear most often is about the top journals. Whether in Cambridge, Edinburgh, Paris, Prague, or Cape Town, promotion to senior positions now requires publishing in top journals, many of which are seen as essentially inaccessible to authors outside the United States. Strangely, these complaints come not only from anxious and frustrated young scholars but also from their department chairs and deans, whose freedom of action is limited by the demands of external evaluation. While I agree that we have a problem (more on this below), I am also old enough to remember the days before metrics and assessments, when professors of very mod-est distinction had great power over appointments in their own departments and, because they were frequently consulted by other universities, over their national professions.

I recall an elderly Italian professor in the early 1970s, well-oiled with Brunello, spluttering with rage over a rejection from a merit-based journal whose editor had dared to cite the comments of an "unknown referee." (Pronounced un-Keh-noan, with the hard k spat out with real hatred.) Even in the United States, it was not long ago that members of the National Academy of Sciences could publish their own papers, as well as those of their friends and students, in the prestigious *Proceedings of the National Academy of Sciences of the United States of America*. I am not sure the world of publishing according to status is entirely gone, and it may even survive in (not so remote) places, but the explosion of metrics and evaluation has diminished its power.

The journals have been kind to me. When I was a very young research assistant at Cambridge in England, I wrote up some results, and a friend suggested I send the paper to a journal. I had no idea that it was even possible and didn't know enough to be surprised when *Econometrica* accepted it. (I had read one of its papers but did not know of its high standing, which would likely have deterred me.) But I *was* surprised when the paper took four years to appear; the professional society that published it was tottering on the verge of bankruptcy (owing to many years of financial mismanagement) and, in the end, could afford to print only on semitransparent paper that had apparently failed East Germany's quality controls even for sanitary purposes. More seriously, *Econometrica*, and the Econometric Society's summer meetings, provided a route to professional recognition for me and for others who were just starting out. The professional societies provided an open ladder of advancement. It would be ironic indeed if the top journals today were to become a barrier to young unknown Europeans who do not have the advantages of graduating from the handful of top schools where senior scholars can advise and guide them.

So what is there to worry about? As in society more generally, the growth of meritocratic evaluation, though it has much to recommend it, has brought new problems and new inequalities.

The top five journals in economics today are usually taken to be the *American Economic Review*, the *Quarterly Journal of Economics*, the *Journal of Political Economy*, *Econometrica*, and the *Review of Economic Studies*, though if you are a specialist in finance or in theory, the journals in those fields count almost as much. Young scholars need to publish in one or more of them if they are to build successful careers. Only one of these journals is under European control, and two of them, the *Quarterly Journal of Economics* and the *Journal of Political Economy*, are *not* under broad-based professional control but are "house" journals of Harvard and Chicago, respectively. These departments, or one or two of their barons (who sometimes act more like warlords), have enormous power over the profession and are accountable to no one other than their immediate colleagues. In some cases, a single individual has retained an editorship for decades, favoring their own students as well as their preferred topics or methodological approaches. Editors of journals run by professional societies typically have term limits, and while editors are encouraged to pursue their likes and dislikes within limits, they would not do so for long if they routinely excluded other approaches within the mainstream.

This is bitterly contested territory, but professional societies are usually capable of dealing with it, with only occasional bloodbaths. I recall a meeting in which one of our editors was asked to step outside for a few moments while their routine reappointment was considered and voted on. The reappointment went through, but it took three hours to do so. Maybe not too much blood, but many hurt feelings.

The editors of the Harvard and Chicago journals have published many important and game-changing papers over the years, and papers in the *Quarterly Journal of Economics* have the highest citation counts of the top five, but their editors face few barriers to pursuing their personal agendas. Even so, it is unclear why the editors—or their graduate students, who referee many of the papers (you are expecting Elvis but you get an Elvis impersonator)—should play such a large part in shaping the profession, not only in North America but in the rest of the world. Among them, the top five journals publish only around three hundred papers a year, fewer than twenty years ago, and even if the number of coauthors of the typical paper is rising, the fraction of active scholars who can publish in these journals has fallen over time; the bar is very high and rising all the time. For those outside of North America, it seems impossibly high.

The undue influence of a small number of journals tends to make economics narrower than it would otherwise be. Women are underrepresented in economics, and there is evidence that female coauthors are given less personal weight than male coauthors when promotion committees evaluate their joint work.[13] Female economists have a different balance of interests than do male economists, and the latter often label fields like health, economic development, or economic history as not "really" economics at all, compared with central (macho?) fields like macroeconomics, econometrics, or economic theory. "I wish she were more of an economist," is a sentiment I have encountered more than once. The words "rigorous" and "penetrating" are often used to describe work in the central fields, in contrast to work in health, development, or history.

Many important, field-changing papers were rejected by the top journals—which is fine if they eventually get discovered, but some are surely missed, or discouraged—and research in "small" fields (economic history, for example) tends to be pushed into field journals, which count for much less at promotion time. I have already noted how few papers on climate change have been published in top journals. Anyone who has been an editor of one of the top journals will relate stories of powerful figures who pressure editors to publish papers by their friends and not to publish papers that criticize their own work. For this behavior, there is no punishment. All of which means that economics journals are much less open than they appear and that there is great pressure on young scholars—who are usually the source of real change—not to stray too far from the mainstream.

There are benefits from excluding nonsense or conclusions that look right but are not. We would like the papers in top journals to be correct. Yet I believe exclusion has gone too far. A standard problem with meritocracies is that the people already judged as meritorious get to define what is or is not of merit.

One of the most striking changes in American economics has been the increasing prevalence of foreign-born economists. More than two dozen countries have been represented in the Princeton economics department over the years (including nontraditional economics powerhouses such as South Korea, Algeria, Mexico, and Belarus), and the third of the faculty who are American born are on average a good deal older. Many of today's public intellectuals in American economics are also foreign born: from Bengal to Jamaica, think of Amartya Sen, Daron Acemoglu, Luigi Zingales, Raghuram Rajan, Abhijit Banerjee, Markus Brunnermeier, Gregory Clark, Esther Duflo, Simon Johnson, Daniel Kahneman, Joel Mokyr, Enrico Moretti, and

Peter Blair Henry, all of whom are fine academics who can and do explain their ideas to a broad audience.

These people came to the United States with very different backgrounds and presumptions than those of the white ex–farm boys from the western and mid-western United States who used to be so prominent in economics. American economics is immensely richer for these immigrants, but it is hard not to wonder what might have happened had they stayed put. Some got their doctorates outside the United States, but many graduated from a handful of top American graduate programs, all of which recruit on a worldwide basis and all of which have similar curricula. If they had stayed home, there might have been a wider range of alternative schools of thought outside the United States. The flow of inward talent is much larger than the outward flow.

Economics, like a species, needs diversity to provide the material for change in times of crisis, and diversity is limited when so many go through almost identical training programs in a small number of universities. Exporting the standards of those schools and the top five journals to programs in the rest of the world, while protecting against the excesses of the worst of the old world, risks a uniformity that diminishes the local approaches that might enhance the future of economics. Heterodox economics is endangered as it is—George Stigler, in the same article where he argued that good economists were conservative, wrote that a believer in the labor theory of value could not get a desirable job, not because of his radicalism but because the members of the hiring committee could not possibly bring themselves to believe that such a person could be both intelligent and honest. A modern American hiring committee might think that there was something to be learned from studying the labor theory of value and would be unlikely to endorse such a monolithic view of economics, but perhaps a committee of external evaluators in France, Germany, or Britain, armed with its metrics, impact factors, and citation counts, might unwittingly do so.

Economics Working on Health, and Health Working on Economics

Historians of science know that scientific developments can change the world but that they are always shaped by the world in which they occur. Economists are no exception, and one recent external influence on American economics is hard to miss: health and healthcare. The United States today spends nearly a fifth of national income on health, and so health economists have always helped think about the organization of healthcare—how much it costs, whether it is competitive, who gets it and who does not—just as they have thought about the organization of any other large industry. Economists have made important contributions to understanding how insurance works and to thinking about how the healthcare industry is organized. A famous example is the RAND insurance experiment that began in 1974 and found that even modest cost-sharing reduced the use of healthcare services. One of the earliest large-scale social policy experiments, it randomized thousands of Americans into insurance schemes with differing coverage.[14]

A new focus has recently emerged, driven by one of the most fundamental forces in current American life: the aging of the baby boom generation. As the boomers have moved into retirement, financial dependency, and ever-closer encounters with disease and death, the pressure for political and economic action has grown stronger. The twin terrors are lack of wealth and lack of health or, worst of all, lack of both. Money and political pressure have worked before, so why not here? Most Americans find it both implausible and unacceptable that money can't buy years of life or even immortality, and with the decline of religion, there isn't much else to try.

The command and control center for the war on morbidity and mortality is the National Institutes of Health (NIH), most of which is on a sprawling university-like campus in Bethesda, Maryland, outside of Washington, a few miles to the north of the Pentagon. The Institutes, many named after body parts (the National Eye Institute, the National Heart, Lung, and Blood Institute) or diseases (the National Institute of Allergy and Infectious Diseases, the National Institute of Neurological Disorders and Stroke), currently spend about $42 billion a year on research. If this is modest compared with the Pentagon ($750 billion), a more telling comparison is the National Science Foundation, whose budget of around $9 billion provides for the other sciences, including physics, as well as economics.

The NIH's own budget requests, even before COVID-19, have often been *added to* by Congress. In a press release in 2019, the NIH modestly noted that life expectancy in twentieth-century America increased by thirty years, "an accomplishment realized, in part, by research-based improvements in health."[15] (Though I wonder if that statement was itself research based.) The recent *decrease* in life expectancy during the pandemic was an even more persuasive fund-raiser! It's always nice to win, whether the coin falls heads or tails. Spending on healthcare is like that.

The largest budgets—for the National Cancer Institute and the National Heart, Lung, and Blood Institute—match the chronic conditions that most threaten the lives of the baby boomers, though they have recently been joined at the top of the big spenders by the National Institute on Aging, which leads the fight against Alzheimer's, and the National Institute of

Allergy and Infectious Diseases, which covers COVID-19 and, until the end of 2022, was headed by Dr. Anthony Fauci. In recent decades, there has been an increasing recognition of a role for social and behavioral research. The National Institute on Aging (NIA) and the National Institute of Child Health and Human Development have been particularly open to economics, and the funds available dwarf those of the National Science Foundation, the traditional source of research funding for American economists, whose budget for social and economic science in 2020 was a mere $100 *million*.

Economists have continued to work on their traditional areas of health expertise, but, not surprisingly in view of the funds involved, there have been real changes of emphasis. It is good to live longer, but life is expensive, and boomers are almost as concerned with their wealth as they are with their health. In response, the National Institute on Aging funded a great deal of the work by economists on Social Security, Medicare, pensions, and the adequacy of funding for consumption and medical care during retirement.

NIH resources have also encouraged economists to seek new intellectual partnerships, particularly with doctors, epidemiologists, demographers, and psychologists, and their joint efforts are shaping economics as a discipline. Even the reverse is beginning to be true: it is no longer unusual for economists to be asked to team up with doctors who fear that their research will not be funded without the presence of economists and their insights into behavior—for example, about smoking or alcohol consumption, about the use of illegal drugs, or, most recently, about why some people are reluctant to be vaccinated. These partnerships involve real mutual learning and are more evenly balanced than the once one-way imperialist excursions of economics into other social sciences. Economists now regularly publish in the top medical and science journals, sometimes jointly with doctors, and sometimes on their own. A recent prominent study, published in the *New England Journal of Medicine*, is an analysis of the effects of providing public health insurance to a random sample of low-income Oregonians on an oversubscribed waiting list.[16] The study on income and health by Raj Chetty and his collaborators was published in the other top medical journal, the *Journal of the American Medical Association*.[17] Economics may be the six-hundred-pound gorilla in the social sciences, but it's still a small creature in the Bethesda Zoo.

The National Institute on Aging has spent large sums of money on research infrastructure for research by economists. It has helped add questions about health to long-running surveys that have previously focused on economic measurement, and has spent much more on new, national panels that collect data on economics and health from middle age to death. One survey even reaches beyond death, ending with an "exit" interview with the decedent's kin, as a result of which we now know that in spite of the high cost of medical care in the United States, most Americans manage to die without incurring any out-of-pocket expenditures.

For at least two hundred years, it has been known that social conditions play a part in determining health, so economists may be able to help reveal the secrets of longevity along with molecular biologists, geneticists, or biochemists. There is much interest in the link between income and longevity. Individuals surveyed around 1980 whose family income was less than $5,000 could expect to live about 25 percent fewer years than those whose family income was greater than $50,000, which for a twenty-five-year-old amounted to a difference of about a decade.[18] More recently, Raj Chetty and his colleagues have merged the tax and death records, finding a gap of 14.6 years in life expectancy between the top 1 percent and the bottom 1 percent of the income distribution.[19] (These estimates are exaggerated because they assume that people's incomes or income ranks do not change as they age.) Smoking contributes to these differences, but it is not easy to point to a link with differential access to medical care. Ill health limits earnings opportunities, and ill health in childhood can compromise earnings throughout life, which no doubt explains some of the link. In studies that allow for both income and education, the credit is about equally shared. In recent years, even before the pandemic, U.S. life expectancy at age twenty-five has been falling among those without a four-year college degree while continuing to rise among those with a degree. During COVID-19, both groups saw higher mortality, but the difference continued to increase.

It will be a long time before the dismal science absorbs the life sciences, before the sick come to economists instead of doctors, and before television dramas move from the emergency room to the seminar room. In the end, economics may make only a modest contribution to the life span of a typical baby boomer, though economists' work on cigarette taxes and on child welfare are candidates for recognition. But the well-funded and powerfully supported desire for immortality of boomers and their political representatives has certainly changed economics.

The happy symbiosis between economics and health was partially disrupted by politics. In 2013, Republicans in the House of Representatives were unhappy about social scientists receiving public funds that had been tagged for health and were determined to stop it. According to Eric Cantor, then House majority leader, "Funds currently spent by the government on social science—including on politics of all things—would be better spent on trying to find the cures for diseases."[20] (It is hard not to admire the chutzpah of a politician who can summon support based on the public's detestation of his own profession.) The immediate, but unstated, target was likely any research that might show the effectiveness of Obamacare, which the Republicans were then determined to abolish. In the long term, the deeper force is likely the richly funded lobbying machine of pharmaceutical firms and medical equipment manufacturers that see cost-effectiveness analysis as potentially leading to cost control, their archenemy. Economists, who might discover that public health insurance is good for people, or who might argue that some treatments enrich suppliers without helping patients, are decidedly unwelcome at the party, particularly when financed by public money. (Another defense is to put economists on the payroll of the healthcare industry, which happens too.)

Economists and other social scientists organized in opposition to Cantor's plans, but it was difficult to get politicians to support the effort. In the end, eighty-three (Democratic) congressmen, led by Representative Lucille Roybal-Allard from California, signed a letter to Francis Collins, then director of the Institutes, making the case for health economics and urging that funding be continued. NIH funding for social and behavioral research went on, though there has been a cutback on some topics. Economists have done a great deal of excellent work on the financial wellbeing of elderly Americans and on the design of schemes that will help them live well during their lengthening periods of retirement. This work has been declared out of bounds, or at least ineligible, for funding. To get NIH funding, economists must direct their efforts toward understanding death and disease, and physical, not financial, wellbeing. So, in the end, Cantor achieved some of what he wanted, although we lost a great deal of important work that might otherwise have been done.

Perhaps ironically, Eric Cantor was unexpectedly ousted by a Tea Party candidate in the Republican primary in 2014. The victor was Dave Brat, a professor of economics at Randolph-Macon College. Despite his profession, his platform did not endorse health funding for economists.

Enron, the Universities, and Economists

The corporate scandals of the 1990s long filled the newspapers' business pages, which daily presented the travails of their erstwhile heroes, now villains, whose previous farsightedness about their enterprises had become, in court, an account of equally incredible myopia and lack of understanding about the rules and practices of corporate accounting and accountability. These scandals provoked new thinking about corporate governance, as well as new legislation, particularly the Sarbanes-Oxley Act of 2002.

Although most universities are not profit-making corporations, there are those, including the editorial page of the *Wall Street Journal*, that believe that "greed is not confined to Wall St., and that when it comes to accountability, the business world has much to teach our universities."[21] That "teaching" became evident in the early 2000s, leaving many universities and their administrators unhappy. And economists and economics departments were, as usual, on the front line.

American universities (and other nonprofit institutions) shifted their internal financial procedures from lax to draconian. Before I left Britain for the United States in 1983, my university required that all telephone calls made before 1:00 p.m. have advance authorization from the vice chancellor's office. Princeton, with an endowment of around $8 billion at the time, required the dean of the faculty's advance authorization for travel by anything other than the cheapest available mode, including rail travel, so the all-business-class Acela train was banned, irrespective of faculty time constraints or convenience. The working assumption by university financial controllers that professors are criminals certainly prevents administrators from being surprised when they turn out to be so, but what once was an extraordinarily positive relationship, in which administrators saw it as their primary task to advance teaching and research, has soured as administrators assumed a police function, a long ongoing process in which the federal government issues rules and unfunded mandates that universities must enforce. And of course, there were some genuine problems from time to time.

Economists can earn substantial fees for their outside activities. The movie *Inside Job*, directed by Charles Ferguson (narrated by Matt Damon), won the 2011 Oscar for Best Documentary. It excoriates several senior economists for not disclosing fees when making recommendations on policy in their papers and in newspaper articles. I know most of the people portrayed, and I believe that the movie did a lot of work with innuendo or by withholding full information. Those who had things to hide, or were just wise, chose not to cooperate with the movie, leaving some innocents, who knew no better, bitterly regretting their helpfulness. In one scene, Glenn Hubbard, dean of the Columbia Business School, who is far from helpless, argues that there should be full disclosure of conflicts of interest whenever anybody does research on a topic, but then makes the astounding claim "I cannot imagine anybody not doing that. . . . There would be significant professional sanction for failure to do that." If only.

Accurate or not, the movie did great harm to the public image of economists who were seen as benefiting mightily from an economy that they were claiming to research in a neutral, scientific way. After the movie, financial reporting requirements on economists were tightened, so that, for example, interests of $5,000 and up typically must be disclosed on published work. (At the AEA, a vocal minority was arguing for $50,000 instead.) I would not argue against this transparency, but it generates a burden of reporting, as well as the need for more administrators. This is all well and good, and we can afford it, but there is little evidence that it reduces wrongdoing or improves the public perception that economists are apologists for capitalism or that they are shills for greedy and immoral corporations. Indeed, disclosures can make things worse by creating a false impression of openness; in medicine, doctors who have warned their patients can feel free to present biased information, behavior known as moral licensing.[22] There are certainly many economists who are well remunerated for legal work—for example, in lawsuits between firms and workers or in antitrust work. My sense is that conflict of interest declarations are usually cast narrowly so that, for example, there is no bar to health economists sitting on the boards of pharmaceutical companies, provided that their work does not directly benefit the companies. Of course, it is hard to think ill of the hand that feeds you, and harder still to police the unconscious biases that might result.

Even without their moonlighting activities, economists are extremely well paid, at least in top private universities. Top new PhDs in economics starting out as professors in 2022 can expect a *starting* salary between $180,000 and $220,000 for nine months ($40,000 more in a business school), plus a guaranteed summer salary of two-ninths more, in exchange for which they are required to teach *three* (thirty-six hour) courses spread over the next *four* years—and for the most attractive prospects, whose offer is enriched by an initial year as a postdoctoral researcher at an only somewhat lower salary, *three* courses spread over the next *five* years. Over the past twenty-five years, remuneration in the financial sector has spilled over into not only corporate boardrooms but also salaries in business schools, many of which employ economists, and academic economists' earnings have risen in their wake. As salaries have risen, workloads have fallen as university administrators have struggled to minimize intrafaculty income inequality by permitting (arguably less visible) inequalities in teaching. "We can't pay you that much, but you only have to teach half as much as a historian or an English professor."

How do universities pay for all this as well as the much higher salaries of those who have gone on to become successful senior faculty members? They have done this in part by increasing fees, but also through endowments—Harvard's and Princeton's are among the largest—as well as through donors, federal grants, and technological partnerships with private corporations, including pharmaceutical companies. A friend at a California university was appalled to discover locked and guarded buildings on his campus. (Concentration campus?) So much for the free and interdisciplinary interchange of ideas and experience. It is not just the faculty who are out there making money from activities that seem unrelated to the original purposes of institutions of higher learning.

Brief Lives

I have been a working economist since the late 1960s, and I have met, and sometimes known, many economists who are no longer with us. Some were important, and their names are still well known. I am not old enough to have known John Maynard Keynes, but I knew his remarkable disciples Ferdie Khan, Nicholas Kaldor, Austin Robinson, and the redoubtable Joan

Robinson. (In chapter 9 I write about James Meade and Richard Stone, who were of the same generation and who also worked with Keynes.) In 1972, in Moscow, I met the very old A. A. Konüs, who in 1924 published (in Russian) an account of how price indexes can be linked to measures of the cost of living. On the same visit, I met Fritz Machlup, an Austrian economist of great charm and erudition who, according to economists' lore, once dated the beautiful movie star and inventor Hedy Lamarr. At a party in Princeton in 1980, I wondered why none of the women we had invited were there, until I discovered that they had gathered in another room in a tight circle around then seventy-eight-year-old Machlup, hanging on his every word, which gave at least circumstantial credence to the lore.

Here I want to do more (or less) than pass on celebrity gossip or list famous economists I have known. Rather, I write about some remarkable economists who died within a few months of one another—some well known, some not—in part because they were important to me, but also because economists (like accountants) are often seen as faceless or boring. These individuals were not. I could include many other economists, some more famous, some less. But the four described below will give noneconomists a chance to meet a selection of different economists in the wild. Unlike Oscar Wilde's cynic, they knew not just prices but values.

One economist who was never dull was my friend Esra Bennathan, who died in 2016 at the age of ninety-three. Esra spent much of his career in England, at Birmingham, Cambridge, and Bristol, but was born in Berlin, fled to Palestine, and eventually fought in the North African campaign against Field Marshall Rommel in World War 2. He was valued by the army because of his knowledge of which German accents came from which parts of the country, useful information about captive soldiers who refused to give more than their name, rank, and serial number. He worked on transport economics and on development, often with his longtime friend from Birmingham, Alan Walters. (Walters, another nonboring economist, was part of the kitchen cabinet of Margaret Thatcher, whom he once surprisingly described as "kittenish.")

Bennathan was an old-world intellectual of immense (and sometimes obscure) knowledge. He had a deep fund of wisdom and of fun; he was a fine companion and friend. He had the invaluable skill, in academia and later at the World Bank, of leaving people happy even after persuading them to do things they were determined not to. One day, he sold to his Bristol professorial colleagues, many in post since before I was born, the idea that I, a freshly minted twenty-nine-year-old Cambridge PhD, would make a good professor of econometrics. He was known at Bristol as the "silver tongued" professor. Faced with an appointment committee that was about to turn down a candidate whose English, although fluent, was almost incomprehensible, he explained to the abashed group (entirely falsely, and with great feigned reluctance) that the man had just had major dental surgery but was too proud to use it as an excuse. He had a charming small house in Branscombe in Devon, where he loved to don his Wellington boots and a beret to walk the path past the ancient church and down to the English Channel, nodding to the cows and chatting with the farmers along the way.

Farmers were also important to Hans Binswanger-Mkhize, another unforgettable economist who, like Bennathan, spent much of his career at the World Bank. Hans was a leading agricultural economist best known for his influential work on agricultural risk. Many economic theories depend on how people respond to and handle risk; the classic example is a farmer whose harvest depends on unpredictable fluctuations in weather. Financial economics, too, is all about market risk. Hans was one of the first to measure attitudes toward risk using field experiments with farmers in India in the 1970s, and then to use his results to see if the attitudes he had measured affected how they farmed.

He came out as gay, only to discover that he was HIV positive when that was an imminent death sentence. He sold up, and gave away most of the proceeds, but the new therapies arrived, and he lived for another quarter century. He moved to Zimbabwe, a country he had fallen in love with during his work for the World Bank, where he founded and ran a residential school for HIV orphans. He was expelled by the Mugabe government, denounced as a sexual deviant by a disgruntled employee who had been caught stealing, and moved to South Africa, where he married his husband Victor in a traditional multiday Zulu celebration. He continued to run his orphanage from Kwa-Zulu Natal.

Economists are often accused of seeing themselves as a superior species, as masters of policy, if not of the universe. The labor economist John DiNardo was not one such individual. He cared about underdogs, often feeling like one himself. He died in 2017 at the absurdly early age of fifty-six. John had an (occasionally) overwhelming and often scatological sense of humor, with a deep streak of irreverence that he loved to use to deflate the pomposity and pretensions of the sophisticated methods so beloved of many economists. He wrote a memorable paper with Steve Pischke that poked fun at earlier research that had demonstrated that computer literacy paid off in earnings; workers who used computers at work earned more than those who did not. DiNardo and Pischke showed that workers who carried a *pencil* also received higher wages than those who did not, as did workers who worked sitting down compared with those who worked standing up. Their paper has been long affectionately known as "the pencil paper." He was also famous for writing *three* (mostly apoplectically negative) reviews of Levitt and Dubner's best-selling *Freakonomics*.[23]

When he finished his PhD at Princeton, I discovered that the class prejudice I thought I had left behind in Britain was alive and well in the United States. His affect was that of an Italian American working-class guy from Detroit, a smoker who did not care about niceties of dress, and who gave respect only when he thought it was due. All this made it hard for him to land the kind of job that was warranted by the outstanding quality of his doctoral research. In the end, his talent won out, and he moved quickly up the ladder of economics departments.

More widely known than Bennathan, Binswanger, or DiNardo was the British economist Tony Atkinson, who died in 2017 at the age of seventy-two and who did important work up to his death. His last book, *Inequality: What Can Be Done?*, is a testament to a life spent thinking about and measuring inequality. One of his arguments there drew controversy and remains sharply relevant today. He suggested that innovations (think self-driving cars or health-monitoring wearables) be vetted for social desirability before being licensed. This is not Luddism—machines are aborted, not smashed—but the suggestion is heresy to most economists and historians who see technical innovations as the source of rising prosperity. My own doubts are more concerned with who would do the vetting and with preventing the process being controlled by those who want to protect their own innovations. Yet, as with much else that Tony wrote, I predict that this idea will become widely discussed in the near future.

The first professional talk in economics that I ever attended, in Cambridge in 1969, was Tony presenting what became a landmark paper about measuring and interpreting inequality. It made me think that economics was a cool subject. I thought all economics seminars were like this, and it ruined me for a lifetime of such talks. When he became a professor at Essex University at the age of twenty-six, we young researchers were inspired not by the possibility of becoming as learned or creative as Tony, which we knew was out of reach, but by the realization that academic recognition did not have to wait until just before retirement, if then. A few years later, I read an early draft of his book with Joe Stiglitz on public economics and made what I now see as foolish comments. Tony treated them not with disdain but with courtesy and gratitude. In later years, Tony read drafts of two of my own books and wrote extensive comments that greatly changed what I ultimately wrote. In one of his comments, he protested that a method I was then advocating (what economists call instrumental variables) could rarely do what was expected of it. That was heresy to me at the time, as it is to most practicing economists today. But he was right, though it took me a decade or more to absorb and understand. Tony was one of those who, when you catch up with where they were, are just vanishing over the next hill.

I have often wondered why there was no American Atkinson, or even a close equivalent, and what the U.S. profession would have looked like had there been. It is certainly true that British economists, and British society more generally, have long worried about income inequality in a way that was not true for Americans, at least until recently. But I think that if Tony had worked in the United States for the last half century, inequality would have been a public issue earlier, and it is not fanciful to imagine that it might even have grown less rapidly.

CHAPTER 9

NOBEL PRIZES AND NOBEL LAUREATES

EVERY YEAR SINCE 1969, economists have been awarded Nobel Prizes. This chapter is about those prizes, about how they came to be, and about some of the subsequent laureates. The first section is a general overview, the second is about the friendship between two laureates, Richard Stone and James Meade, and the third is about my own prize in 2015. The first two sections are new to this book. The third is a revised and updated version of an account I wrote in 2016.

The Nobel Prizes and the Prize in Economics

When Alfred Nobel left his fortune to establish the Nobel Prizes, he made no mention of economics. Nobel made his fortune from dynamite and wanted to be remembered not as a merchant of death but as a benefactor of mankind, and to that end he established prizes in physics, chemistry, medicine or physiology, literature, and peace. The prizes, first awarded in 1901, were to be awarded annually to those whose work had conferred the greatest benefit to mankind.

The year 1968 was the centenary of the central bank of Sweden, Sveriges Riksbank, and its then governor, Per Åsbrink, advised by the economist Assar Lindbeck, established the Sveriges Riksbank Prize in Economic Sciences in memory of Alfred Nobel. The prize was approved by the Swedish government and, like the other prizes except Peace, is administered by the Nobel Foundation. Although the economics prizes are not among the original Nobel Prizes, they are presented in the same way and at the same time as the other prizes and are handed to the laureates by the King of Sweden in a spectacular ceremony in Stockholm.

The first economics prize was awarded to Ragnar Frisch of Norway and Jan Tinbergen of the Netherlands in 1969. The next year, it was awarded to Paul Samuelson of the United States. Frisch and Tinbergen had pioneered the use of econometrics, using statistical methods and data to understand how the economy changes. Samuelson, a generation younger than Frisch and Tinbergen, was arguably *the* dominant figure in economics in the second half of the twentieth century. His 1947 *Foundations of Economic Analysis* had established the mathematical basis for modern economics, and, over a long career, he made major contributions to almost all areas of the subject.

In the years after 1901, when the first Nobel Prizes were awarded, the selection committees had a backlog of giants of nineteenth-century science to choose from.[1] Their prestige and fame helped establish the prestige and fame of the new prize. At the time, and in most years since, the cash value of the prize was large enough to attract global attention, and Nobel originally wanted not just to recognize the worth of the laureates but to support their subsequent work without the need for external funding. Economics had a backlog of giants too, and the prestige of the first laureates, followed by Simon Kuznets, John

Hicks, and Kenneth Arrow, left no doubt about the distinction of the prize. The members of the committees that choose the winners spend much of their professional time collecting nominations and appraisals, as well as reading and discussing, and eventually writing long and detailed assessments of the laureates' work to be published at the time of the announcement. This careful work, which is a serious burden for Scandinavian economists, is surely necessary to maintain the prestige of the prizes. It is also true that the decisions are not immune to current fashions in the economics profession; after all, the committee is composed of members of the profession and, like the rest of us, is subject to its often-persuasive hot topics or methods. It is foolish to expect any living committee to deliver the judgments of history, even supposing such judgments ever come to pass.

Economics is much closer to politics and public affairs than are physics, chemistry, and medicine, and so the economics prizes give (some) laureates a public platform that is only occasionally open to other laureates. The most famous example was Friedrich von Hayek in 1974. He had battled Keynes in the 1930s and decisively lost—at least according to what we were taught in Cambridge, England—and had vanished from sight. If asked, around 1970, I should have replied that he was probably dead. His Nobel Prize in 1974 resurrected him, intellectually if not literally, and made him famous, giving his work renewed influence with many, including, most famously, Margaret Thatcher. Keynes died in 1946, so he could not respond with his side of the story. Nor could he have been awarded a Nobel in economics, though he was nominated in 1922, 1923, and 1924 for the Nobel *Peace* Prize after the publication of his famous *Economic Consequences of the Peace*.[2]

The politics of the economics prize have long been debated. One account argues that the establishment of the prize was an attempt by Åsbrink and Lindbeck to push Sweden to adopt a more market-friendly posture.[3] This was the era in economics when Keynesian policies were being challenged in many countries, and the virtues of the market were being reassessed; in retrospect, and in today's terminology, it was the end of the Keynesian or New Deal order and the beginning of the neoliberal order.[4] Economists do indeed tend to emphasize the virtues of markets more than do others, and the prestige of the prize in Sweden is sufficiently large that something of the kind is plausible. Hayek could perhaps be regarded as a triumph of the strategy, but he shared the prize with Gunnar Myrdal, and the politics of the pair could not have been further apart. In later years, prizes have gone to both right and left, and it is hard to discern a systematic pattern.

Like Myrdal and Hayek, Sir Arthur Lewis and Theodore Schultz, who shared the prize in 1979, held very different views about economic development, and there is surely some discomfort in sharing a prize with the opposition. More recently, in 2013 when Eugene Fama, Lars Peter Hansen, and Robert Shiller were jointly named for their work in finance, the disagreements among them, especially between Fama and Shiller, were on display in Stockholm in the public lectures that must be delivered as conditions of the awards. Fama believes in markets and that they are good at processing information, while Shiller is much more skeptical about the behavior of both investors and markets.

Awards like these are made for contributions to the field, and indeed much can be learned from (partially) discordant views, each of which brings a hard-earned insight that is a real discovery. Economists often have several different ways of thinking about the same phenomenon, and the best economists have the skill to know which one to use in which context.[5] There are those, including many "hard" scientists, who do not agree but think that prizes should recognize the discovery of truth. Robert Zoellick, a past president of the World Bank who often argued against his own economists, approvingly repeated a comment that he attributed to an unnamed but "excellent physicist" that "in physics, Nobel prizes are awarded for being correct while in economics they are often awarded for being brilliant."[6] In the same vein, Robert Solow is reputed to have said that the way to get ahead in economics is to come up with a brilliant argument in favor of an absurd conclusion. As I will argue later in the last chapter, not all the work that has been recognized in Stockholm has brought much benefit to mankind, or even to the effectiveness of economic policy.

The lack of female winners has long been a concern, and not only in economics. Perhaps the most notorious case is that of the astronomer Dame Jocelyn Bell Burnell, whose discovery of pulsars when she was a graduate student in Cambridge was belittled and obscured by her supervisor, who then received the prize without her.[7] The first woman to win the economics prize was Eleanor Ostrom, whose career was mostly in political science; the second and only other to date was Esther Duflo, the youngest economics laureate ever, who shared the prize in 2019. Joan Robinson should have won the prize for her scholarly work on imperfect competition, including monopsony, a term that she invented, and an idea that is increasingly influential again today. But perhaps her long and vocal support of Mao's China, including the cultural revolution, may not have gone down well with the committee.

Keynes was one of many eminent economists who was excluded because he was dead. Lindbeck, who was chair of the committee for many years, lists Jacob Viner, Michael Kalecki, Frank Knight, and Roy Harrod, who died in 1970, 1970, 1972, and 1978, respectively, as economists who would likely have been laureates had they lived longer.[8] Another is Amos Tversky, the psychologist who would have shared the 2002 prize with Daniel Kahneman had he lived. I have already mentioned my ex-colleague Alan Krueger, whose work with David Card was honored in 2021.

The award of the prize is a big enough event to affect people's lives. George Stigler, in true Chicago fashion, argued that the incentive would distort people's choice of research topics in a less than ideal way. There is also evidence that the maelstrom that follows the award diminishes the scientific production of laureates for several years afterward. Yet the prizes seem to bring happiness, and not just to the awardees. When my Princeton colleague Danny Kahneman won the prize in 2002, he said his lasting impression of the subsequent celebration was the sea of unalloyed happiness around him. My own experience was similar: as an experiment, try telling a taxi driver that you have just been awarded a Nobel Prize, though probably a good idea to run the experiment in October, the month when the announcements are made. There is jealousy too; one pair of economists had been adversaries since graduate school, and when one of them was recognized, the other complained that his antagonist had been given "his" prize. When Robert Lucas won the prize in 1995, his ex-wife cashed in too, having presciently added a clause to their divorce settlement; Lucas had a distinguished exemplar in Albert Einstein, who similarly shared his 1919 prize.

There is also the money. In 2021, each prize was worth 10 million Swedish kroner, a little less than a million U.S. dollars. The amount is awarded to a single winner, split in two, or divided three ways, in which case the division is either thirds or a half and two quarters. The last has happened only once in economics, in 2021. Such prizes contribute to inequality, not just directly but through the subsequent speaking, writing, and career opportunities that become available to those winners who are not too old or decrepit to travel and give talks. Universities advertise their laureates, opening a gap between them and universities without laureates. Perhaps these inequalities are acceptable as just rewards for achievement. But many people dislike inequalities in principle, or at least want to know why they are just.

A Tale of Two Laureates:
Richard Stone and James Meade

Richard Stone, who lived from 1913 to 1991, was a British economist, known for his work on consumer behavior and on national income accounting. He was awarded the Nobel Prize in 1984 for the latter. Simon Kuznets, who won in 1971, was also a pioneer in the development of national income measurement and is most often given the lion's share of the credit, but Stone developed the *systems* of national accounts that underly the architecture of today's national accounts. His friend James Meade was four years older and survived until 1995. They lived and worked in or near Cambridge, England, spending time together as colleagues and often dining together. Meade was awarded the Nobel Prize in 1977 for his work on international trade.

Stone was my mentor, the person I most wanted to be, and although he never taught me—and indeed rarely taught anyone—he led by the example of his writings and the way he lived his life. I knew Meade, too, from his work and from the occasional social gathering—including dinners chez Stone hosted by his wife, Giovanna (née Saffi), a onetime concert pianist who had played under the baton of Carlo Maria Giulini (a Bach keyboard concerto) as part of the celebrations of the liberation of Rome in June 1944. (The concert was attended by then sergeant Robert Solow, who appears several times in this book.) When I knew the Stones, they had a Bösendorfer grand piano in their living room, an instrument that I had only ever read about. Courtesy of the King's College cellar, dinner parties came with great wines. If such a world still exists, it is long since I have seen it.

At the beginning of World War 2, John Maynard Keynes concerned himself with how to pay for the war, and his colleague and friend Austin Robinson (husband of previously mentioned Joan) persuaded the Cabinet office to hire people to improve the inadequate estimates of the national accounts. (National accounts are just what they sound like and provide estimates of what the economy is producing, as well as of imports, exports, and incomes. They provide the instrument panel for measuring and guiding the economy, especially so in wartime.)

Meade and Stone were tasked with improving the estimates of the national accounts, and during six months of intensive work, they provided the numbers, in the process creating the fully balancing double-entry framework that underpins the modern System of National Accounts. The conceptual framework originally came from the older man, but in the process of filling in the empty boxes with numbers—Stone was armed with a Monroe calculator that his parents had given him for his twenty-first birthday—endless conceptual issues had to be dealt with, and so by the end, neither man could separate out his individual contributions (though Meade remembered turning the handle on the calculator). Their comradeship developed into a lifelong friendship. Both would look back on these months as the best time in their lives; they were engaged in important and creative work for a higher purpose, they liked each other, and they were becoming friends.

When Meade was awarded the Nobel Prize in 1977, he learned of the award from a crowd of journalists when he alighted from a bus on his way to give lectures at the then new University of Buckingham. There were no cell phones in 1977. The paparazzi were waiting to hear his comments. He later talked of his disappointment that the award had been given to him jointly with the Swede Bertil Ohlin for their work on international trade and international capital movements, not for the work that he had done with Stone on the national accounts. Meade never enjoyed or welcomed the publicity and public recognition that came with the prize. I recall him saying, only half in jest, that the three worst features of the twentieth century were the "infernal" combustion engine, the population explosion, and the Nobel Prize in Economics.

In that same conversation, he told me that he had faced a quandary when asked by the prize committee making its exploratory discussions whether he would support an award to Richard Stone for his work on national income accounting. He was all in favor but was concerned that if he gave an unqualified yes and Stone were given the award, he would be written out of the story of their joint work. He knew that Nobel Prizes could rewrite history, and indeed there have been several famous subsequent cases, including that of Jocelyn Bell Burnell mentioned above. Meade also did not want to say no, nor did he want to remind the committee that his own and Stone's contributions were inextricably entangled. If he did the latter, he said, they might give him *another* Nobel Prize, compounding what he already thought was a disaster. Eventually, he told me, he wrote to the prize committee to say that if one man deserved the prize for national income accounting, that man was Richard Stone. Which is what happened.

Stone died in December 1991. I spoke briefly at the funeral service; Meade said he would have been unable to compose himself to do so. The next morning, as I waited to fly back to Princeton, I read Stone's obituary in the London *Times*. It was an affectionate tribute that did full justice to the man and to his work. Although obituaries in the *Times* are unsigned and prepared in advance, I believed that it could only have been written by Meade. But when I asked Giovanna, she said no, because Meade would have told her, and he had not. She thought perhaps someone in the statistical community wrote it; Stone was much loved among that group.

Several months later I had the chance to ask Meade directly what he thought of the obituary. "I thought it was outrageous," was his response. I replied, "But it is so kind, so well informed, and so affectionate, I had assumed that you had written it." "I did," he said.

What had happened is exactly what Meade had dreaded; the obituary he had written, and which became the property of the newspaper, had been slightly edited. He had explained, in only a few words, how they had worked together in the winter of 1940. Those few words were edited to remove Meade's name, and so he had been written out of the history of the national accounts.

There was likely no conspiracy, and perhaps the editors of the newspaper were primed to look for what might be taken to be self-serving references in commissioned obituaries. Yet there remains the responsibility to the historical record of the Nobel committee, a responsibility that they take very seriously. It is why the Swedish economics profession devotes so much time to trying to get their selections right. They and the other committees often do, perhaps even usually so. And perhaps the altering of history cannot be avoided given the prestige of the prizes. Richard Stone was himself taught by the now almost forgotten Colin Clark, a pioneer of national and international accounting whose work went uncredited.[9] Nor has there been recognition of the related work by Angus Maddison on historical international accounts or of that by Irving Kravis, Alan Heston, and Robert Summers, who constructed the international accounts—the Penn World Table—that are among the most heavily used data in economics.

As to teachers and their students, David Card and Joshua Angrist were advised as graduate students at Princeton by Orley Ashenfelter, whose long-held views on experiments and on credible empirical analysis are deeply imprinted in their work and who is the ultimate source of much of modern empirical practice in economics. Sometimes, teaching must be its own reward.

What Is It Like to Win a Nobel Prize?

In October 2015, I got the famous early-morning phone call and learned to my delight that I was the recipient of the 2015 Nobel Prize in Economics. As many previous recipients have reported, the experience is both exhilarating and overwhelming. I often think of the story of the dog that liked to chase buses but had little idea of what it would be like to catch one. The Nobel is not just catching the bus but being run over by it. Over and over again.

While the bus was driving backward and forward over me, just a month later, Anne Case and I published a paper in the *Proceedings of the National Academy of Sciences* showing a reversal of the long-established decline in mortality among middle-aged whites in the United States, especially those without a four-year college degree, and that the fastest-rising causes of death were suicides, accidental poisonings (mostly from drug overdoses, both legal and illegal), and alcoholic liver disease.[10] These are the deaths that Anne later labeled "deaths of despair," a term that has now entered the language.[11] We had discovered these results in May 2015, and every time we showed them to economists or physicians, jaws would drop. Even so, we failed to interest either of the major medical journals, one of which rejected it so quickly that I thought I must have sent the paper to a bad email address. But once it appeared in the *PNAS* in early November, the storm of publicity exceeded by an order of magnitude the still-ongoing publicity about the Nobel. Now there were several buses driving backward and forward over both of us. Pleasant enough to have such recognition, but we were gasping for breath.

Of course, the Nobel and "the paper" became entangled. Although the authors were (deliberately) listed on the paper as Anne Case and Angus Deaton, the order was typically reversed in the media, and in several cases became "Nobel economist Angus Deaton and his wife, Anne Case, who is also a researcher," a designation that the Alexander Stewart 1886 Professor of Economics and Public Affairs was not happy about. Economist Justin Wolfers wrote a piece in the *New York Times* on similar cases of blatant sexism in economics, including Ralph Nader's extraordinary suggestion that Janet Yellen (then chairman of the Federal Reserve, currently secretary of the Treasury) sit down with her Nobel Prize–winning economist husband (George Akerlof) before she decided what to do about interest rates. But some of the entanglements were much more positive.

A splendid tradition in the United States, which, as mentioned earlier, was abandoned in 2016, and has not subsequently been revived, is that American Nobelists are invited to the Oval Office. We went with two remarkable chemists who worked on

DNA repair (one of whom, Aziz Sancar, was born in Turkey to illiterate parents) and the infinitely charming Bill Campbell, born in Ireland, who found a cure for river blindness (and invented ivermectin, of recent fame as a possible cure for COVID-19). Three out of the four of us were immigrants to the United States, and the fourth, Paul Modrich, is the son of an immigrant. For Anne and me, the high point was when President Obama opened the door to the Oval Office and, when I tried to introduce her, said, "Professor Case needs no introduction to me." He continued, "We have got to talk about this paper that you have written," the paper that had appeared only days before. He had clearly read it in detail. He had comments about earlier similar events in the African American community and made some suggestions, some of which made it into the book that we published in 2020; we were delighted to acknowledge the assistance. It was unusual for an academic paper to receive such attention, and all of this before we had got to Stockholm.

Many have written about the splendors of Stockholm, and the videos and photographs on the Nobel website give a good idea of the colors, the flowers, the pomp, the dresses (Anne's scarlet sheath could be seen from outer space), the jewelry, the king and queen, and the princes and princesses. Being treated like a head of state, even for a week, is a memorable experience. Laureates are met at the door of the plane by the president of the National Academy of Sciences and, after a brief wait in a quiet lounge while someone else deals with passports and the like, are whisked away to the Grand Hotel in a chauffer-driven limosine that was theirs for the week.

Laureates can bring guests to the ceremonies, so I could invite and thus acknowledge the many outstanding scholars with whom I had worked. Family, too, are invited, and the biggest surprise for me was that the week became an extended family holiday with my two children and three grandchildren. My grandchildren were the only young children among the families of the 2015 laureates, and the three Deaton *barnbarn* became television darlings. Nine-year-old grandson Julian wore white tie and tails and was charmingly interviewed on Swedish television while flirting outrageously with the TV interviewer. For the Swedish people, the Nobel ceremony and the banquet that follows it play a role similar to that of the Oscars in the United States. People make dates with friends, they buy food and drink, and they watch it all on TV. I told my immediate neighbor at the banquet, Finance Minister Magdalena Andersson (who later became prime minister), that the banquet was not the kind of thing that happened to me, but that she, as a cabinet minister, must find such things routine, or even tedious. Absolutely not, she told me; this banquet is so important for Swedes that it is only tonight, when my mother sees me here on television, that she will believe that I am an important person.

All of this, amazingly, is to honor not movie star charisma, not athletic prowess, but intellectual achievement. Alfred Nobel himself was determined to be remembered for intellectual achievement, and the Swedish people have long honored his vision. And although the Swedes have their share of suicides, they have among the lowest all-cause mortality rates in the world, with no signs of rising mortality in middle age.

CHAPTER 10

DID ECONOMISTS BREAK
THE ECONOMY?

THE FINANCIAL CRISIS that began in 2008 with the collapse of Lehman Brothers was a pivotal event, not just for those who were harmed in the subsequent recession but also for stimulating discussion about whether the American and global economies were fit for purpose. The discussion has gone on long after the crisis itself. Many serious commentators continue to worry that democracy is incompatible with capitalism, at least capitalism as currently practiced and regulated. The rich whose actions had caused the crisis made off with hundreds of millions of dollars and were never punished, while many ordinary people lost their jobs and their homes. Most economists, including forecasting institutions such as the International Monetary Fund and the Organisation for Economic Co-operation and Development, did not predict the crisis, a public failure that inspired the Queen on a visit to the London School of Economics to ask, "Why did no one see it coming?" Before the crisis, many economists had promoted the elaborate financial engineering that underlay the collapse, confident in the power of financial markets to create wealth and to regulate themselves.

Once it happened, economists were far from united on what to do about it.

Alan Blinder wrote in 2022, "The financial crisis was the result of a series of grievous errors, misjudgments, and even frauds by private-sector companies and individuals, aided and abetted by leaders such as George W. Bush and Alan Greenspan, who were unduly enamored of laissez-faire and viscerally attached to the vaunted wisdom of the market."[1] This is a tale that cannot be told too often, of government-enabled rent seeking and destruction supported by the ideology of market fundamentalism. Not all economists supported that ideology, but many did and still do.

An epidemic of what Anne Case and I called "deaths of despair"—deaths from suicide, drug overdose, and alcohol abuse—began before the Financial Crisis and continues to this day. For Americans without a college degree, life expectancy at age twenty-five has been falling since 2010. Among the worst villains of this story are rich pharma companies that exploited the despair in an economy and a society that was no longer serving the majority, and enriched themselves by promoting addiction and death. Yet the background of despair, into which addiction enriched the pharma companies, came from decades of an economy that was not delivering a good life for the two-thirds of the population without a four-year college degree.

Not entirely unrelated to these events came a populist upsurge that brought the election of Donald Trump in 2016, his failure to acknowledge his defeat by Joe Biden in 2020, and an ongoing threat to American electoral democracy. One can perhaps understand why so many are unfazed by a threat to democracy as it is currently working, given that it has long failed to work for them.

Economists did not cause the Financial Crisis, nor did they bring deaths of despair. But many would assign them a good deal of responsibility for their reckless enthusiasm for markets in general and financial markets in particular, and they were often relaxed about the growing inequality that markets were generating. As to health, there is always a ready supply of economists denouncing government interference or price control in a healthcare system whose exorbitant costs are destroying good jobs and spreading despair.

The big question is whether today's American capitalism—and to a lesser extent capitalism in other rich countries—continues to be compatible with liberal democracy. I do not have the answer to this question, but I do want to explore the question of the responsibility (if any) of my profession in bringing us to this pass.

Here, I start with the crisis, and with economists' reaction to it. Throughout the crisis, economics had its critics, both internal and external. I continue with a brief account of deaths of despair and of the flaws in current American capitalism that are responsible for them. Finally, in the next and final Chapter, I come back to the question that began this book, which is the part that economists played in creating the forces that threaten to swamp us today.

Economists Struggling

Business cycles have long been a central topic in economics, and many individuals in the generation before mine, who came of age in the Great Depression, became economists to better understand the horrors of mass unemployment, and dedicated their professional lives to ensuring that it would never happen again. To a large extent, they, and we, thought that they had succeeded, if not perfectly, then close enough. The crash in the fall of 2008 was a great surprise, rather like being told that the plague was back. Then, in the spring of 2020, the plague did come back (though that is a different story).

Encountering the Financial Crisis, or the Great Recession as it was called both to echo and to separate it from the Great Depression, was therefore rather like meeting a dinosaur or attending the premiere of a Shakespeare play instead of reading about them in history books. As always, textbooks leave things out, and so the experience seemed fresh. When I was an undergraduate, my Cambridge teachers explained how the Great Depression need never have happened, if the benighted policymakers had only understood John Maynard Keynes's insight that government spending—stimulus policies—could cure unemployment and restart the factories, just as diabetics need never have died if they had only known about insulin. As in too much of the economics we learned, politics was little mentioned, but in 2007 and 2008, the politics came back with a vengeance.

The Republican Party is unanimously anti-Keynesian and robustly challenged the postcrisis stimulus policies. Republicans accused the Obama administration of printing money, debasing the dollar, stealing from future generations, and turning the USA into the USSA—the first S stands for socialist. A sinister purpose was even read into the visit to Washington in March 2009 of Britain's *socialist* prime minister Gordon Brown, leader of the Labour Party, who had previously been a successful and orthodox finance minister. Such talk would not have been unfamiliar eighty years ago. Many politicians and much of the media take it as obvious that the stock market measures social welfare and that the job of any administration is to keep it high. As a result, the fall in the market in the early days of the Obama administration was taken as showing that its policies had failed.

Most American economists—including many who have advised and worked with Republican administrations—did not argue against government stimulus spending in and of itself. Yet there has been no unanimity in the profession. Robert Barro of Harvard, who is one of the top ten most cited economists in the world, wrote about what he called "Voodoo multipliers" and sounded a common theme, that the crisis does "not invalidate everything we have learned about macroeconomics since 1936."[2] The multiplier refers to the factor by which stimulus spending will add to national income, a number that the administration's economists believed was greater than one; after all, the postcrash unemployment of labor and capital left unused resources that could be brought into play. Barro, by contrast, argued that the multiplier is zero, because the government cannot do anything that the market cannot do better, and will simply replace private spending that would otherwise have taken place. Barro is most famous for his argument that deficit spending generates offsetting saving by consumers. He argues that people realize that, in the end, the government will have to pay the money back, that the repayment will have to be financed by higher taxes, and so they will save in anticipation of the day that they or their descendants will have to make restitution by paying those taxes.

For most economists, including me, this insanity is an embarrassment, and the fact that Barro is taken seriously—and is a professor at Harvard, rather than a fringe blogger—is a sure indication that, indeed, macroeconomics has regressed, not progressed, since 1936. Still, there is some justice to the claim that it is possible to find some well-credentialed economist who will support *any* policy. And that Barro's ideas on this are taken seriously does not redound to the credit of the profession.

Instead of a stimulus, Barro recommended that the elimination of the corporate income tax would be a "brilliant" way to address the crisis. The late Ed Prescott of Arizona State noted that it is not true that all economists agree on the effectiveness of a fiscal stimulus, though "if you go down to the third-tier schools, yes, but they are not the people advancing the science."[3] Prescott won the Nobel Prize in 2004 for advancing the science, and specifically for understanding "the driving forces behind business cycles." But even his presence does not propel Arizona State into the top tier. According to *U.S. News and World Report*, the graduate program there is tied for thirty-eighth place, far behind Harvard, MIT, Stanford, and Princeton, many of whose economists are fans of fiscal stimulus.[4]

The (libertarian) Cato Institute, one of whose cofounders was Charles Koch, found two hundred economists to sign a full-page advertisement stating that government expenditure had not stimulated economies in the past, and would not do so then. Prominently absent from the signatories were professors of economics at the "third-tier schools" such as Harvard, MIT, and Princeton, perhaps because so many of their faculty were in Washington, helping to construct the stimulus. It is not clear how many of the two hundred signers agreed with Barro's or Prescott's economic analysis, and many may simply be skeptical of the effectiveness of large government programs under American political conditions. Yet many economists do not appear to recognize that such programs might act differently in an economy in a slump rather than at full employment, which was Keynes's point, nor would they learn such a thing in many of today's graduate courses in macroeconomics.

Most of the economists I know and talk to do not take Prescott's or Barro's work as a serious guide to policy. They accept that it is clever, is original, and has opened up avenues that were not previously explored, even if those avenues would perhaps have been better left that way. The same is true of the other recent innovative approaches to macroeconomics, several of which have earned Nobel Prizes but have had little or no impact on policymaking in Washington.[5] Perhaps it would have been good if they had had more impact, though I believe not. Either way, whether it is the profession or the policymakers who are to blame, it is a distressing fact about my profession that eighty years of work in macroeconomics, much of which earned the highest accolades, has had so little effect on the policies that it nominally addressed. I also find it profoundly depressing that, at least as far as macroeconomic policy is concerned, there is no consensus that would convince an intelligent but skeptical layperson. Indeed, it is worse than that. Paul Krugman's discussion of why economists got it so wrong, with which I am largely in sympathy, points to the huge divides among macroeconomists but is honest enough to admit that even those on the opposite side from Barro and Prescott have nothing like the coherent understanding of the aggregate economy that would support sound policymaking.[6]

Lest I am taken as claiming that only macroeconomics is in trouble, there are other areas that are doing equally badly. In December 2008, I attended a meeting to "celebrate" thirty years of research on economic development at the World Bank, followed immediately by the American Economic Association (AEA) meetings in San Francisco. (Full disclosure: I organized the program at the AEA meetings.) Both had a feeling of crisis. At the Bank, it was clear that the model of economic development through aid or concessionary lending was broken, and that the research agenda that supports those loans and is financed out of them has become untethered from any chance of promoting development around the world. The atmosphere was dreary, the gloom unrelieved. It seems that the idea that the international organizations, guided by economics, could promote growth in the world and eliminate poverty, an idea born after World War 2 and midwifed by Keynes among others, is dead.

The AEA meetings were not engineered to talk about crises in financial markets or in the profession, if only because the program was set nine months ahead and before the crisis. Yet much could be arranged at the last minute, and instead of gloom and depression there was a sense of invigoration, of a task to be done, and of the talent to deal with it. Over and over again people happily argued that, at last, macroeconomics would change. Perhaps so, and at the time of writing in early 2023, there is a great ferment of debate, with many mainstream economists challenging ideas that would not have been challenged fifteen years ago.

Deaths of Despair

One of the most important divisions in America today is between those who have a four-year college degree and those who do not. The bachelor's degree has increasingly become a passport not only to a good job—the kind of job that is worth doing and whose rewards have steadily increased over the last half century—but also to good health, to longevity, and to a flourishing social life. Without it, you risk being a second-class citizen, with implications for life at home and at work, and in time spent with others. Michael Sandel notes that "the idea that a college degree is a condition of dignified work and social esteem has a corrosive effect on democratic life. It devalues the contributions of those without the diploma, fuels prejudice against less-educated members of society, effectively excludes most working people from representative government, and provokes political backlash."[7]

In our book, *Deaths of Despair and the Future of Capitalism*, Anne Case and I tell the story of how the lives of Americans without a college degree have, on average, and in many dimensions, fallen behind those with a college degree.[8] The gap began opening fifty years ago (around 1970), and has continued since, including the last few years of the pandemic. Keep in mind that, even today, when educational attainment is much more widespread than it used to be, only a third of American adults have a four-year college degree.

Perhaps the most prominent gaps are seen in mortality and in life expectancy. After a century of increasing life expectancy—not only an indicator of health but, as many argue, a sensitive indicator of the state of the economy and society[9]—life expectancy in the United States fell for three years in a row, from 2014 through to 2017, something that had not happened in the century since the last pandemic in 1918–1919. The rising mortality came not only from rising deaths of despair—suicide, drug overdose, and alcoholic liver disease—but from a simultaneous slowdown and eventual cessation of the decline in deaths from cardiovascular disease that had been the main engine of mortality improvement in the last quarter of the twentieth century.

Remarkably, this rising epidemic of deaths has almost entirely spared those with a four-year college degree. For those without that qualification, we draw a parallel to Emil Durkheim's analysis of suicide, where people found themselves in an economy and society that no longer worked for them and no longer provided the support that they needed to make their lives worth living.

Even in normal times, there are suicides, drug overdoses, and deaths from alcoholism among both the more and less educated, and indeed, until the last part of the twentieth century, it had been believed that suicide was more common among those with more education. But the increase in deaths of despair, around one hundred thousand every year since the mid-1990s, is confined to those without a college degree. It is as if those without the degree must wear a scarlet badge denoting their inferior status. Suicide itself is now more common among those without a college degree, those wearing the badge.

Death is the terminus at the end of the long road of despair. The starting point is a labor market that increasingly excludes those without a four-year college degree from good jobs. The fraction of nonelderly adults who are employed has been declining for less educated men for half a century, and for less educated women since 2000. Participation in work increases in boom times and falls back in recessions, but the rise in the next boom never attains the previous peak. The same is true for the real value of wages, falling and rising around a falling trend. For men, even in the boom leading into the pandemic—when the rise in wages for less educated men was being loudly celebrated—the purchasing power of wages for men without the degree was lower than at *any* date in the 1980s.

The failing labor market spills over into the rest of life. Unions are now almost nonexistent in the private sector. Unions not only raised wages for their members, as well as for many nonmembers, but also kept an eye on working conditions—federal authorities are not always effective in preventing even illegal practices—and were often a center for social life. Bob Putnam's famous solitary bowler was bowling in a union hall; neither would likely be there today.[10] Unions provided countervailing power for working people not only at work but in local and national politics.[11] Unions have little power in Washington today, and even the most powerful union lobbies are outspent by several individual corporations like Facebook and Google.

Marriage has declined among the less educated, but not among those with college degrees. Instead of marrying, many Americans participate in serial cohabitations, often having children, with the result that men in middle age, although often father to several children, do not know their kids who are living with their mothers or perhaps other men. These nontraditional family and childbearing patterns may appear to promise personal and sexual liberty for the young, but for those who are middle aged and older, they cannot provide the comfort and stability of traditional arrangements, at least when they work well.

Morbidity has risen alongside mortality. In an extraordinary reversal of a law of nature, middle-aged Americans now report more pain than do elderly Americans.[12] Once again, this is true only for those without a four-year college degree and is not in fact a reversal of the process of aging but happens because those in midlife today have experienced more pain throughout their lives than have today's elderly.

The largest part of the increase in deaths of despair comes from opioid overdoses. For this, pharmaceutical companies bear huge blame; the initial wave of opioid deaths was a result of wealth-seeking pharma companies seeking profits by addicting people. Pharma knew to target the less educated, because it was the less educated whose lives were in disorder; more broadly, historical opioid epidemics have happened in places and at times of social turmoil and disintegration. Pharma and their distributors were supported and defended by politicians, some "representing" the places most deeply affected. Money speaks very loudly in American politics, and when it comes to choosing between the interests of your voters and campaign finance, the selection is often the latter.

Meanwhile, suicide rates rose to levels that used to characterize only the worst societies on earth: the former Soviet Union and its satellites, as well as women in China, especially rural China. Even in those countries, as throughout the world, suicide rates have been falling. American suicide rates—especially those for less educated Americans—are a notable and disgraceful exception.

Economists and Deaths of Despair

Economists are perhaps less split over the causes of deaths of despair than they are over the causes of the Financial Crisis. Yet, the familiar divides between right and left soon appeared. The facts themselves are not in dispute, and the National Center for Health Statistics (part of the Centers for Disease Control and Prevention) confirmed Anne Case's and my calculations soon after our first publications, but different writers assign blame differently.

Our own story sees the decline in good jobs for less educated Americans as the key. This decline, in response to globalization and, more importantly, technical change (robots), is made much worse in the United States than elsewhere by the grotesquely exorbitant cost of healthcare. Much of the cost is financed through health insurance premiums paid by employers, premiums that are much the same for low- and high-income workers, making the former much more expensive relative to their contribution to the firm. Beyond that, when bad things happen and people need help, the safety net in the United States is fragmentary compared with those in other rich countries.

Others lay the blame on the victims themselves. Although he does not explicitly write about deaths of despair, Charles Murray identifies the same rising gaps between the more and less educated but attributes them to a decline in virtue among the latter, particularly the virtue of industriousness.[13] They are not working because they are lazy. Murray previously made the same argument about the African American community in the 1960s and 1970s.[14] But there was a more compelling story from William Julius Wilson, who saw the loss of jobs as the key, just as Anne Case and I argue today.[15] Indeed, if ever-lazier workers were turning down jobs, we would expect wages to rise, not fall, as workers became scarcer relative to available jobs. Nicholas Eberstadt tells a story similar to Murray's, that less educated workers are choosing not to work, with their choice enabled by government benefits, particularly disability benefits.[16]

It was not long before those arguments were brought to bear on the opioid crisis, and once again, some on the right argue that government benefits are making things worse. The story begins with work by Alan Krueger on the long-term decline in employment. He reports survey evidence that half of those not employed were using pain medication, and that two-thirds of those were using prescription pain medication.[17] Nicholas Eberstadt quoted this study in an article in *Commentary*, in which he wondered how these people, out of employment, could afford to be "stoned," given that painkillers like OxyContin are not cheap.[18] The answer, according to Eberstadt, is Medicaid. It was the government providing subsidized opioids through Medicaid. He wryly comments, "In 21st century America, 'dependence on government' has come to take on an entirely new meaning."

President Trump's Council of Economic Advisers, while recognizing the role of pharma companies pressing doctors to write prescriptions, focused on the prices of opioid drugs, arguing that the expansion of government healthcare programs, particularly Medicare Part D (which covers prescription drugs), had made opioids cheaper and encouraged their consumption.[19] The Senate Committee on Homeland Security and Government Affairs, chaired by the execrable Senator Ron Johnson of Wisconsin, issued a 164-page report whose message is summarized by its title, *Drugs for Dollars: How Medicaid Helps Fuel the Opioid Epidemic.*[20] Yet, according to a leading healthcare information company, only 8 percent of opioid prescriptions between 2006 and 2015 were paid for by Medicaid.[21]

We might wonder how it is that rich European countries, which subsidize or even have free prescription drugs, have managed to avoid opioid epidemics. Perhaps it is because those countries' governments do not allow opioids to be used outside of hospitals or clinical settings. Nor are pharma companies allowed to send their representatives to doctors' offices to persuade them to prescribe opioids, often bringing misleading information. The U.S. government does indeed bear much responsibility for the epidemic. But its guilt lies in yielding to relentless and well-funded lobbying by pharma and their distributors to write favorable laws and to hamper investigations that attempt to counter abuse. In a better regulatory environment, providing cheaper drugs to consumers would be a good thing, not a bad thing.

Once the COVID-19 pandemic arrived, deaths of despair were used as an argument for not imposing lockdowns. President Trump argued that stay-at-home orders would be worse for people's health than the virus: "You're going to have suicides by the thousands." Others, including Health Secretary Alex Azar, pointed to the likelihood of mass casualties from alcoholism and opioid overdoses, and warned about deaths from postponing medical screenings and treatment.[22] But in fact, suicides fell at the beginning of the pandemic, not just in the United States but around the world. Perhaps this could not have been predicted, but the studies linking unemployment and suicide had broken down long before the pandemic (for example, during the Financial Crisis).[23] Drug overdoses rose rapidly during the pandemic, as did deaths from alcoholic liver disease, and Casey Mulligan, who served as the chairman of President Trump's Council of Economic Advisers, has long argued that the pandemic, and government responses to it, is largely responsible. Yet opioid overdoses were rising rapidly in January and February 2020, and there is no obvious increase in the upward trend at the time of the emergency. Later, it is certainly possible that some of the benefit checks were spent on street drugs.

But Mulligan's argument linking unemployment and unemployment benefits to deaths from alcohol is an almost perfect caricature of the kind of economic story that only economists could love.[24] Here it is. Before the pandemic, people liked to go to bars, drink, and hang out with friends and other drinkers. With bars closed, that is impossible, so people have to drink at home. Alcohol at home is cheaper than in a bar; there are no markups and no time costs of going out. When prices fall, people drink more, leading to the sort of lock-down casualties that the Trump administration predicted. Perhaps. But what people care about—or at least most people—is the experience of having a drink; otherwise, they would behave like "stoned" people who sleep and drink on the street, dosing themselves with the cheapest alcohol they can find. So, using Mulligan's version of price theory, what would I actually expect? Even if the "price" of a drink is lower, the "price" of socializing with alcohol is now *higher* than before. Consumption should fall. Do

I believe this? I don't know, but the problem with this sort of theorizing is that, once we depart from the actual observable prices in the store or in a bar, we can make up any story we like about the "price" that we think is relevant.

What I find so distressing in these alternative accounts of deaths of despair is the deflection of blame, away from the pharmaceutical companies and their enablers in Congress, where it rightfully belongs, toward the victims themselves. Policy is helpless, government is always the problem, and never the solution, and the best that we can do is to tell people to be more virtuous. Economics does not have to be like this.

CHAPTER 11

FINALE: IS ECONOMIC FAILURE A FAILURE OF ECONOMICS?

MY SKETCHES OF economists in these pages have not always been flattering. A reader might be forgiven for thinking we are scoundrels concerned only with our own financial gain. That we are lobbyists and apologists for the rich, who reward us generously for our work. That our profession has cast off its early roots in eugenics, nativism, and racism, only to become a tribe of misogynists that admits few women into its inner circles and then treats them badly when it does. That we care little about climate change. That we are a group of "camp-following whores" whose pronouncements are entirely predictable from their politics. Whenever a group of several hundred economists signs a petition in support of a policy, within days there are another several hundred who condemn it. We often assume a mantle of policy expertise for which we have no qualification, with predictably disastrous outcomes. Yet we command high salaries and give each other prizes for work that does little to improve the world and would likely harm it if it were taken seriously. At worst, economics seems devoid of scientific content, simply tracking political splits.

We have certainly made too little progress on central policy questions that ought to be amenable to scientific inquiry. Is economic growth compromised by higher tax rates? And if so, just how? Does the near record high of foreign-born people in the United States harm the lives and working conditions of Americans, especially less educated Americans? Many economists believe that they have settled these issues, but they have not built a social or even professional consensus around their answers. Perhaps people simply will not hear results that threaten their interests, but I believe that the profession also bears responsibility for insisting on a methodological purity that artificially limits the applicability and acceptance of their results.

Yet there are economists who do everything that good scientists should do, and I have described some of them in this book. Many economists have well-developed ethical systems and a sense of justice. Many worry about inequality. They work to better understand the world, making honest attempts to interpret evidence objectively, to get their analyses right. These are economists who change their minds in the light of their work, whose findings often surprise themselves, and whose empirical results cannot be predicted from their political beliefs. They produce new, previously unknown facts and findings that are persuasive across the spectrum of opinion and that change the national conversation. There are thinkers in economics who come up with new ideas, who are good at taking apart long-believed stories that, with enough thought, turn out to be incoherent, or can demonstrate that even the accepted wisdom can have surprising and unanticipated implications that no one has thought of before.

That there are good and bad economists is hardly a surprise and does not address their possible responsibility for the state of the economy. When a bridge falls into the river or a rocket explodes in space, we ask hard questions of the engineers, and it is reasonable to ask whether economists had some role in leading us into our current difficulties. Certainly, there is much to answer for. American democratic capitalism as currently practiced is serving only a minority of the population, and the majority is not happy with either democracy or capitalism. The fable that letting financiers get rich helped grow the economy and benefited everyone was exposed by the Financial Crisis. Meanwhile, deaths of despair were (and are) killing less educated Americans, who have turned to populism and given up on a political system that is not helping them. Economists are seen by many as both experts on and apologists for markets, yet they did not predict the crisis and, by some reasonable accounts, encouraged it. They are apostles for the globalization and technical change that have enriched an elite and have redistributed income and wealth from labor to capital, all the while destroying millions of jobs, hollowing out communities, and worsening the lives of their occupants. And when confronted with deaths of despair, they can blame the victims and those who try to help them.

Many economists have worked in Washington and advised on policy. My friend and colleague Alan Blinder, who has done so in several capacities, has written about lampposts in his well-titled book *Advice and Dissent*.[1] He argues that politicians rarely do what economists suggest—sometimes for good reasons, sometimes for bad; they use economic analysis as a drunk uses a lamppost, for support, not illumination. Politicians are happy enough to accept an intellectual or technical endorsement of what they were about to do in any case, but they are rarely swayed by economists' arguments. This does not mean economists are paid hacks who adopt postures pleasing to their masters—though there are plenty of those—but that even good work can be selectively misused. Jason Furman, chief of President Obama's Council of Economic Advisers (CEA), in a rebuttal to Elizabeth Popp Berman's argument that economists have too much sway,[2] has written that he "could only dream of having the power" that is attributed to economists.[3]

Furman notes that even outstanding expertise can be ignored. He reports a 2015 conversation with Kenneth Arrow, the great economist and our greatest thinker about health economics, who reported that, although he was a member of the CEA when Medicare and Medicaid were being designed in the early 1960s, he played no part in the process. Other administration economists have claimed that, at best, they play a negative role, stopping bad things from happening. This, I am sure, is correct. Even politicians face budget constraints but like to live in fantasy worlds in which their pet schemes pay for themselves. Economists in the CEA or Congressional Budget Office play a valuable role in bringing some realism to these fantasies. In Britain in September 2022, when the new government introduced large-scale unfunded tax cuts, one of the main criticisms was that the plan was unaccompanied by any detailed costing of its implications.[4]

I believe that Blinder and Furman are correct in noting the limits to the power of economists in Washington, but not always. When Larry Summers was Treasury secretary from 1999 to 2001, he used his enormous intellect, knowledge, and persuasiveness to weaken restrictions on the international flow of speculative funds, as well as on derivatives and other more exotic instruments on Wall Street. Those decisions were fiercely opposed by other distinguished economists, including Blinder and Joe Stiglitz.[5] According to many assessments, these changes contributed to both the Asian financial crisis and the (global) financial crisis. Earlier, when Robert Rubin was Treasury secretary, Summers was his deputy, and the libertarian business economist Alan Greenspan was chairman of the Federal Reserve, the three appeared on the cover of *Time magazine* as the "committee to save the world," over text describing how "the three marketeers have prevented a global economic meltdown—so far."[6] I think it is probably true to say that, in February 1999, when *Time* did the profile, most of us in the profession felt more admiration than apprehension. To a greater or lesser extent, we bought into the notion that modern economics had given us the tools to sweep away the growth-restricting regulations of the past, many of which were based on prejudice and myth, not science. Mea culpa.

I should note that I have known Summers for more than forty years and that there is no other economist of my acquaintance who knows so much or who is so creatively original; several times he has come up with ideas about my own area of expertise that I would not have thought of and that have changed the way I think. A lunch with Summers can advance your work faster than months of solitary thought. Perhaps we could be forgiven for our enthusiasm or bedazzlement, or perhaps we should be criticized for the common academic fallacy that superb intelligence—the "best and the brightest" syndrome[7]—can make up for other qualities needed in statecraft.

Yet the Rubin/Summers/Greenspan period was exceptional. Janet Yellen, an immensely distinguished economist, is Treasury secretary as I write but does not have the same influence or power. Ezra Klein has written that she "holds real weight in internal discussions, and so do some others, but economists are one of many voices at the table, not the dominant voices."[8] Joe Biden does not listen to economists in the way that Obama or Clinton did, something that arguably makes him a better president. Or possibly not. Obama's signature achievement,

Obamacare, which is likely to have long-lasting benefits, was pushed hard by his economic advisors, often against those more focused on politics. Note too that both Yellen and Summers are themselves exceptional. Academic economists do not usually get to be secretary of the Treasury.

Keynes, who spent much of his life advising policymakers, had a different view of the power of economists. According to him, "The ideas of economists and political philosophers, both when they are right and when they are wrong, are more powerful than is commonly understood. Indeed the world is ruled by little else."[9] Note the "wrong" here; it is not just good ideas that survive and prosper. I have repeatedly told stories in this book about politicians who were in the thrall of bad economics, or, perhaps more commonly, of good economics only half understood, when a full understanding would reverse the conclusion. A good example is the Texas Republican Jeb Hensarling, who chaired the House Financial Services Committee from 2013 to 2019 and who became a politician to "further the cause of the free market" because "free market economics provided the maximum good to the maximum number."[10] Hensarling's view is an example of what James Kwak calls "economism," the idea that the world operates exactly as described in elementary economics textbooks.[11] Not incidentally, Hensarling studied economics with then professor and future Senator Phil Gramm.

Of course, there is folly on the left too. If the right cannot see the flaws in markets, the left can be equally blind to the flaws in government that prevent it from acting reliably to fix the flaws in markets. Government, or at least American government, is not at all well described as a representative body (elected by fully informed citizens) whose job is to correct the flaws in markets, whether it is the tendency toward monopoly, exploitation of workers, or excesses of income distribution. In practice, governments often make things worse and are captured in part by those who are the beneficiaries of the system and who they are not about to rein in. Of course, they are happy to use Blinder's textbook lamppost to justify their failure to interfere—after all, free markets provide the maximum good.

If it is impossible to police the production of future lampposts, we could perhaps be more careful with our basic textbooks. Forty percent of college students take at least one course in economics, so teaching is important, no more so than at elite colleges that train so many future lawyers, legislators, and CEOs.[12] Indeed, there is a powerful movement to broaden the syllabus, initially led by dissatisfied students, with high-quality free textbooks that are available online and that cover many topics that are absent from the standard fare.[13] And there is something to be said for economic research that is designed to act as illumination, not now, but in the future. Milton Friedman argued that real change happens only in times of crisis and argued to his fellow economists, "That, I believe, is our basic function: to develop alternatives to existing policies, to keep them alive and available until the politically impossible becomes the politically inevitable."[14] That Friedman was writing about keeping neoliberalism alive to await the collapse of Keynesian economics does not undermine the basic point.

In my own view, a central problem of modern mainstream economics is its limited range and subject matter. The discipline has become unmoored from its proper basis, which is the study of human welfare. Amartya Sen[15] argues that Lionel Robbins's famous definition of economics—the allocation of scarce resources among competing ends—was a wrong turn, a terrible narrowing of scope compared with what Hilary Putnam calls the "reasoned and humane evaluation of the social wellbeing that Adam Smith saw as essential to the task of the economist."[16]

This was not only Adam Smith's view but that of his successors, who were philosophers as well as economists. Sen contrasts Robbins's definition with that of Arthur Cecil Pigou, who wrote that "it is not wonder, but rather the social enthusiasm which revolts from the sordidness of mean streets and the joylessness of withered lives, that is the beginning of economic science."[17] Economics should be about understanding the reasons for and doing away with the sordidness and joylessness that come with poverty and deprivation. Keynes had a good summary too: "the political problem of mankind: how to combine three things: economic efficiency, social justice and individual liberty."[18]

That we have lost our focus on liberty and justice at the expense of efficiency has also been eloquently argued and meticulously documented by the sociologist Elizabeth Popp Berman, who mourns the sidelining of other philosophical approaches to public policy.[19] Popp Berman's book is persuasive, and I find it useful to divide mainstream economists into two broad groups. I label the first group "conservative economists"; they are concerned with efficiency and believe in the power of markets to promote it, and are concerned that attempts to interfere with the market will compromise current or future prosperity. These conservatives recognize the legitimacy of calls to do something about poverty. The second group I label "progressive economists"; they too are concerned with efficiency and they, too, believe in the power of markets to promote it and are concerned that attempts to interfere with the market will compromise current or future prosperity. They also care about poverty. The difference—and remember I am talking about the mainstream here—is that the progressives worry about inequality and are willing to use redistribution to correct the failures of the market, even at the expense of some loss of efficiency. They are also more skeptical than are conservatives that markets are self-regulating and, on those grounds too, are more willing to interfere even if they counsel caution.

For progressives, there is a trade-off between efficiency and equality, what Arthur Okun called "the big trade-off."[20] Yet the two groups have a vast amount in common, especially in their endorsement of efficiency and of the effectiveness of markets in promoting efficiency, aggregating information, and delivering prosperity. Both groups see themselves as guardians of the national interest—not entirely unfairly defined as per capita national income—with the progressive group willing to trade in some of the total for a more equal society. Of course, they want to do so in the most efficient way, giving up the least for the most, and have developed ideas of how that can be done.

Economists like economic growth because it makes it possible for everyone to be materially better off. While there is no unanimity on a comprehensive story of growth, new and more efficient ways of doing things are widely seen to be key. Such change involves much destruction of existing jobs—for example, replacing workers with machines, closing whole industries in favor of new ones, or switching production from the United States to cheaper sources around the world. And now we get to the rub. Progressive economists are typically in favor of compensating losers, either by making direct compensation to those who lose their jobs to trade or by expanding our relatively weak safety net to catch those who have been harmed. Yet such compensation hardly ever happens, prevented by a coalition of conservative economists who hate interference in the market and of those who have benefited from the changes—for example, capital over labor in the case of globalization and automation—and do not want to give up any of their gains.

What to do? In the past, perhaps until half a century ago, and despite the lack of compensation, things seem to have worked out, at least eventually. Or that is the story that economists traditionally tell, and that many continue to tell. One part of the argument is that at least some of the efficiency gains come to everyone—for example, through cheap Chinese goods at Walmart or Target. More important is the argument that when NAFTA (North American Free Trade Agreement), China's accession to the World Trade Organization, or technical advances destroy their jobs, people are angry and dispirited but eventually move to better jobs elsewhere, go back to school, or upgrade their work. In effect, furniture makers in South Carolina become airplane makers in Seattle just as handloom weavers in Britain before the Industrial Revolution became factory workers afterward (or more realistically, their children or grandchildren did). Even when this process works, it takes time, and there is a marked increase in inequality in the short run. Eventually, the overall gains percolate around, not necessarily to everyone, but widely enough to make the whole process both economically and socially acceptable, as well as politically stable.

It is this strategy that is currently broken and has been broken for several decades. Economists who continue to endorse it are both out of date and thinking too narrowly. There has been growth, albeit at slower rates than before, but those who have lost have gone on losing. We do not know why, but one reason is that moving to a new place is more difficult than it once was because prices, especially house prices, are too high in successful cities to allow less skilled workers to move there. Another reason is the educational divide. Most of the new jobs require something that those who have lost their jobs do not have: a four-year college degree. So, we are left with falling wages and a falling share of the population in employment, the background conditions for deaths of despair and for the rejection of a system that is not working.

Neither conservative nor progressive economists have a solution. Matters are made worse by both groups, meaning all mainstream economists, thinking of human welfare in terms of money. This is where the difference between Pigou (or Adam Smith) and Robbins comes home to roost. What deaths of despair and the associated catastrophes tell us is that people care about their jobs, about the meaning they get from them, and, even more, about their families, their children, and their communities. They care about leading a dignified life in a functioning community in a democratic society, all things that are being lost for people without a college degree. Perhaps we need to think more about *predistribution*—the mechanisms that determine the distribution of income in the market itself, before taxes and transfers—and less about a redistribution that is not going to happen and is not what people want in any case. We need rules and policies that prevent the distress in the first place, all of which takes economists into uncomfortable territory: promoting unions, place-based policies, immigration control, tariffs, job preservation, industrial policy, and the like. We need to promote a more realistic understanding of how governments and markets work. We need to abandon our sole fixation on money as a measure of human wellbeing. We need a better acquaintance with the way that sociologists think about these issues. And above all, we need to spend more time with philosophers, recapturing the philosophical territory that used to be central to economics.

ACKNOWLEDGMENTS

SOME CHAPTERS in this book are adapted from pieces first written for the *Royal Economic Society Newsletter* between 1997 and 2022; a few are adapted from essays for Project Syndicate. The late Thelma Seward Liesner first suggested that I write for the *Newsletter*, and for that I owe her a great debt; she encouraged me to write in a way that was new for me and brought me an often appreciative audience. She was succeeded by Peter Howells, who was a model editor for many years, and very recently by Jon Temple. I am grateful to the many colleagues and friends who commented on the original pieces. More recently, Helen Epstein, Hank Farber, and Leif Wenar read the book in draft and helped me find its current form and structure. I thank them. My work on health was financed by awards from the National Institute on Aging to the National Bureau of Economic Research, most recently award numbers R01AG05339605 and P01AG00505842. I would like to thank all of those at Princeton University Press, led by my editor Joe Jackson and his assistant Emma Wagh. Most of all I want to acknowledge Anne Case, who lived through a quarter century of newsletters, who has occasionally appeared in them, and who read and critiqued each and every one. Several chapters are about the work that we have done together. She also helped me with the harder than anticipated task of turning sometimes disparate material into a coherent book.

NOTES

Preface

1. John Maynard Keynes, 1936, *The general theory of employment, interest and money*, Palgrave Macmillan, ch. 24, p. 383.

2. I particularly recommend Binyamin Appelbaum, *The Economists' Hour: False prophets, free markets, and the fracture of society*, Little, Brown, 2019; Elizabeth Popp Berman, *Thinking like an economist: How efficiency replaced equality in US public policy*, Princeton, 2022; Stefanie L. Mudge, *Leftism reinvented: Western parties from socialism to neoliberalism*, Harvard, 2018; Diane Coyle, *Cogs and monsters: What economics is, and what it should be*, Princeton, 2021.

Chapter One

1. Kungl Vetenskaps-Akadamien (Royal Swedish Academy of Sciences), 2021, "The Prize in Economic Sciences 2021: Natural experiments help answer important questions," https://www.nobelprize.org/uploads/2021/10/popular-economicsciences prize2021-2.pdf.

2. Pew Research Center, 2019, "The growing partisan divide in views of higher education," https://www.pewresearch.org/social-trends/2019/08/19/the-growing -partisan-divide-in-views-of-higher-education-2/.

3. Richard Hofstadter, 1963, *Anti-intellectualism in American life*, Knopf, p. 59.

4. Congressional Record Volume 143, Number 37 (Thursday, March 20, 1997), https://www.govinfo.gov/content/pkg/CREC-1997-03-20/html/CREC-1997-03 -20-pt1-PgE541.htm.

5. Jackie Calmes, 1996, "Minimum wage hike will have minimum effect," *Wall Street Journal*, April 19. https://www.wsj.com/articles/SB829876049733093500.

6. David Card and Alan B. Krueger, 1995, *Myth and measurement*, Princeton University Press.

7. David Card and Alan B. Krueger, 1994, "Minimum wages and employment: A case study of the fast food industry in New Jersey and Pennsylvania," *American Economic Review*, 84(4), 772–93.

8. Paul Craig Roberts, 1995, "A minimum wage study with minimum credibility," *Business Week*, April 24. https://www.bloomberg.com/news/articles/1995-04-23/a-minimum-wage-study-with-minimum-credibility#xj4y7vzkg.

9. Thomas Sowell, 1995, "Repealing the law of gravity," *Forbes*, May 22, 82.

10. Finis Welch, 1995, "Review symposium," *Industrial and Labor Relations Review*, 48(4), 827.

11. James A. Buchanan, 1996, "Minimum wage addendum", *Wall Street Journal*, April 25, p. A20.

12. Confirmed in private correspondence on March 9, 2023.

13. One of the most thorough and convincing is Doruk Cenzig, Arindrajit Dube, Attilla Lindner, and Ben Zipperer, 2019, "The effect of minimum wages on low wage jobs," *The Quarterly Journal of Economics*, 114(3), 1405–54.

14. Joan Robinson, 1933, *The economics of imperfect competition*, Macmillan.

15. A review of monopsony is David Card, 2022, "Who set *your* wage?," *American Economic* Review, 112(4), 1075–90.

16. Adam Smith, 2021, *An inquiry into the nature and cause of the wealth of nations*, Delhi Open Books, p. 652.

17. The Nobel Prize, "The Sveriges Riksbank Prize in Economic Sciences in Memory of Alfred Nobel 2021," https://www.nobelprize.org/prizes/economic-sciences/2021/summary/.

18. Kungl Vetenskaps-Akademien, 2021, "The Prize in Economic Sciences 2021: Natural experiments help answer important questions", https://www.nobelprize.org/prizes/economic-sciences/2021/popular-information/.

Chapter Two

1. Hilal Maradit Kremers, Dirk R. Larson, Cynthia S. Crowson, Walter K. Kremers, Raynard E. Washington, Claudia A. Steiner, William A. Jiranek, and Daniel J. Berry, 2015, "Prevalence of total hip and knee replacement in the United States," *Journal of Bone and Joint Surgery*, 97(17), 1386–97. https://www.ncbi.nlm.nih.gov/pmc/articles/PMC4551172/.

2. Kristen Fischer, 2022, "How much does a hip replacement cost?, *GoodRx Health*, August 29. https://www.goodrx.com/conditions/musculoskeletal-conditions/how-much-does-a-hip-replacement-cost.

3. Uwe Reinhardt, 2006, "The pricing of U.S. hospital services: Chaos behind a veil of secrecy," *Health Affairs*, 25(1), 57–69.

4. Glenn Hubbard, 2006, "Health care, heal thyself," *National Review*, January 30. https://www.nationalreview.com/2006/01/health-care-heal-thyself-r-glenn-hubbard/.

5. Sherry A. Glied, Dahlia K. Remler, and Mikaela Springsteen, 2022, "Health savings accounts no longer promote consumer cost-consciousness," *Health Affairs*, 41(6), 814–20.

6. Amitabh Chandra, Even Flack, and Ziad Obermeyer, 2021, "The health costs of cost sharing," NBER Working Paper No. 28439, February.

7. Organisation for Economic Co-operation and Development, 2017, *Health at a glance: Access times for elective surgery*, https://www.oecd-ilibrary.org/docserver/health_glance-2017-28-en.pdf?expires=1678387104&id=id&accname=guest&checksum=5218223DFFA3EC6024A90722BE015131.

8. Aaron Kiersh, 2009, "Baucus-led 'coalition' receives health sector dollars," June 26. *Open Secrets*, https://www.opensecrets.org/news/2009/06/baucusled-coalition-receives-h/.

9. Ryan T. Bell, 2009, "Obama wets a line in Montana," *Outside Magazine*, August 17. https://outsidemagazine.typepad.com/blog/page/407/.

10. Kenneth J. Arrow, 1963, "Uncertainty and the welfare economics of medical care," *American Economic Review*, 53(5), 941–73.

11. National Public Radio, 2012, "Chief Justice Roberts jokes that he's headed to 'an impregnable fortress,'" June 29, https://www.npr.org/sections/thetwo-way/2012/06/29/155987648/chief-justice-roberts-jokes-hes-headed-to-an-impregnable-fortress.

12. The video of Gruber's remarks was played on several news channels. For the CNN feed, see https://www.youtube.com/watch?v=AEjr9WchNkg.

13. The biographer is Lisa Duggan, 2019, *Mean girl: Ayn Rand and the culture of greed*, University of California Press, and the quote comes from the review by Cass Sunstein, 2020, "The siren of selfishness," *New York Review of Books*, April 9.

14. Jane C. Timm, 2013, "POLL: More oppose 'Obamacare' than 'Affordable Care Act,'" Sep 27. NBC News, https://www.nbcnews.com/id/wbna53122899.

15. Katie Reilly, 2017, "Republican lawmaker: Buy health insurance instead of a new iPhone," March 7. *Time*, https://time.com/4693313/jason-chaffetz-health-care-coverage-iphones/.

16. Kenneth J. Arrow, 1963, *op cit*, p. 967.

17. See this statement from the Substance Abuse and Mental Health Services Administration, the branch of the National Institutes of Health that deals with suicide and substance abuse: "Learn about marijuana risks: Know the risks of marijuana" updated Feb 27, 2023. https://www.samhsa.gov/marijuana, accessed March 9, 2023.

18. David M. Cutler, Jonathan Gruber, Raymond S. Hartman, Mary Beth Landrum, Joseph P. Newhouse, and Meredith B. Rosenthal, 2002, "The economic impacts of the tobacco settlement," *Journal of Policy Analysis and Management*, 21(1), 1–19.

Chapter Three

1. USAID, "USAID history," https://www.usaid.gov/who-we-are/usaid-history, accessed July 13, 2022.

2. Ibid.

3. Bill and Melinda Gates Foundation, "Foundation fact sheet," https://www.gatesfoundation.org/about/foundation-fact-sheet, accessed July 13, 2022.

4. Derek Parfit, 1997, "Equality and priority," *Ratio*, 10, 202–21.

5. John Rawls, 1971, *A theory of justice*, Harvard University Press. On why not to extend the argument internationally, see John Rawls, 1993, *The law of peoples*, Harvard University Press. Arguing for the extension is Thomas W. Pogge, 2002, *World poverty and human rights, cosmopolitan responsibilities and reforms*, Polity.

6. The World Bank numbers are organized into an excellent array of charts and maps at the *Our World in Data* website, see Joe Hasell, Max Roser, Esteban Ortiz-Ospana, and Pablo Arriagada, 2022, "Poverty," *Our World in Data*, https://ourworldindata.org/poverty.

7. Kathryn J. Edin and H. Luke Shaefer, 2015, *$2.00 a day: Living on almost nothing in America*, Houghton, Mifflin, Harcourt. Farah Stockman, 2021, *American made: What happens to people when work disappears*, Random House.

8. Anne Case and Angus Deaton, 2020, *Deaths of despair and the future of capitalism*, Princeton University Press.

9. Kim Parker, Anthony Cilluffo, and Renée Stepler, 2017, "6 facts about the U.S. military and its changing demographics," Pew Research Center, Apr 13. https://www.pewresearch.org/fact-tank/2017/04/13/6-facts-about-the-u-s-military-and-its-changing-demographics/.

10. Kwame Anthony Appiah, 2019, "The importance of elsewhere: In defense of cosmopolitanism," *Foreign Affairs*, 98(2), 20–6.

11. Jørgen Juel Andersen, Niels Johannesen, and Bob Rijkers, 2022, "Elite capture of foreign aid: Evidence from offshore bank accounts," *Journal of Political Economy*, 130(2), 388–425.

12. William J. Easterly, 2001, *The elusive quest for growth: Economists' adventures and misadventures in the tropics*, MIT Press.

13. Joseph E. Stiglitz, 2002, *Globalization and its discontents*, Norton.

14. Kenneth Rogoff, 2002, "An open letter to Joseph Stiglitz, by Kenneth Rogoff, Economic Counsellor and Director of the Research Department, IMF," July, http://faculty.nps.edu/relooney/IMF_Defense_1.

15. "Joseph Stiglitz and Kenneth Rogoff discuss *Globalization and its discontents*," YouTube, June 28, 2002, https://www.youtube.com/watch?v=fv2N4nAqj_I.

16. Jeffrey D. Sachs, 2005, *The end of poverty: Economic possibilities for our time*, Penguin.

17. William J. Easterly, 2005, "A modest proposal," *Washington Post*, March 13, https://www.washingtonpost.com/archive/entertainment/books/2005/03/13/a-modest-proposal/cf219afc-22f9-4f1f-97b4-ffba7f7a058a/.

18. The exchange is in the Letters section of the *Washington Post* of March 27, 2005. https://www.washingtonpost.com/archive/entertainment/books/2005/03/27/letters/a30b218f-6763-4c98-a3f1-e8bad06b3ac0/.

19. Nina Munk, 2013, *The idealist: Jeffrey Sachs and the quest to end poverty*, Doubleday.

20. For an excellent review of the controversy and the lessons, see Michael Clemens and Gabriel Demombynes, 2013, "The new transparency in development economics," *World Economics*, 14(4), 77–99.

21. The Census Bureau has developed a supplementary poverty measure that, while not the government's official count, is much to be preferred and shows much larger poverty decline, see https://www.census.gov/content/dam/Census/library/visualizations/2021/demo/p60-275/figure4.pdf.

22. Council of Economic Advisers, 2018, "Expanding work requirements in non-cash welfare programs," https://trumpwhitehouse.archives.gov/wp-content/uploads/2018/07/Expanding-Work-Requirements-in-Non-Cash-Welfare-Programs.pdf, p. 29.

23. Philip Alston, 2018, *Report of the special rapporteur on extreme poverty and human rights on his mission to the United States of America*, https://digitallibrary.un.org/record/1629536?ln=en.

24. The World Bank has subsequently changed the way it calculates poverty, so that it is no longer possible to reproduce my calculations.

25. Jamie Hall and Robert Rector, 2018, *Examining extreme and deep poverty in the United States*, February 20, https://www.heritage.org/poverty-and-inequality/report/examining-extreme-and-deep-poverty-the-united-states.

26. Paul Theroux, 2015, "The hypocrisy of helping the poor," *New York Times*, October 2, https://www.nytimes.com/2015/10/04/opinion/sunday/the-hypocrisy-of-helping-the-poor.html.

27. Gordon Graham, 2023, *The hope of the poor: Philosophy, religion, and economic development*, Imprint Academic.

28. Bernie Sanders, 2018, "U.N. ambassador dismisses report on extreme poverty in America in letter to Sanders," press release, June 21, https://www.sanders.senate.gov/press-releases/u-n-ambassador-dismisses-report-on-extreme-poverty-in-america-in-letter-to-sanders/.

29. U.S. Mission to International Organizations in Geneva, 2018, "Country concerned statement in response to SR Alston's country report on the United States," June 22. https://geneva.usmission.gov/2018/06/22/country-concerned-statement-in-response-to-sr-alstons-country-report-on-the-united-states.

30. Amy Mackinnon, Robbie Gramer, and Simon Ostrovsky, 2018, "Internal documents show how Trump administration misled public on poverty," *Foreign Policy*, August 2, https://foreignpolicy.com/2018/08/02/internal-documents-show-how-trump-administration-state-department-misled-public-on-poverty/.

Chapter Four

1. Catherine Rampell, 2020, "A number cruncher told the truth. He became his country's public enemy No. 1," *Washington Post*, January 2, https://www.washingtonpost.com/opinions/global-opinions/a-number-cruncher-told-the-truth-he-became-his-countrys-public-enemy-no-1/2020/01/02/06a484c4-2d8e-11ea-bcd4-24597950008f_story.html.

2. Katharine G. Abraham, 1996, "Statistics in the spotlight: Improving the consumer price index: a statement," Economic News Release, Bureau of Labor Statistics, August 6, https://www.bls.gov/news.release/cpi.br12396.a09.htm.

3. Advisory Commission to Study the Consumer Price Index, 1996, *Toward a more accurate measure of the cost of living*, final report to the Senate Finance Committee, December 4, https://www.ssa.gov/history/reports/boskinrpt.html.

4. Jerry A. Hausman, 1996, "Valuation of new goods under perfect and imperfect competition," in Timothy F. Bresnahan and Robert J. Gordon, editors, *The economics of new goods*. Chicago. University of Chicago Press for NBERR, 207–48. https://www.nber.org/system/files/chapters/c6068/c6068.pdf.

5. Timothy F. Bresnahan, n.d., "The Apple-Cinnamon Cheerios war," https://web.stanford.edu/~tbres/Unpublished_Papers/hausman%20recomment.pdf, accessed Mar 10, 2023.

6. Brent R. Moulton, 1996, "Bias in the consumer price index: What is the evidence?," *Journal of Economic Perspectives*, 10(4), 159–77.

7. Jeff Madrick, 1997, "The cost of living: A new myth," *The New York Review of Books*, March 6.

8. Advisory Commission to Study the Consumer Price Index, 1996.

9. David M. Cutler, Angus Deaton, and Adriana Lleras-Muney, 2006, "The determinants of mortality," *Journal of Economic Perspectives*, 20(3), 97–120.

10. Angus Deaton and John Muellbauer, 1980, *Economics and consumer behavior*, Cambridge University Press.

11. Louis Uchitelle, 1996, "How should the price index change when consumers pay more but get more?" *New York Times*, Dec 18.

Chapter Five

1. Martin Feldstein, 1998, "Income inequality and poverty," NBER Working Paper No. 6670, October. Harry G. Frankfurt, 2015, *On inequality*, Princeton University Press. Thomas M. Scanlon, 2018, *Why does inequality matter*, Oxford University Press.

2. Amartya K. Sen, 2022, *Home in the world: A memoir*, Liveright. Kenneth J. Arrow, 1951, *Social choice and individual values*, Yale University Press.

3. James A. Mirrlees, 1971, "An exploration in the theory of optimal income taxation," *Review of Economic Studies*, 38(2), 175–208.

4. Ian M. D. Little and James A. Mirrlees, 1974, *Project appraisal and planning for developing countries*, Heinemann.

5. Lyn Squire and Herman G. van der Tak, 1975, *Economic analysis of projects*, Johns Hopkins for the World Bank.

6. Anthony B. Atkinson, 1970, "On the measurement of inequality," *Journal of Economic Theory*, 2, 244–63.

7. George Stigler, 1959, "The politics of political economists," *Quarterly Journal of Economics*, 73(4), 522–32.

8. Milton Friedman, n.d. *An open letter from economists on the estate tax*, http://friedmanletter.org/wp-content/uploads/2017/08/Milton-Friedman-Open-Letter-on-the-Estate-Tax.pdf, accessed Mar 10, 2023.

9. Eileen Applebaum and Rosemary Batt, 2019, "Private equity and surprise medical billing," Institute for New Economic Thinking, Sep 4. https://www.ineteconomics.org/perspectives/blog/private-equity-and-surprise-medical-billing.

10. For an example from West Virginia, see Evan Osnos, 2021, *Wildland: The making of America's fury*, Bloomsbury.

11. Binyamin Applebaum, 2019, *The economists' hour: False prophets, free markets, and the fracture of society*, Little, Brown and Company.

12. Kim Parker, Anthony Cilluffo, and Renée Stepler, 2017, "6 Facts about the military and its changing demographics," Pew Research Center, Apr 13. https://www.pewresearch.org/fact-tank/2017/04/13/6-facts-about-the-u-s-military-and-its-changing-demographics/.

13. Jason Lyall, 2020, *Divided armies: Inequality and battlefield performance in modern war*, Princeton University Press.

14. Anne Case and Angus Deaton, 2020, *Deaths of despair and the future of capitalism*, Princeton University Press.

15. Annual Review Conversations presents Robert M. Solow in conversation with Peter Berck, https://www.youtube.com/watch?v=umV81FFl1RE, accessed Mar 10, 2023.

16. Henry Aaron, 1978, *Politics and the professors*, Brookings.

17. Thomas Piketty and Emmanuel Saez, 2003, "Income inequality in the United States, 1913–1998," *The Quarterly Journal of Economics*, 118(1), 1–41.

18. The White House Office of the Press Secretary, 2013, "Remarks by the President on Economic Mobility," Dec. 4, https://obamawhitehouse.archives.gov/the-press-office/2013/12/04/remarks-president-economic-mobility.

19. Feldstein, "Income inequality and poverty," Abstract.

20. N. Greg Mankiw, 2012, "Capital income, ordinary income and shades of gray," *New York Times*, March 3.

21. Doris Kearns Goodwin, 2013, *The bully pulpit: Theodore Roosevelt, William Howard Taft, and the golden age of journalism*, Simon and Schuster.

22. A. Scott Berg, 2013, "Wilson," *Putnam's Magazine*, p. 135.

23. Kenneth Pomeranz, 2000, *The great divergence: China, Europe, and the making of the modern world economy*, Princeton University Press. Sidney W. Mintz, 1985, *Sweetness and power: The place of sugar in modern history*, Viking. Sven Beckert, 2014, *Empire of cotton: A global history*, Knopf.

24. Philippe Aghion and Peter Howitt, 2022, "Creative destruction and US economic growth," *Capitalism and Society*, 16(1), article 2.

25. Open Secrets.org, "Lobbying, top spenders," 2021, https://www.opensecrets.org/federal-lobbying/top-spenders?cycle=2021, accessed July 28, 2022.

26. Thomas Philippon, 2019, *The great reversal: How America gave up on free markets*, Belknap Press of Harvard University Press.

Chapter Six

1. Michael Walzer, 1983, *Spheres of justice: A defense of pluralism and equality*, Basic Books.

2. Christopher Caldwell, 2020, *The age of entitlement: America since the sixties*, Simon and Schuster.

3. Barack Obama, 2020. *A promised land*, Crown, 610.

4. US Bureau of Labor Statistics, 2023, "Usual weekly earnings of wage and salary workers fourth quarter 2022," Jan 19. https://www.bls.gov/news.release/pdf/wkyeng.pdf, accessed March 10, 2023.

5. US Bureau of Labor Statistics, 2021, "Labor force characteristics by race and ethnicity, 2020," November. https://www.bls.gov/opub/reports/race-and-ethnicity/2020/home.htm, accessed August 8, 2022.

6. US Bureau of the Census, 2021, "Income and poverty in the United States : 2020," Sep. 14. https://www.census.gov/library/publications/2021/demo/p60-273.html#:~:text=Among%20non%2DHispanic%20Whites%2C%208.2,a%20signifi-cant%20change%20from%202019, accessed August 8, 2022.

7. Board of Governors of the Federal Reserve System, 2020, "Disparities in wealth by race and ethnicity in the 2019 Survey of Consumer Finances," September 28. https://www.federalreserve.gov/econres/notes/feds-notes/disparities-in-wealth-by

-race-and-ethnicity-in-the-2019-survey-of-consumer-finances-20200928.htm, accessed August 8, 2022.

8. Ember Smith and Richard V. Reeves, 2020, "SAT math scores mirror and maintain racial inequity," Dec 1. https://www.brookings.edu/blog/up-front/2020/12/01/sat-math-scores-mirror-and-maintain-racial-inequity/#:~:text=Portion%20of%20test%20takers%20meeting%20college%20readiness%20benchmarks&text=Of%20those%20scoring%20above%20700,or%20Latino%20and%2026%25%20Black, accessed August 8, 2022.

9. Michele J. K. Osterman, Brady E. Hamilton, Joyce A. Martin, Anne K. Driscoll, and Claudia P Valenzuela, "Births: Final data for 2020," *National Vital Statistical Reports*, 70(17), Feb 7, https://www.cdc.gov/nchs/data/nvsr/nvsr70/nvsr70-17.pdf.

10. Federal Bureau of Investigation, 2016, Crime in the US 2016, Expanded homicide data Table 3, https://ucr.fbi.gov/crime-in-the-u.s/2016/crime-in-the-u.s.-2016/tables/expanded-homicide-data-table-3.xls, accessed August 8, 2022.

11. E. Ann Carson, 2020, "Prisoners in 2019," U.S. Department of Justice, October, https://bjs.ojp.gov/content/pub/pdf/p19.pdf.

12. Elizabeth Arias, Betzaida Tejada-Vera, Farida Ahmad, and Kenneth D. Kochanek, 2021, *Provisional life expectancy estimates for 2020*, Centers for Disease Control, NVSS Vital Statistics Rapid Release, Report 015, July, https://stacks.cdc.gov/view/cdc/118999.

13. Institute of Medicine (U.S.) Committee on Understanding and Eliminating Racial and Ethnic Disparities in Health Care, 2003, *Unequal treatment: Confronting racial and ethnic disparities in health care*, ed. B. D. Smedley, A. Y. Stith, and A. R. Nelson, National Academies Press, PMID: 25032386.

14. Keith Wailoo, 2014, *Pain: A political history*, Johns Hopkins University Press.

15. Keith Wailoo, 2011, *How cancer crossed the color line*, Oxford University Press.

16. Richard G. Wilkinson and Kate Pickett, 2009, *The spirit level: Why greater equality makes societies stronger*, Bloomsbury.

17. Richard G. Wilkinson, 2000, *Mind the gap: An evolutionary view of health and inequality*, Orion.

18. Alberto Alesina and Edward L. Glaeser, 2004, *Fighting poverty in the US and Europe: A world of difference*, Oxford University Press.

19. Jennifer Karas Montez, 2020, "US state polarization, policymaking, power, and population health," *Millbank Quarterly*, 98(4), 1033–52.

20. Peter B. Bach, Hongmai H. Pham, Deborah Schrag, Ramsey Tate, and J. Lee Hargraves, 2004, "Primary care physicians who treat blacks and whites," *New England Journal of Medicine*, 351, 575–84.

21. Amitabh Chandra and Jonathan Skinner, 2003, "Geography and racial health disparities," NBER Working Paper No. 9513, February.

22. Anne Case and Angus Deaton, 2021, "Life expectancy in adulthood is falling for those without a BA degree, but as educational gaps have widened, racial gaps have narrowed," *Proceedings of the National Academy of Sciences of the United States of America*, 118(11), https://doi.org/10.1073/pnas.2024777118.

23. Nicholas Stern, 2007, *The economics of climate change: The Stern review*, Cambridge University Press. (Originally commissioned by British Government and presented in October 2006 under the title *Stern Review on the economics of climate change*.)

24. Martin L. Weitzman, 2007, "A review of the Stern review on the economics of climate change," *Journal of Economic Literature*, XLV, Sep. 704–24.

25. William D. Nordhaus, 2007, "A review of the Stern review on the economics of climate change," *Journal of Economic Literature*, XLV, Sep. 686–702.

26. Martin L. Weitzman, 2007, "A review of the Stern review on the economics of climate change," *Journal of Economic Literature*, XLV, Sep. 707.

27. Bjorn Lømborg, editor, 2006, *How to spend $50 billion to make the world a better place*, Cambridge University Press.

28. Nicholas Stern and Andrew Oswald, 2019, "Why are economists letting down the world on climate change?," VOXEU, Sept. 17, https://cepr.org/voxeu/columns/why-are-economists-letting-down-world-climate-change.

29. Tony Judt, 2010, "Meritocrats," *New York Review of Books*, August 10.

30. Michael Sandel, 2020, *The tyranny of merit: Can we find the common good?*, Macmillan.

31. Chris Hayes, 2012, *The twilight of the elites: America after meritocracy*, Crown.

32. Sandel, *The tyranny of merit*.

33. Pew Research Center, 2019, "The growing partisan divide in views of higher education," Aug 19. https://www.pewresearch.org/social-trends/2019/08/19/the-growing-partisan-divide-in-views-of-higher-education-2/.

34. William Easterly, 2014, *The tyranny of experts: Economists, dictators, and the forgotten rights of the poor*, Basic Books.

Chapter Seven

1. Evan Osnos, 2021, *Wildland: The making of America's fury*, Farrar, Straus, and Giroux.

2. Organisation for Economic Cooperation and Development, Global pension statistics, online database, queried March 11, 2023. https://www.oecd.org/finance/private-pensions/globalpensionstatistics.htm.

3. Lee Drutman, 2015, *The business of America is lobbying*, Oxford University Press, 64–65.

4. The President's Commission to Strengthen Social Security, 2001, *Strengthening social security and creating personal wealth for all Americans*, December, https://www.ssa.gov/history/reports/pcsss/Final_report.pdf.

5. Albert Rees and Sharon P. Smith, 1991, *Faculty retirement in the arts and sciences*, Princeton University Press.

6. National Research Council, 1991, *Ending mandatory retirement for tenured faculty: The consequences for higher education*, National Academies Press, https://nap.nationalacademies.org/read/1795/chapter/1.

7. Orley Ashenfelter and David Card, 2002, "Did the elimination of mandatory retirement affect faculty retirement?" *American Economic Review*, 92(4), 957–80.

8. Orley Ashenfelter and David Card, 2002.

9. Congressional Research Service, 2021, "A visual depiction of the shift from Defined Benefit (DB) to Defined Contribution (DC) pension plans in the private sector," https://crsreports.congress.gov/product/pdf/IF/IF12007.

10. David Fertig, 1996, "Interview with James Tobin," Federal Reserve Bank of Minneapolis, Dec 1. https://www.minneapolisfed.org/article/1996/interview-with-james-tobin.

11. Jacob S. Hacker, 2019, *The great risk shift: The new economic insecurity and the decline of the American dream*, 2nd ed., Oxford University Press.

12. Congressional Budget Office, 2012, "Actual ARRA spending over the 2009–2011 period quite close to CBO's original estimate," Blog, Jan. 5, https://www.cbo.gov/publication/42682.

13. Michael H. Keller and David D. Kirkpatrick, 2022, "Their America is vanishing: Like Trump, they insist they were cheated," *New York Times*, October 27, https://www.nytimes.com/2022/10/23/us/politics/republican-election-objectors-demographics.html.

14. Jeffrey R. Brown, Stephen G. Dimmock, Jun-Koo Kang, and Scott J. Weisbenner, 2014, "How university endowments respond to financial market shocks: Evidence and implications," *American Economic Review*, 104(3), 931–62.

15. Mickey Koss, 2022, "Pension funds must adopt bitcoin or risk insolvency," *Bitcoin Magazine*, Nov 18. https://bitcoinmagazine.com/markets/pension-funds-must-adopt-bitcoin.

16. US Department of Labor, 2022, Compliance assistance release No. 2022–01, "401(k) plan investments in 'cryptocurrencies'," Mar 10. https://www.dol.gov/agencies/ebsa/employers-and-advisers/plan-administration-and-compliance/compliance-assistance-releases/2022-01.

17. Josephine Cumbo and Joshua Franklin, 2022, "Virginia pension fund invests in crypto lending to boost returns," *Financial Times*, Aug. 4. https://www.ft.com/content/7cb3f87d-7cb3-4429-952a-ba122efdda3b.

18. John B. Shoven and David A. Wise, 1996, "The taxation of pensions: A shelter can become a trap," NBER Working Paper No. 5815, November.

19. Christopher Byron, 1997, "The tax time bomb," *Esquire*, 128(1), July, 88–9.

Chapter Eight

1. Martin Cripps, Andrea Galeotti, Rachel Griffith, Morten Ravn, Kjell Salvanes, Frederic Vermuelen, 2015, *Economic Journal 125th special issue*, Mar 29, *Economic Journal*, 125(583), 203–8.

2. Austin Robinson, 1948, "Review of 'What I remember' by Mary Paley Marshall," *Economic Journal*, 58(229), 122–24.

3. Robinson, 1948, page 124.

4. Rohini Pande and Helena Roy, 2021, "'If you compete with us, we shan't marry you': The (Mary Paley and) Alfred Marshall lecture," *Journal of the European Economic Association*, 19(6), 2992–3024.

5. Richard T. Ely, 1886, "Report of the organization of the American Economic Association," *Publications of the American Economic Association*, Mar. 1(1), page 7.

6. This paragraph is based on Benjamin M. Friedman's splendid 2021 book, *Religion and the rise of capitalism*, Deckle Edge.

7. Ram Abramitzky and Leah Boustan, 2022, *Streets of gold: America's untold story of immigrant success*, Public Affairs.

8. Thomas C. Leonard, 2005, "Retrospectives: Eugenics and economics in the Progressive Era," *Journal of Economic Perspectives*, 19(4), 207–24.

9. Matthew Connelly, 2010, *Fatal misconception: The struggle to control world population*, Belknap Press of Harvard University Press.

10. Leonard, "Retrospectives."

11. American Economic Association, "Committee recommendation regarding renaming the Ely lecture series," https://www.aeaweb.org/resources/member-docs/renaming-lecture.

12. Pascaline Dupas, Alicia Sasser Modestino, Muriel Niederle, Justin Wolfers, and the Seminar Dynamics Collective, 2021, "Gender and the dynamics of economics seminars," page 1, https://web.stanford.edu/~pdupas/Gender&SeminarDynamics.pdf, accessed August 25, 2022.

13. Heather Sarsons, Klarita Gerxhani, Ernesto Reuben, and Arthur Schram, 2021, "Gender differences in recognition of group work," *Journal of Political Economy*, 129(1), 101–47.

14. W. G. Manning, J. P. Newhouse, N. Duan, E. Keeler, A. Leibowitz, M. A. Marquis, and J. Zwanziger, 1987, *Health insurance and the demand for medical care: Evidence from a randomized experiment*, RAND, Santa Monica, CA.

15. Government Scientific Source, 2019, Trade show: NIH research festival exhibit, Sep 12–13. https://resources.govsci.com/event/nih-research-festival-exhibit/, accessed March 11, 2023.

16. Katherine Baicker, Sarah L. Tubman, Heidi Allen, Mira Bernstein, Jonathan H. Gruber, Joseph P. Newhouse, Eric C. Schneider, Bill J. Wright, Alan M. Zaslavsky, and Amy N. Finkelstein, for the Oregon Health Study Group, 2013, "The Oregon experiment—Effects of Medicaid on clinical outcomes," *New England Journal of Medicine*, 368, 1713–22.

17. Raj Chetty, Michael Stepner, Sarah Abraham, Shelby Lin, Benjamin Scuderi, Nicholas Turner, Augustin Bergeron, and David Cutler, 2016, "The association between income and life expectancy in the United States, 2001–2014," *Journal of the American Medical Association*, 315(16), 1750–66.

18. E. Rogot, P. D. Sorlie, and N. J. Johnson, 1992, "Life expectancy by employment status, income, and education in the National Longitudinal Mortality Study," *Public Health Reports*, 107(4), 457–61.

19. Chetty et al, 2016.

20. Ezra Klein, 2013, "Full text: Eric Cantor's 'make life work' speech," *Washington Post*, Feb 5. https://www.washingtonpost.com/news/wonk/wp/2013/02/05/full-text-eric-cantors-make-life-work-speech/.

21. *The Wall Street Journal*, "Follow the money," July 19, 2002.

22. George Loewenstein, Sunita Sah, and Daylian M. Cain, 2012, "The unintended consequences of conflict of interest disclosures," *Journal of the American Medical Association*, 307(7), 669–70.

23. John DiNardo, n.d., "Reviews of Freakonomics," http://www-personal.umich.edu/~jdinardo/Freak/freak.html, accessed Mar 11, 2023.

Chapter Nine

1. Harriet Zuckerman, 1995, *Scientific elite: Nobel laureates in the United States*, reprint edition, Routledge.

2. Lars Jonung, 2021, "Why was Keynes not awarded the Nobel Peace Prize after writing *The economic consequences of the peace*," *Scandinavian Journal of Economics*, doi: 10.1111/sjoe.12467.

3. Avner Offer and Gabriel Söderberg, 2016, *The Nobel factor: The prize in economics, social democracy, and the market turn*, Princeton University Press.

4. Gary Gerstle, 2022, *The rise and fall of the neoliberal order: America and the world in the free market era*, Oxford University Press.

5. Dani Rodrik, 2015, *Economics rules: The rights and wrongs of the dismal science*, Norton.

6. Robert B. Zoellick, 2010, "Democratizing development economics," Speech at Georgetown University, Sept. 29, p. 2. https://documents1.worldbank.org/curated /en/919061521627731460/pdf/Democratizing-development-economics-by -Robert-B-Zoellick-President-World-Bank-Group.pdf.

7. Sarah Kaplan and Antonia Noori Fazan, 2018, "She made the discovery, but a man got the Nobel: A half-century later, she's won a $3 million prize," *Washington Post*, Sept. 8. Ben Proudfoot, 2021, "She changed astronomy forever: He won the Nobel prize for it," *New York Times*, July 27.

8. Assar Lindbeck, 1985, "The prize in economic science in memory of Alfred Nobel," *Journal of Economic Literature* 23(1), 37–56.

9. Fortunately, there is now a fine biography by Alex Millmow, 2021, *The gypsy economist: The life and times of Colin Clark*, Palgrave Macmillan.

10. Anne Case and Angus Deaton, 2015, "Rising morbidity and mortality among non-Hispanic Americans in the 21st century," *Proceedings of the National Academy of Sciences of the United States of America*, 112(49), 15078–83.

11. Anne Case, 2015, "'Deaths of despair' are killing America's white working class," *Quartz*, December 30.

Chapter Ten

1. Alan S. Blinder, 2022, *A monetary and fiscal history of the United States, 1961–2021*, Princeton University Press, p. 305.

2. Robert J. Barro, 2009, "Voodoo multipliers," *Economists' Voice*, February, 1–4.

3. For this and other similar quotes, see the collection by Brad DeLong at https:// delong.typepad.com/sdj/2009/09/a-magnificent-seven.html.

4. *US News and World Report*, 2023 Best Economics Schools, https://www .usnews.com/best-graduate-schools/top-humanities-schools/economics-rankings ?_sort=rank-asc, accessed March 11, 2023.

5. Blinder, *A monetary and fiscal history of the United States*.

6. Paul Krugman, 2009, "How did economists get it so wrong?" *New York Times*, September 2, https://www.nytimes.com/2009/09/06/magazine/06Economic-t.html.

7. Michael Sandel, 2020, *The tyranny of merit: What's become of the common good?* Farrar, Straus and Giroux, p. 104.

8. Anne Case and Angus Deaton, 2020, *Deaths of despair and the future of capitalism*, Princeton University Press.

9. Amartya Sen, 1998, "Mortality as an indicator of economic success and failure," *Economic Journal*, 108(446), 1–25.

10. Robert D. Putnam, 2000, *Bowling alone: The collapse and revival of American community*, Simon and Schuster.

11. John Kenneth Galbraith, 1952, *American capitalism: The concept of countervailing power*, Houghton Mifflin.

12. Anne Case and Angus Deaton, 2020, "Decoding the mystery of American pain reveals a warning for the future," *Proceedings of the National Academy of Sciences of the United States of America*, 117(40), 24785–789.

13. Charles Murray, 2012, *Coming apart: The state of white America, 1960–2010*, Crown Forum.

14. Charles Murray, 1984, *Losing ground: American social policy, 1950–1980*, Basic Books.

15. William Julius Wilson, 1987, *The truly disadvantaged: The inner city, the underclass, and public policy*, University of Chicago Press.

16. Nicholas Eberstadt, 2016, *Men without work: America's invisible crisis*, Templeton Press.

17. Alan Krueger, 2017, "Where have all the workers gone? An enquiry into the decline of the US labor force participation rate," *Brookings Papers on Economic Activity*, Fall, 1–87.

18. Nicholas Eberstadt, 2017, "Our miserable 21st century," *Commentary*, March.

19. Council of Economic Advisers, 2019, *The role of opioid prices in the evolving opioid crisis*, https://trumpwhitehouse.archives.gov/wp-content/uploads/2019/04/The-Role-of-Opioid-Prices-in-the-Evolving-Opioid-Crisis.pdf.

20. United States Senate, Committee on Homeland Security and Government Affairs, 2018, *Drugs for dollars: How Medicaid helps fuel the opioid epidemic*, https://www.hsgac.senate.gov/imo/media/doc/2018-01-17%20Drugs%20for%20Dollars%20How%20Medicaid%20Helps%20Fuel%20the%20Opioid%20Epidemic.pdf.

21. Anne Case and Angus Deaton, 2017, "The media gets the opioid crisis wrong; Here is the truth," *Washington Post*, September 12.

22. Alex Azar, 2020, "We have to reopen—for our health," *Washington Post*, May 21, https://www.washingtonpost.com/opinions/reopening-isnt-a-question-of-health-vs-economy-when-a-bad-economy-kills-too/2020/05/21/c126deb6-9b7d-11ea-ad09-8da7ec214672_story.html.

23. Anne Case and Angus Deaton, 2020, "Trump's pet theory about the fatal dangers of quarantine is very wrong," *Washington Post*, June 1, https://www.washingtonpost.com/outlook/suicide-coronavirus-opioids-deaths-shutdown/2020/05/31/bf6ddd94-a060-11ea-81bb-c2f70f01034b_story.html.

24. Casey B. Mulligan, 2022, "Lethal unemployment bonuses? Substitution and income effects on substance abuse, 2020–21," NBER Working Paper No. 29719, February.

Chapter Eleven

1. Alan S. Blinder, 2018, *Advice and dissent: Why America suffers when economics and politics coincide*, Basic Books.

2. Elizabeth Popp Berman, 2022, *Thinking like an economist: How efficiency replaced equality in U.S. public policy*, Princeton University Press.

3. Jason Furman, 2022, "The quants in the room: How much power do economists really have?," *Foreign Affairs*, July/August 1–14, p. 184.

4. Martin Wolf, 2022, "Kwarteng is risking serious economic instability," *Financial Times*, September 23, https://www.ft.com/content/52abf1de-10c2-4c15-a0d7-6f3f8f297fbd.

5. Michael Hirsh and National Journal, 2013, "The case against Larry Summers," *Atlantic*, Sep 13. https://www.theatlantic.com/business/archive/2013/09/the-comprehensive-case-against-larry-summers/279651/.

6. See the cover here: http://content.time.com/time/covers/0,16641,19990215,00.html.

7. David Halberstam, 1992, *The best and the brightest*, Random House.

8. Ezra Klein, 2021, "Four ways of looking at the radicalism of Joe Biden," *New York Times*, April 8, https://www.nytimes.com/2021/04/08/opinion/biden-jobs-infrastructure-economy.html.

9. John Maynard Keynes, 1936, *The general theory of employment, interest and money*, Palgrave Macmillan, ch. 24, 383.

10. James Kwak, 2016, "Jeb Hensarling and the allure of economism," *Economist's View*, December 20, https://economistsview.typepad.com/economistsview/2016/12/jeb-hensarling-and-the-allure-of-economism.html.

11. James Kwak, 2017, *Economism: Bad economics and the rise of inequality*, Pantheon.

12. John J. Siegfried, 2000, "How many college students are exposed to economics?," *Journal of Economic Education*, 31(2), 202–4.

13. CoreEcon: Economics for a changing world, https://www.core-econ.org/.

14. Milton Friedman, 2002, *Capitalism and freedom: Preface*, fortieth anniversary edition, 1982 preface, University of Chicago Press, xiv.

15. Amartya K. Sen, 2020, "Economics with a moral compass? Welfare economics: Past, present, and future," *Annual Review of Economics*, 12, 1–21.

16. Hilary Putnam, 2002, *The collapse of the fact/value dichotomy and other essays*, Harvard University Press, 60.

17. Arthur Cecil Pigou, 1932, *The economics of welfare*, 4th edition, ch. 1, 10.

18. John Maynard Keynes, 1933, *Essays in persuasion* (popular edition), Macmillan, 344.

19. Popp Berman, *Thinking like an economist*.

20. Arthur Okun, 1975, *Equality and efficiency: The big tradeoff*, Brookings.

INDEX